# ONE OF OUR AIRCRAFT

# ONE OF OUR AIRCRAFT

*The Story of 'R for Robert'*
*The Loch Ness Wellington*

Robin Holmes

Foreword by HRH Prince Michael of Kent

'Only another thousand miles, Charlie, and we'll be home'

QUILLER PRESS
for
The Brooklands Museum

*For my wife Annabelle with much love*

First published by
Quiller Press Ltd
46 Lillie Road
London SW6 1TN



ISBN: 1-870948-56-4



Produced by Hugh Tempest-Radford *Book Producers*
Typeset by Galleon Photosetting
Printed in Great Britain by St Edmundsbury Press

# *Contents*

'I'm coming to Old Yellowstain. Coming to him. See, while I was studying law 'n' old Keefer here was writing his play for the Theatre Guild, and Willie here was on the playing fields of Prinshton, all that time these birds we call regulars – these stuffy, stupid Prussians, in the Navy and the Army – were manning guns. Course they weren't doing it to save my mom from Hitler, they were doing it for dough, like everybody else does what they do. Question is, in the last analysis – last analysis – *what* do you do for dough? Old Yellowstain, for dough, was standing guard on this fat dumb and happy country of ours. Meantime me, I was advancing my little free non-Prussian life for dough. Of course, we figured in those days, only fools go into armed service. Bad pay, no millionaire future, and you can't call your mind or body your own. Not for sensitive intellectuals. So when all hell broke loose and the Germans started running out of soap and figured, well it's time to come over and melt down old Mrs Greenwald – who's gonna stop them? Not her boy Barney. Can't stop a Nazi with a lawbook. So I dropped the lawbooks and ran to learn how to fly. Stout fellow. Meantime, and it took a year and a half before I was any good, who was keeping Mama out of the soap-dish? Captain Queeg.'

*The 'Caine' Mutiny* by Herman Wouk, published by Jonathan Cape

**KENSINGTON PALACE,**
**LONDON,W.8.**

FOREWORD

What must have been one of the most complex underwater salvage operations ever undertaken was successfully completed just six years ago when the Vickers Wellington Mk 1A N.2980 "R for Robert" finally broke the surface of Loch Ness after over 44 years in its watery grave.

It was on New Year's Eve 1940 when the pilot, David Marwood-Elton, nursed his crippled bomber through the gloom of a Scottish winter afternoon and skilfully landed it on the only flat surface in the vicinity - the waters of Loch Ness. The Wellington rapidly sank to the muddy bottom of the Loch, some 70 metres below, and lay there undisturbed until discovered during a "monster hunt" 36 years later.

We are much indebted to Mr. Holmes, who was responsible for the initial discovery and identification of "R for Robert", for setting up a charitable trust to finance the salvage operation. The money will also be used to recruit the skilled team of divers and salvage experts and to find a final resting place for this historic old warrior with the facilities and manpower to carry out the long-term restoration work.

The author is also to be congratulated on producing such a fascinating and readable account of the RAF-service career, the salvage operation and the restoration work now taking place at Brooklands on "R for Robert". It is, after all, the last surviving example of a Wellington bomber which saw active service during World War II and which is now one of the star attractions at Brooklands Museum.

I am delighted to have been asked to write this foreword and I wish the book every success.

Michael

# *Picture Acknowledgements*

*Plates (Picture Numbers)* by courtesy of:

R. T. Holmes: 4, 5, 6, 7, 8, 10, 12, 13, 14, 73, 74, 75, 79, 99, 104, 108
P. I. Harris: 1, 28, 47, 62
N. W. D. Marwood-Elton: 2
Academy of Applied Science, and Klein Associates: 3
Scottish Marine Biological Association (SMBA): 9, 11
Aeromodeller: 15
W. Wright: 17
Mrs J. Tarry: 16
Imperial War Museum (IWM): 19, 21, 22, 23, 25, 33, 34, 41–46, 48
Royal Air Force Museum (RAFM): 20
Mrs S. Richardson: 36, 41–46
Vickers: 29, 30, 72
Quadrant Picture Library, *Flight International*: 18, 24, 71
*The Second Great War a Standard History*, published by The Amalgamated Press Ltd, 1939–40: 26, 27, 31, 66
*Wellington Special*, by Alec Lumsden. Published by Ian Allan Ltd, 1974: 37
R. Kellett: 39
The Rev. Canon M.C.G. Sherwood: 35, 40
Public Records Office, Kew Richmond, Surrey, Ref. No. CN 5/15: 49
*Die Ritterkreuztrager der Luftwaffe, Jagdflieger 1939–1945*, by Ernst Obermaier. Published by Verlag Dieter Hoffmann, Mains 1966: 51, 52, 53, 54, 58, 59
W. Falck: 50, 55, 56, 63, 64, 65, 68, 81
Photo Cinema Video des Armees, Fort d'Ivry, Paris: 57
*Bomber Command*, by Max Hastings. Published by Michael Joseph Ltd, 1979: 60, 69
H. Jones: 61, 70
The British Library, Newspaper Library, Colindale Avenue, London: 67
Mrs S. Hamilton: 77
Brooklands Museum: 96, 97
British Aerospace: 76, 78, 80, 83, 88, 90, 92, 93, 95, 98, 103, 106, 109
C. Stuart: 82
R. L. Allwood: 101
P. Grant: 94
Oceaneering International: 85
Solo Syndication and Literary Agency: 84, 87, 89, 91
BBC television documentary, 'One of our bombers is no longer missing': 86
D. Morgan: 102
J. Wise: 105
H. Tyrer: 107
RAF Kinloss: 100

*Maps in text*:

Reproduction from the 1978 Ordnance Survey (1:25,000) map, 1964 Ordnance Survey (1:2,500) map and the 1981 Ordnance Survey (1:50,000) map, with the permission of the Controller of Her Majesty's Stationary Office, © Crown Copyright.

Vickers Wellington Mk III cutaway drawing and key reproduced by courtesy of William Green from *Famous Bombers of the Second World War*, published in 1975 by Macdonald and Jane's. Copyright Greenborough Associates.

# *Preface*

*by*
*Group Captain P. I. Harris, DFC*

This book records the history of 'R for Robert', a battered and beaten-up old Wimpy that lay for forty-five years on the bottom of Loch Ness. Like all Wellingtons, she was a joy to fly and an object of affection to her crew. Much is owed to the genius of the late Sir Barnes Wallis, who gave us this superb aeroplane to help us through the dark and difficult times of the early war years. I flew her on that fateful raid to Wilhelmshaven on 18th December 1939, an intensely exciting experience that shattered the long held belief that 'the bomber will always get through'. I was fortunate that day to survive the battle, one of the first major clashes between the Royal Air Force and the *Luftwaffe*. We survived simply because Wing Commander (as he was then) Richard Kellett's leading was immaculate, our ten Wellingtons stuck closely together in tight formation, our guns worked and our very young crews exhibited the true 'bulldog spirit'. In those early days we lumbered along at about two hundred miles an hour and defended ourselves with guns that were little better than pea-shooters. Today, the young men who guard our island fly at twice the speed of sound and tackle the enemy with sophisticated guided missiles. How different things were in 1939. All our operations in those days were overshadowed by the 'Phoney War', when very strict orders forbade us from attacking anything that might result in German civilians being hurt, the last vestige of a decade of appeasement thinking.

In July 1934 the Government announced its modest five-year plan to increase the Royal Air Force by forty-one squadrons. There was immediate opposition and Motions of Censure were put down in both Houses, charging the Government with 'a policy of rearmament that was neither necessary nor calculated to add to the security of the nation'. Had these Motions of Censure not been defeated by the Government, the Battle of Britain would have been lost and the world today would have been a very different place. Our museums are well provided with Spitfires and Hurricanes to remind us of those stirring days of the Battle of Britain. There are Lancasters, Mosquitoes, and even bits of a Halifax to recall the retribution meted out on the *Third Reich*. But an old Wimpy that has survived from the earliest days of the Phoney War must be unique.

After the excitement of the Wilhelmshaven raid, I well remember landing 'R for Robert' safely at Coltishall, the nearest airfield I could find, because we had the dinghy stuck on our tail-plane. I was met by a very irate site engineer who told me that I had no right to land on his aerodrome because it was not yet finished. After a few well chosen words in his ear, he ran us all back to Mildenhall in his big Rover. One of my happiest recollections is of meeting my wife, Kit, in the 'Bird in Hand' when we got back. She had pints of beer lined up on the bar for me and Sandy Innes, my able second pilot. It had been a long hard day; but we were still able to raise a laugh as we listened to 'Lord Haw-Haw' on the German wireless telling us that, from our force of 22 Wellingtons, they had shot down 38. It was not till later that we learned of the terrible losses suffered by 9 and 37 Squadrons. Sandy Innes had a narrow escape a couple of weeks later when a squadron of Messerschmitts attacked three Wellingtons on a daylight armed reconnaissance sweep over the North Sea. After the disaster of the Battle of Heligoland Bight, this was the last nail in the coffin of Bomber Command's cherished philosophy of daylight precision raids by self-defending bomber formations. Wisely, the veil of darkness was thereafter drawn over our bombers that flew to Germany. A whole new technology had to be learned. The public image of Bomber Command in World War II is one of huge dark shapes taking off at dusk with the survivors limping home at the break of dawn. *One of our Aircraft* tells us why it had to be done that way – by night.

# Introduction

'A long time ago in a Galaxy far, far away . . .' So begins one of the most successful films of the seventies – *Star Wars*, a conflict of epic proportions between the eternal forces of good and evil, a science-fiction spectacular set in some bygone era, safely removed by light years from all our own humdrum little squabbles here on earth; well – not exactly.

How many elderly gentlemen sitting in cinema audiences on both sides of the Atlantic, dutifully escorting their grandchildren perhaps, identified instantly with Hans Solo and Luke Skywalker as they swung into their computerised gun turrets to blaze away with laser cannon at Imperial Tie fighters pursuing the *Millennium Falcon*? How many among that grey-haired audience recalled swinging into infinitely less sophisticated gun turrets to blaze away with Brownings at 109s, 110s and 190s pursuing their bombers over Germany? AC1 Jimmy Mullineaux would have remembered because he was one of the first turret gunners to win a DFM for defending his Wimpy against hordes of pursuing enemy fighters.

'A war-worn man known to the younger pilots only as Blue Leader' marshalled his X-Wing and Y-Wing craft as they prepared to attack the *Death Star*. 'Good shooting Blue Six, watch out you've got one on your tail.' Flight Lieutenant George Pinkerton DFC would have remembered because he *was* Blue Leader when he shot down one of the first German raiders over Britain in 1939.

Perhaps the spectacle of Luke Skywalker doggedly holding his X-Wing Incom T-65 straight and level down the trench through a barrage of 'flak' to release his Proton Torpedo at just the precise instant necessary to hit the vulnerable exhaust port struck a chord. Wing Commander Guy Gibson VC would have remembered and no doubt smiled quietly to himself.

*Star Wars*, that forerunner in a spate of space fantasies, drew heavily on the images and dialogue from a conflict much more recent and closer to home – World War II. That the images of aerial combat and accompanying service jargon should still be so familiar to cinema and television audiences, the vast majority of whom can have no first-hand knowledge of the events alluded to, is a measure of the legacy left by our own conflict of epic proportions that we staged here on earth between 1939 and 1945.

In the fantasy of *Star Wars* and the reality of World War II, final victory was won by a single bomber delivering a single bomb. The *Death Star* was destroyed by an Incom T-65. Nagasaki was destroyed by a Boeing B-29.

The contribution of the bomber to the defeat of Nazi Germany was significant, but in securing the unconditional surrender of Imperial Japan it was decisive. The curtain fell on the Second World War to the drone of a Superfortress over Nagasaki, a curtain that had been raised almost exactly six years earlier to the roar of Wellingtons over Brunsbüttel and Blenheims over Wilhelmshaven. Whereas the story of Colonel Tibbets' *Enola Gay* over Hiroshima on 6th August 1945 and Major Sweeney's *Bock's Car* over Nagasaki on 9th August 1945 is legend, the story of Squadron Leader P. I. Harris and Squadron Leader L. S. Lamb over Brunsbüttel and Flight Lieutenant K. C. Doran over Wilhelmshaven on 4th September 1939 is virtually unknown.

> 'With hindsight, it is possible to see that there were two wars between 1939 and 1945. The first was the last war of a past generation. The second was the first of the new era. Technology was coming of age: radar and the atomic bomb, the jeep and the high-performance aircraft. Somehow even the faces in the photographs look different. A Bomber Command group from, say, Honington in 1939 merges imperceptibly into the sepia shades of Camels and "Archie" and the old Royal Flying Corps. But then study the faces of the Lancaster crews of Harris's Bomber Command (ironically, for he himself was anything but a modern man): so many of the faces are already those of the knowing, professional young technocrats of the post-war era, children who have lost their innocence thirty times over Germany, who will vote for the Welfare State in 1945, who are the most highly trained front-line fighters in the history of warfare.'[1]

Exactly when the sepia shades of Camels and 'Archie' started to merge into the starker black and whites of the young technocrat era is hard to pin-point. Perhaps the change came with the appointment on 22nd February 1942 of Air Marshal A. T. Harris as AOC-in-C Bomber Command; perhaps it came on the night of 30/31st May 1942 when Harris launched the first of his three 1,000 bomber raids on the Ruhr; perhaps the change was more gradual as the Whitleys, Blenheims and Hampdens were pensioned off throughout 1942 to other Commands and Operational Training Units. What can be said with certainty is that after 1942 the shapes in the night sky over Germany were bigger and more lethal. The glare from the burning cities of the *Third Reich* was increasingly reflected from shapes like Stirlings, Halifaxes and Lancasters. One aircraft alone was good enough to bridge the gap between the two eras and that was the Wellington. For almost five years the RAF's heavies cloaked themselves in darkness as they wreaked their retribution on Hitler. That RAF Bomber Command operated almost exclusively by night is a well known historical fact. What is less well known is why.

On 2nd September 1945, four hundred and sixty-two B-29s staged a fly-past over the USS *Missouri* during the Japanese surrender ceremonies.

With a bomb load of 20,000 lbs and a defensive armament of twelve 0.5 inch machine guns and a 20 mm cannon, the Boeing Superfortress was the most modern and efficient Allied bomber when World War II finished. On 2nd September 1939 the Royal Air Force was placed on War Establishment. With a bomb load of 4,500 lbs and a defensive armament of six 0.303 inch machine guns, the Vickers Wellington Mk1A was the most modern and efficient British bomber when World War II started.

The stories of the first British raid of the war, of why Bomber Command flew by night and of the Wellington Mk1A are all closely linked together. It is a story of the Stone Age of Strategic Bombing, very much sepia tinted, decidedly Camels and 'Archie'. On 4th September 1939 Squadron Leader P. I. Harris led No. 149 Squadron to Brunsbüttel in a Mk1 Wellington L4302 whose guns didn't work. On 18th December 1939 Paul Harris flew to Wilhelmshaven in a Mk1A Wellington N2980 whose guns got red hot. That particular raid proved so disastrous that Bomber Command was forced to change its entire bombing strategy from daylight operations to night raids only.

Out of a total of 11,461 produced, N2980 – 'R for Robert' – is the *only* Wellington bomber that fought back against Nazi tyranny to survive intact from World War II.* All the others were shot down, ditched in the sea, crashed on training flights or melted down into saucepans.

* Wellington bomber MF628, beautifully preserved in the Royal Air Force Museum at Hendon, is a late TMk10 trainer that saw no active service in the war.

# 1

## *'Hidden away for all time'*

Just after 3 p.m. on New Year's Eve 1940, Squadron Leader David Marwood-Elton, his co-pilot, Pilot Officer Slatter, and six young trainee navigators took off from RAF Lossiemouth on the Moray Firth in a battle-weary Wellington bomber, just retired from active service to an Operational Training Unit. Their route took them south west to Fort Augustus when they encountered heavy snow squalls at 8,000 ft over the Monadhliath Mountains. Suddenly the starboard engine spluttered and failed. The aircraft began to lose height, and all around were cloud covered peaks. The pilot gave the order to bail out and the six young trainees jumped from the stricken aircraft. One pulled his ripcord too soon; his 'chute' was damaged on striking the aircraft and failed to open properly. The other five landed safely. The Wellington continued to lose height and, through a break in the cloud, the pilot spotted a long stretch of water and decided to ditch. As the plane came down the port propeller sent up a great spray of water. Marwood-Elton and Slatter struggled out on to the starboard wing, released the dinghy from its housing behind the engine, clambered aboard and paddled to the shore. As he watched his aircraft sink the thought crossed Marwood-Elton's mind that his plane was 'hidden away for all time' at the bottom of Loch Ness. The incident was all over in 90 seconds.

The trauma of the Second World War passed into history and Loch Ness settled back into its peacetime role as host to legions of intrepid monster-hunters. At first they came armed only with binoculars and cameras. Slowly, as time passed and technology advanced, more sophisticated equipment started to appear around the shores of the loch. Wing Commander Ken Wallis tried searching from the air in his diminutive James Bond-type autogyro. Dan Taylor from America tried looking beneath the surface in his tiny yellow submarine *Viper Fish*. The answer however does not lie with the 'MkI Eyeball' either above or below the surface. High-frequency sound waves penetrate with ease the murkiest of waters. In 1968 Professor Tucker from Birmingham University caused a sensation by reporting large underwater moving objects in the vicinity of his experimental sonar equipment in Urquhart Bay. This was the answer, and two years later a team from the Academy of Applied Sciences in Boston, Massachusetts, arrived with the latest high-definition side-scan sonar and reported finding major targets in Urquhart Bay and near Fort Augustus. Over the next six years many different types of sonar were tried out in the loch, producing such controversial results as the now famous 'flipper' and 'head' photographs. Parliament was petitioned to declare *Nessie* an endangered species, but only samples of carcass or bones from a deceased animal could provide the proof necessary for such legislation. Marty Klein, president of Klein Associates Inc. of Salem, New Hampshire, arrived at Drumnadrochit in the summer of 1976 equipped with his new combined side-scan sonar/sub-bottom profiler. After tests in a lake in New Hampshire, when his equipment successfully detected mammoth bones placed in a pattern on the bottom by divers, Marty Klein was ready to repeat the experiment in Loch Ness, with the object of locating the skeletal remains of a long-necked plesiosaur. During the ensuing survey in 1976 many strange and unexplained objects were found on the bottom: an old sailing barge in Urquhart Bay; deep undercuts (caves?) in the steep walls near Invermoriston; an open sided square structure near Cherry Island (Thomas Telford's steam barge?); large stone circles at Lochend; a long, unidentified object nicknamed 'The Average Plesiosaur' and last, but by no means least, what seemed to be a Catalina aircraft that went down during World War II. To publicise these results together with new photographs taken by Dr Robert H. Rines of the Academy of Applied Sciences in 1975, a public lecture entitled 'In Search of Nessie' was organised by the World Wildlife Fund at the Eden Court Theatre in Inverness on 27th June 1977. The speakers were Dr Robert Rines and Sir Peter Scott, CBE, DSC.

As Heriot-Watt University had been granted its Charter only in 1966, it had the opportunity to embark upon new lines of research unhampered by the restraint of established traditions. In 1969 Heriot-Watt carried out a survey to identify possible areas for future research. One of the facts highlighted by this survey was the almost total lack of involvement of British Universities in the engineering aspects of the underwater environment. In 1970 an Underwater Technology Group (UTG) was set up within the Department of Electrical and Electronic Engineering to carry out research into methods of visually surveying the sea bed. As manned submersibles were prohibitively expensive for a university to operate, the Underwater Technology Group decided to design and build an unmanned submersible controlled remotely from the surface by a long electrical cable. The name chosen for the project was A Navigable General-purpose Underwater Surveyor or ANGUS for short. By 1977 the UTG had successfully built and operated two unmanned cable-controlled submersibles called ANGUS 001 and ANGUS 002. Learning of the forthcoming lecture 'In search of Nessie', the author and a colleague, Robin Dunbar, decided to attend because of interest in the latest techniques for locating objects on the sea bed. Distributed at the lecture were copies of a paper entitled 'Sonar Serendipity in Loch Ness' published by Marty Klein in 1976[1], describing all the interesting things that he had found during his side-scan sonar survey that year. Of particular interest was the reported

American PBY Catalina aircraft lying in 34 metres of water. The UTG had just taken delivery of a new 35mm underwater photographic camera and this was an ideal chance to learn how to find an object underwater and take photographs of it. For many years the Scottish Marine Biological Association at Oban has cooperated with the University by providing ship time to help test our submersibles. In 1978, once again, the SMBA kindly agreed to provide us with a small research vessel called *Seol Mara* equipped with side-scan sonar. In September 1978 the UTG went up to Loch Ness to learn how to search for underwater objects and, if possible, photograph them.

While giving the depth of the Catalina as thirty-four metres, Klein's paper did not divulge the location of the aircraft. The paper however did refer to a local surveyor, George Reid, who had assisted with the 1976 survey. To find the exact position of the aircraft Mr Reid was tracked down and asked for his assistance. Once convinced of our *bona fides* and assured that we had no intention of harming *Nessie,* he showed us the spot on the chart where the aircraft lay. The *Seol Mara* started to search along the thirty-metre contour at the given chart co-ordinates. After several passes over the reported position the side-scan sonar showed nothing. We then moved out to the forty metre contour and started our search procedure again. On the third pass there it was, a tiny little 'T' shape at the extreme range of our sonar. Two more passes confirmed that we had indeed found the Catalina lying, not as we had anticipated in thirty-four metres of water, but in seventy metres, well below diver depths. We were at a loss to know what to do next when Alex Souter and Willie Ritchie, the crew of the *Seol Mara,* took over and laid marker buoys either side of the wreck. The boat was held in position between the marker floats and our camera frame called PK1 was hoisted over the stern and lowered carefully into the water. In the normal course of events such a search can be tedious and prolonged and the team was prepared for this eventuality. As the lowering wire was fed out over the depth recorder and the dials approached seventy metres, a totally unexpected picture suddenly appeared on the surface television monitor. Bright shiny metal strips connected together like a garden trellis showed up on the screen. By a thousand-to-one chance we had landed right on top of the aircraft – first time. As the *Seol Mara* drifted with the wind, PK1 was pulled gently along this framework and the underwater television camera observed pieces of material being dislodged to float away into the darkness. The structure was covered with some form of fabric. The port wing became visible. Again the construction was in the form of a lattice of metal formers and it was a mid-wing aircraft. From somewhere deep in the recesses of my memory came school-boy recollections of scrounging souvenirs from a similar wrecked aircraft at a dump close to my school during the war. This was not a Catalina with its high parasol wing and metal skin. Geodetics was the name that suddenly sprang to mind. The aircraft we had found was a twin-engined, mid-wing aircraft with a fabric covered geodetic framework, and could therefore only be the creation of the late Sir Barnes Wallis. We had found a Wellington bomber. By manoeuvring *Seol Mara* and tugging the wire to PK1 we were able to see that the aircraft was in mint condition, as good as the day it settled on the bottom. Photographs were taken of the rudder, fuselage geodetics, astrodome hatch, port engine and front guns. Because PK1 was suspended seventy metres below the *Seol Mara* it was impossible to carry out a systematic survey of the aircraft and we could only study those parts of the structure that the vagaries of wind and current permitted.

Upon returning to Edinburgh a letter was sent to the Ministry of Defence informing them of our find. In reply, the Air Historical Branch suggested that the aircraft could be a very early Mk 1A Wellington bomber, number N2980, that had ditched on New Year's Eve 1940. This was subsequently confirmed when the Royal Navy Deep Diving team from HMS *Vernon* in Portsmouth searched the wreck in 1979 at the request of the Air Ministry and found traces of the serial number on the fuselage fabric. The aircraft that Squadron Leader Marwood-Elton thought he had 'hidden away for all time' at the bottom of Loch Ness had been found.

The opportunity to return to Loch Ness did not present itself for another two years. In 1980 the Underwater Technology Group took delivery of a sophisticated underwater navigation system for use with ANGUS 002. This time the Scottish Marine Biological Association provided their brand new research vessel *Calanus* to carry ANGUS and our new navigation equipment. Borlum Bay, close by Fort Augustus, provided an ideal location for our scientific work, with deep sheltered water a few minutes' steaming time from our base. When we had completed our scientific programme, *Calanus* headed up the loch for the remaining few days of our charter. The object was to try a practical experiment to see if the underwater navigation system could be used to navigate a submersible around a wreck. It was also hoped to check the accuracy of the equipment against the precisely known dimensions of the aircraft. Jack Bruce, Keeper of the Royal Air Force Museum at Hendon, and Eric Morgan, an authority on Vickers aircraft from the British Aircraft Corporation at Weybridge (where the Wellington was built in 1939), had been invited up to give their advice and study the condition of the aircraft during the last few days of the exercise.

ANGUS 002 was lifted over the stern into the water and driven down onto the bottom. The August sun beamed down and a gentle breeze blew up the loch. On the bottom the visibility was about a metre, not too good but acceptable. For over two hours ANGUS searched the area where the aircraft should have been, the stirred up silt helping to obscure the visibility. Dark clouds drifted over the sun and, looking down the loch, the sky appeared grey and forbidding. It started to rain. Another half hour went by and still ANGUS had not found the Wellington. *Calanus* started to roll and pitch about a bit. Suddenly a bright object was spotted on the television screen and ANGUS was steered towards it. The submersible's lights were being reflected from the shiny metal of the port engine's exhaust collector ring. At long last we had found the aircraft and were ready to start taking measurements and video-taping the structure. Without warning, ANGUS was dragged away from the Wellington by the umbilical cable. By now *Calanus* was really heaving about as the waves increased in height. The ship was caught in the middle of a squall. ANGUS was brought to the surface and recovered as quickly as possible. With ANGUS and its umbilical cable safely out of the water, *Calanus* was able to get under way and head for the shelter of Urquhart Bay. The squall developed into a full blown gale and the few days allocated to the Wellington were spent sheltering under the lee of Urquhart Castle.

The following year, 1981, saw the end of the University's programme of research into cable controlled submersibles. At Dunstaffnage near Oban, ANGUS 002 was linked to a computer on board *Calanus* which took over control from the pilot and drove the vehicle automatically over the sea bed in a series of predetermined search patterns. Our ten years of work on Remotely Operated Vehicles had been crowned with success. Now, however, there was no longer any justification for returning to Loch Ness with ANGUS to finish off the photographic survey interrupted the previous summer. An alternative solution had to be found, and this materialised as an offer from the Officer in charge of the Fleet Clearance Diving Team. Royal Navy divers had been using the Wellington since 1979 for training purposes, and offered to carry out any filming or photography that was required during their forthcoming visit to Loch Ness in early June 1981. The Navy team requested the assistance of the research vessel from the marine laboratory, equipped with a deck compression chamber and electrical power for underwater lights. This request called for external funding, and in February a major oil company was approached to see if they would sponsor the project.

To take maximum advantage of the Navy's offer, two companies, Osprey Electronics and Underwater Marine Equipment Ltd, were contacted to see if they would supply, on free loan, the latest underwater colour television cameras and high-quality underwater photographic equipment. Both companies responded immediately with offers of the necessary gear. At the beginning of April the oil company replied to the effect that it could not support the project due to other commitments, but at the end of April the Navy said they would provide their own surface support ship with all the necessary safety equipment on board, and it was 'all systems go' for the survey at the beginning of June. On 20th May the Officer in charge of the Navy team telephoned to say that the whole operation had been cancelled due to financial cutbacks. Once again, two small companies, UMEL and Oceonics Ltd, stepped into the breach and offered the services of their little ROV* called 'Sea Pup'.

The problem of a suitable surface support ship still remained. Out of the blue, Adrian Shine, the Field Leader of the Loch Ness and Morar Project, telephoned to say that he had heard we were looking for assistance and offered, free of charge, the services of his survey pontoon. Two organisations provided the finance for the project, the Royal Air Force Museum at Hendon, and *Fly Past* magazine. On the tightest of shoestring budgets the underwater survey of the Wellington was successfully carried out and the results recorded

* ROV – Remotely Operated Vehicle.

on videotape during the two weeks from 13th to 24th July 1981.

Gremlins were mischievous, pixy-like creatures that inhabited all RAF aircraft during the war. They got up to all sorts of tricks and were blamed for everything that went wrong with an aircraft or its equipment. They were thought to have become extinct many years ago, but one survived and lived on somewhere in the Loch Ness Wellington. No sooner had Sea Pup been launched over the side of the support craft, reached the bottom and found the Wellington, than things started to go wrong. Fuses blew, shear-pins sheared and the joystick controller went haywire.

The whole of the first week of the survey was spent trying to find the elusive little gremlin that had beamed aboard Sea Pup. He surpassed himself on the Friday of the first week just as the team were about to pack up and go home for the weekend; he wrapped the Sea Pup's umbilical cable firmly round the wreck so that it could not be pulled free. After hours of tugging and heaving, with the surface support craft firmly anchored to the bottom by the umbilical cable, it was decided to uncouple the cable at the top end and take it ashore. Fortunately it was long enough to reach the side of the loch, where it was secured and hidden in a large bush at the water's edge. It was a worried and dispirited team that headed for home that weekend. Monday morning, and the Heriot-Watt and Oceonics teams arrived at the base camp, boarded the pontoon and were ferried out across the loch to the dive site. As Oceonics fitted a new joystick, the crew of the pontoon recovered the end of the umbilical cable from its hiding place under the bush at the water's edge. The cable was hauled in, hand over hand, until the pontoon was pulled directly over the aircraft's position.

After all our trials and tribulations of the first week, *Nessie* must have realised that we meant her no harm and whispered to our gremlin to let Sea Pup go. A couple of half-hearted tugs and the cable suddenly went slack as the little submersible floated back to the surface.

Just as the first week had provided every frustration imaginable, the second week saw Sea Pup perform to perfection. The aircraft was located on the first dive and the survey commenced. Looking at the front gun turret with its twin 0.303 inch Browning machine guns pointing out into the darkness, triggered, once again, long forgotten memories of school boy ecstasy, of sitting in just such a turret at an RAF Open Day during the War shooting down squadrons of imaginary Me 109s and Me 110s.* As Sea Pup moved back to the starboard wing we came upon the empty dinghy compartment at the rear of the engine nacelle from which Marwood-Elton and Slatter had struggled to release and inflate the dinghy before their aircraft sank beneath them. The propeller blades of the starboard engine appeared to be perfectly straight, witness to the fact that the engine had packed up before it hit the

* The correct designation is Bf 109 and Bf 110, the Bf standing for Bayerische Flugzeugwerke (Bavarian Aircraft Company). As a sop to nostalgia they will be given their war-time names – Me 109 and Me 110.

water. The port engine propeller blades were bent backwards as they sent up the 'great splash of water' witnessed by Mrs Helen Massie from the shore. Sea Pup travelled slowly over the huge wings and the wash from the horizontal thrusters blew away forty years of sediment from the fabric to reveal the RAF roundels, still clearly visible. For four days we surveyed the aircraft and recorded our findings on videotape. The submersible's pilot, Bill Carver, became so adept at manoeuvring the vehicle about the wreck that it took only a few moments to select a particular feature for closer study and then proceed to that precise location on the structure. Close inspection of the metalwork of the geodetics showed each rivet as bright and shiny as the day it was punched home at Vickers Armstrongs at Weybridge in 1939. The rear gun turret, in which AC1 Mullineaux earned a DFM over Wilhelmshaven, was fully traversed to starboard indicating that, before ditching, the gunner had bailed out backwards through the open turret door. The strangest sensation of all however was gazing into the cockpit and imagining the pilot sitting there at the controls struggling to hold 'R for Robert' in tight formation over Wilhelmshaven as German Me 109s and Me 110s swarmed into the attack, but more of that later.

The saddest thing about the 1981 survey was the realisation that our old warrior from World War II had been extensively vandalised. In 1978, when we found the aircraft, the entire fuselage was intact and in mint condition. Three years later the fuselage aft of the trailing edge main frame had been torn apart. The port and starboard upper longerons, the strength members, were broken and bent outwards. The astrodome hatch had disappeared and in its place was a great gaping hole. The Direction Finding Loop had been torn off and lay on the port mid wing. By a strange coincidence N2980 now looked remarkably like the 1941 cartoon by Freddie, extolling the durability of Wellingtons.

Our gremlin, having behaved himself for almost a week, could restrain his natural impulses no longer. The next step, with the videotaping complete, was to take a set of colour photographs of the Wellington. Sea Pup was placed in position and the remote camera button pressed – nothing happened. The 35mm still camera would not function. The submersible was recovered, the camera batteries charged overnight, and the camera tested out next day ashore. Everything worked perfectly. Back down to the aircraft again, the button was pressed and nothing happened. Time had run out, our gremlin's honour had been satisfied, and so we decided to pack up and head for home.

The survey that started out as a chaotic shambles developed into a smoothly run and highly efficient operation. The pontoon that seemed at first sight small and unstable, proved to be absolutely ideal for the job. Sea Pup was off-loaded at Temple Pier late on the afternoon of Friday the 24th July 1981, bringing to an end what may possibly be the first underwater archaeological 'dig' by an ROV.

The crew of N2980 when it ditched on Loch Ness were:

| | | |
|---|---|---|
| S/Leader N. W. D. Marwood-Elton | Pilot | Survived the war. |
| Pilot Officer Slatter | Co-pilot | Killed in action 5/2/44. |
| Pilot Officer Lucton | Tr./Nav. | No trace of his record. |
| Sergeant Wright | W.Op./A.G. | Survived the war. |
| Sergeant Chandler | Tr./Nav. | Killed in action 2/8/41. |
| Sergeant Little | Tr./Nav. | Killed in action 26/6/42. |
| Sergeant Ford | Tr./Nav. | Killed in action 31/5/42. |
| Sergeant Fensome | Rear Gunner | Killed 31/12/40 when N2980 ditched. |

Tr./Nav. – Trainee Navigator.
W.Op./A.G. – Wireless Operator/Air Gunner.

# 2

## *'A very good cottage on the foundations of a castle'*

'G for George' skims the surface of the water, lower and lower until the two spotlights meet and the bomb aimer peers through his sights at the twin towers of the Möhne dam. Streams of tracers arc up towards his Lancaster as Wing Commander Guy Gibson steadies his aircraft on its run up to the target. As Barnes Wallis's bouncing bomb skips across the surface, the Lancaster claws itself upwards through a hail of flak. A mighty explosion is followed by a huge fountain of water. The dam holds. The rest of 617 Squadron take their turn, and there are more explosions, more fountains of water, till finally the dam face cracks and the deluge pours through. Every time they re-run *The Dam Busters* you get a lump in your throat, but by May 1943 the writing was on the wall for Nazi Germany. By then Bomber Command was a truly formidable organisation equipped with the most efficient aerial sledgehammers – the Lancaster and the Halifax. From then on, in partnership with the US Eighth Airforce's Liberators and Flying Fortresses, the cities of Germany were subjected to an ever-increasing pounding that eventually resulted in vast areas being reduced to piles of rubble, the bomber's contribution to the final defeat of Nazi Germany. Nostalgia, however, tends to distort our view of history by recalling the better times at the expense of the bad ones. Perhaps that is why the Lancaster and Mosquito are remembered with such affection. Big, tough and menacing – fast, daring and deadly – these two epitomise today's image of Bomber Command during the Second World War. They belong to the better times when our backs were no longer against the wall and when, with the help of our American and Russian allies, victory was on the horizon. Model shops abound with plastic kits of Lancasters, Mosquitoes, Halifaxes, Flying Fortresses and Liberators. You have to search hard to find a model of a Whitley or a Wellington. They belong to the dark days when Britain stood alone, invasion and defeat staring us in the face. The 'Flying Barn Door' and the 'Wimpy' however were the two aircraft that laid down the firm foundation upon which both Bomber Command *and* the US Eighth Airforce built their huge self-defending bomber formations, a concept that relied upon a major British advance in armament technology – the power-operated gun turret. More than any other bomber, the Wellington proved the power-operated gun turret to be a formidable defensive weapon.

Until the advent of long-range escort fighters in 1944, big bomber formations had to rely for their survival upon mutual supportive cross-fire from their power-operated gun turrets.

The *raison d'être* for the big bomber formations that were later to become such familiar sights as they headed out over the sea towards Germany, night after night, can be traced right back to the very beginnings of the RAF in 1918. Its founder, Sir Hugh Trenchard, was a fervent advocate of the philosophy that 'offence is the best form of defence'. Through the lean years of the twenties and early thirties this was the guiding light that motivated senior officers in the RAF, officers who were finally given the go-ahead to rebuild their run-down service in July 1934 when it eventually dawned on a reluctant British Government that Herr Hitler meant business. Just prior to leaving to present a new British disarmament plan to the Reduction and Limitation of Armaments Conference at the League of Nations in Geneva, Stanley Baldwin expressed his growing concern to the House of Commons on 10th November 1932.

> I think it well also for the man in the street to realise there is no power on earth that can protect him from bombing, whatever people may tell him. The bomber will always get through, . . .

'In those days everyone believed that aerial bombardment would reduce the cities of Europe to ruin within a few weeks. European civilisation would come to an end.' So wrote the famous historian A. J. P. Taylor in his book, *History of World War II*.

Baldwin, oft accused of having an 'Air Armada' complex, was not alone in fearing the growing power of the bomber. Memories of the raids by German Gothas on London in 1917 and the predictions of doom from H. G. Wells in his book *The War in the Air* combined to stir up strong anti-bomber feelings. Throughout Europe (with the exception of Germany, where freedom of speech was in the process of being extinguished) and in the United States of America, groups of vocal women organised petitions and presented them to the League of Nations with the clear message 'Ban the Bomber'. In response to Hitler's growing strength in the air the cry went up for Britain to give a moral lead and set an example by adopting a policy of unilateral disarmament.

Hitler's answer to this universal cry for peace and stability was to withdraw from the League of Nations, repudiate the Treaty of Versailles, reintroduce conscription and reveal to the world, on the 1st March 1935, his new *Luftwaffe* which he claimed had already reached parity with the RAF. For those with eyes to see, the reality was now terrifyingly apparent. War in Europe was inevitable – Britain and France *had* to set about defending themselves from Hitler's bombers, but how?

The answer was given at the time by C. G. Grey in an article in *The Aeroplane*. 'The real defence of this country must rest on counter-offensives by which the enemy is prevented from leaving his aerodromes, and his supplies of aircraft and armaments destroyed.' The Royal Air Force was in complete agreement with this sentiment but was unsure as to how it could be implemented.

> In theory, there were three principal methods by which the day bombers might hope to pass safely through the opposing air defences. Firstly, they might travel at such great speed that the opposing fighters and flak would seldom be able to get on terms with them. In this way they would also be able to exploit the element of surprise to the full. A 'speed bomber' did not, however, exist in 1939. . . .
>
> Secondly, the bombers might be covered by long-range fighter escort but, as in the case of the 'speed bomber', no long-range fighter existed in 1939, and the years which followed were to show the difficulties of producing one. It was possible that Spitfires might afford support in an attack on the Ruhr, if flight over the Low Countries was possible, but it was unlikely that any would be available for this purpose.
>
> Thirdly, and this was the only immediately practical proposition, the bombers might concentrate in tight tactical formations and rely for their protection upon collective fire power. The defensive strength of these formations might be increased by equipping some aircraft with more guns or guns of larger calibre and, possibly, by providing them with special armour plating. 'Self-defending' bomber formations might also, of course, gain a certain advantage by surprise, or at times they might be protected by cloud cover.
>
> The success of self-defending formation tactics would depend upon whether the necessary concentration of fire power could be generated and sustained. This, in turn, would depend upon whether the bombers could keep station in the face of enemy attack from the air and the ground and after manoeuvring over the target. Any advantage to be gained from cloud cover might be a disadvantage to station keeping, and whether surprise could be achieved or not would largely depend upon the extent to which the Germans had developed a system of radar early warning. These problems and many others, such as the performance and armament of the German fighters, the accuracy and strength of their anti-aircraft fire and the comparative advantages and dangers of high- and low-level attack, were either unknown or untested when, on the 4th September 1939, fifteen Blenheims and fourteen Wellingtons took off between three and four o'clock in the afternoon to attack German warships reported to be off Brunsbüttel and in Wilhelmshaven.[1]

Having settled on the 'means', the next decision that had to be faced was the 'end' to which it should all be directed, i.e. the target. Before the war, the RAF considered themselves capable of hitting a specified target from 10,000 feet with an average bombing error of no more than 225 yards. It goes without saying of course that this was in good weather, with no cloud, no opposition and above all in *daylight*. The possibility of having to hit a precision target at night was not considered because it was thought that 'appreciable results' would not be forthcoming.*

The Air Ministry duly formulated a whole series of proposals which culminated in the Ruhr Plan. This envisioned a strike at the heart of German industry in the Ruhr valley to destroy precision targets like power stations, synthetic oil plants and aircraft factories. When first informed of this plan, the Air Minister, Sir Kingsley Wood, declared with affronted decency that factories were private property. Later, the German *blitzkrieg* on Warsaw demonstrated that Hitler did not concern himself with such niceties.

The four corner-stones on which pre-war Bomber Command was built were ideas that offence was the best form of defence, that the bomber would always get through, that bomber formations would be self-defending and that attacks on precision targets would be made in daylight.

To implement these four policies the organisation and equipment of the RAF were completely overhauled. Safe behind their Maginot Line, the French reaction to Hitler's sabre-rattling was different. From 1933 to '35 the French Government placed panic orders with their aircraft industry (nationalised in 1936) which resulted, by 1938, in the French Air Force being stocked with obsolete machines unfit to fly against the Germans. The 'family firms' of the British aircraft industry on the other hand resisted the pressures from Government to produce unimaginative bomber designs to the undemanding specifications issued by the Air Ministry. One firm in particular was working on a revolutionary new form of construction against considerable opposition from the traditionalists. Vickers Armstrongs at Weybridge had come up with an idea for 'knitting holes together' called geodetics, and its inventor, Barnes Wallis, was so convinced of its merits that the company went ahead and built a prototype at their own expense and called it the Wellesley. So good was the geodetic design concept that, in 1938, two Wellesley aircraft won the world long distance record for Britain.[2] That same year their big brother, the Wellington, entered squadron service with the RAF when a Mk1, number L4215, was taken on charge by No. 99 Squadron at Mildenhall. Barnes Wallis's faith in his geodetics was later to be fully justified when hundreds of aircrew were brought back safely from over Germany by Wimpys with battle damage that would have destroyed lesser machines.

Nineteen thirty-eight was a momentous year in European politics. In March, Hitler annexed Austria and called it *Anschluss*. Later the Führer announced his intention of doing the same thing to the Sudetenland in Czechoslovakia. In an unprecedented diplomatic initiative, the British Prime Minister, Neville Chamberlain, flew to Berchtesgaden in September to dissuade the Führer from further territorial acquisitions. Though not a phrase in use at the time, Chamberlain started 'shuttle diplomacy' between Britain and Germany. His third and last meeting with Hitler took place in Munich, and he succeeded in getting joint signatures on a document symbolising the desire of

* Minutes of Air Ministry Conference (ACAS in chair), 30th Nov. 1938.

Britain, France, Germany and Italy never to go to war with one another again. Upon his return to Britain, Chamberlain alighted from his aircraft at Heston aerodrome and, in the midst of a tumultuous welcome, waved aloft the piece of paper that was to bring 'peace for our time'.

Historians have argued at length over Chamberlain's motives for his policy of appeasement that culminated in the Munich Agreement. The rapturous welcome he received from the British public, however, testifies to the mood of the nation that September, and a few Members of Parliament were even observed to weep openly with relief upon hearing the news. Hopelessly outmatched and later accused of being hoodwinked by the devious Adolph, Chamberlain was to see everything he had worked for crash in ruins, but as to whether or not he was fooled by Hitler can be judged from his speech to the House of Commons on 3rd October 1938, four days after he returned from Germany.[3]

> Let no one think that because we have signed this agreement between these four Powers at Munich we can afford to relax our efforts in regard to that programme (i.e. rearmament) at this moment. Disarmament on the part of this country can never be unilateral again. We have tried that once, and we very nearly brought ourselves to disaster. If disarmament is to come it must come by steps, and it must come by agreement and the active co-operation of other countries. Until we know that we have obtained that co-operation and until we have agreed upon the actual steps to be taken, we here must remain on guard.

There is no argument however about the outcome of Neville Chamberlain's initiative at Munich – it bought the Royal Air Force the year it so desperately needed to 'gird up its loins' and face what was becoming increasingly apparent as 1939 wore on, even to the most ardent supporters of appeasement, that Britain and Germany were set on a collision course.

Ten years after he relinquished his post as Chief of Air Staff, Lord Trenchard watched the fruits of his labour at an RAF display in the spring of 1939. As the squadrons of fighters and bombers flew in formation overhead, the Father of the Royal Air Force looked up secure in the knowledge that he had provided, as he said in his own words, 'a very good cottage on the foundations of a castle'.

When the siren first sounded over London our shield had been greatly strengthened. Fighter Command stood ready to enter the lists with five hundred Hurricanes and Spitfires and pick up the gauntlet thrown down by the challenger with the swastika-emblazoned fuselage.

While the shield was to prove only just adequate, the lance was as yet no more than a toothpick. Bomber Command could not contemplate a thrust at the heart of German industry. More time had to be bought. Sir Edgar Ludlow-Hewitt, its Commander-in-Chief, had at his disposal only a fraction of the enemy's strength.

Recalling the devastation visited on London, Coventry and Clydebank, it is hard to comprehend that Hitler had made no preparations for a bombing war. The *Luftwaffe* was never intended as a strategic (destruction of cities and civilian population) weapon. Its intended function was to act as handmaiden to the German army. There was plenty of time to build up the *Luftwaffe* into a strategic force, should it prove necessary, for Hitler had promised Göring in 1938 that his beloved *Luftwaffe* would not be required for such a role before 1942; any earlier war with Britain, the Führer had positively assured him, could be ruled out. Born in secret and nurtured at a clandestine base called Lipetsk in Russia, the *Luftwaffe* was above all a propaganda weapon intended to intimidate those who opposed Germany's expansionist policies. In 1936 the Spanish Civil War provided an ideal opportunity to test the aircraft, equipment and organisation of the new *Luftwaffe* under the most rigorous operational conditions. Many deficiencies were brought to light and rectified. For instance in 1937, a year after the war started, it was found that the *Luftwaffe* (like the RAF) did not possess a single modern bomb. Steps were taken to rectify this omission, and new aircraft such as the Heinkel 111, Dornier 17, Junkers 87 dive bomber and the incomparable Messerschmitt 109 received their baptism of fire in the Condor Legion. In the skies over Spain they reigned supreme.

The Heinkel 111 was similar to the Wellington and proved ideal in Continental operations, but it had to struggle to reach targets in the north of England, where its lack of fighter escort and power-operated turrets proved fatal. The Dornier 17, nicknamed the 'Flying Pencil', was similar in appearance and performance to the Hampden and it suffered the same fate; neither could defend themselves against fast, well-armed fighters. The Junkers 87, frequently referred to as 'the scourge of Europe' or 'the aircraft that conquered nations', proved as big a disaster as the Fairey Battle, for the gull-winged 'Stuka' fell easy prey to RAF fighters and was quickly withdrawn to less well-defended theatres.

All-in-all, as August 1939 drew to a close, the scales were just about equally balanced as regards quality, performance, range and bomb-load on the opposing sides.

The big disparity lay in numbers. Sir Edgar Ludlow-Hewitt could muster a maximum of 17 operational squadrons of strategic bombers (Whitleys, Hampdens and Wellingtons), a total of 272 aircraft (Battles and Blenheims were considered tactical bombers). Availability of crews reduced this even further to an average of 140 bombers. Ranged against this, Jeschonnek, Göring's Chief-of-Staff, had at his disposal between 1,200 and 1,600 bombers and this did not include hundreds of dive bombers. The Royal Air Force desperately needed a *deus ex machina* (a divine intervention) and it came on the day Germany invaded Poland. The President of the United States, Franklin D. Roosevelt, appealed to the belligerents to refrain from unrestricted aerial bombardment of civilian populations. The British accepted this restriction that same day. The Germans, for their own good reasons, welcomed the appeal eighteen days later, once their victory in Poland had been assured.

To Chamberlain's government the logic was sound. The RAF desperately needed to conserve its precious aircrews and bombers while new machines issued from the factories and men were trained to fly them. The Ruhr Plan was placed temporarily on the shelf. New targets had to be found that would not provoke instant retaliation on British civilians. A glance at the map of Europe reveals Bomber Command's dilemma. Holland and Belgium wanted nothing to do with the looming hostilities and opted for neutrality, thereby denying Bomber Command direct access to Germany's industrial heartland via their airspace.* The French requested the British to refrain from attacking land targets in Germany because *L'armée de l'Air* had precious few modern bombers to deter an attack or fighters to defend their cities. While they were confident that the Maginot Line would stop the *Wehrmacht*, French politicians, like all other European leaders, were haunted by the spectre of skies darkened by hordes of enemy bombers intent on destroying their cities.

At the Air Ministry they had prepared numerous thick files of possible targets in the event of war with Germany. One of these plans, Western Air Plan 7B, called for the bombing of the German fleet in and around its base at Wilhelmshaven. In the German battleships, the British saw the biggest threat to their vital ocean supply arteries. Besides this, battleships were obviously legitimate targets and, if they could be found clear of land, they could be attacked without the risk of stray bombs killing civilians. Denied direct access to the Ruhr over France and the Low Countries, and fearful of the repercussions from being the first to harm civilians, the British Government seized enthusiastically upon WAP 7B.

The only way into Germany then was via the Heligoland Bight and the only unmistakable military targets were battleships. At the Air Ministry it became fashionable to view this new situation as 'keeping the gloves on'. Let the Germans incur the odium of being the first to break Roosevelt's humanitarian appeal; the Royal Air Force would go for the *Scharnhorst, Gneisenau, Emden, Admiral von Scheer, Nürnberg, Leipzig* and the rest of the German fleet at Wilhelmshaven.

A quarter of a century before, as August 1914 drew to its close, HMS *Arethusa* engaged the German light cruisers *Stettin* and *Frauenlob* in what developed into the first full scale fleet engagement of World War I. In history books this is referred to as the first Battle of Heligoland Bight.

* The Royal Air Force had strict instructions not to overfly neutral territory.

# 3

## *'La Drôle de Guerre'*

Early on the morning of September the first, 1939, Hitler unleashed his Stukas on Poland. The Germans called their new form of warfare *Blitzkrieg*. In support of their *Panzer* divisions the *Luftwaffe* rained down death and destruction, first on the airfields, later on the cities. The Poles resisted gallantly for twenty seven days but, with half their obsolete airforce destroyed on the ground, cavalry pitted against tanks and Warsaw ablaze from end to end, resistance soon crumbled.

In accordance with treaty obligations, the British Ambassador delivered our ultimatum in Berlin at 9.00 a.m. on 3rd September. It is reported that Hitler, Göring and Goebbels received it with stunned surprise. An answer was demanded within two hours. None was received.

> Everything that I have worked for, everything that I have hoped for, everything that I have believed in during my public life, has crashed in ruins.

So said the British Prime Minister to a silent House of Commons at noon. That evening Chamberlain re-formed his Cabinet with Churchill as First Lord of the Admiralty.

Forty-eight minutes after Chamberlain broke the news to the world, a MkIV Blenheim bomber, N6215, took off from Wyton to reconnoitre the great German naval base at Wilhelmshaven. Several enemy warships were spotted, but when the pilot tried to transmit this information back to base he found that the intense cold at 24,000 feet had frozen up his wireless transmitter. By the time he returned to Wyton it was too late in the day to do anything about it. Early next morning Flying Officer McPherson took off once again and headed his Blenheim towards the great naval base. As he approached his target low cloud forced him to fly at only 300 feet above the waves. He photographed warships lying in the Schillig Roads near Wilhelmshaven and at Brunsbüttel at the mouth of the River Elbe. Immediately he transmitted this information by wireless but only a garbled account was received back at base. When the Blenheim eventually touched down, just before noon, the aerial photographs were processed to reveal two battle cruisers, the *Gneisenau* and *Scharnhorst* at Brunsbüttel and the 'pocket battleship' *Admiral von Scheer*, with cruisers and destroyers, anchored in the Schillig Roads.

The time had come to test Stanley Baldwin's oft repeated maxim: 'The bomber will always get through'.

The Royal Air Force launched their first bombing raid of the Second World War shortly before 3.00 p.m. on 4th September 1939. In response to Flying Officer McPherson's photographic reconnaissance, eight Wellington bombers of No. 149 Squadron, under the command of Squadron Leader P. I. Harris, took off from Mildenhall to be joined by a further six Wellingtons of No. 9 Squadron from Honington under the command of Squadron Leader L. S. Lamb. Their targets were the battleships *Scharnhorst* and *Gneisenau* at Brunsbüttel.

Ten Blenheim bombers of No. 110 and No. 107 Squadrons under the command of Flight Lieutenant K. C. Doran also took off from Wattisham, to be joined by a further five Blenheims of No. 139 Squadron from Wyton. Their target was the 'pocket battleship' *Admiral von Scheer* at Wilhelmshaven. In Doran's words, 'The weather in the Heligoland Bight was bloody, a solid wall of cloud seemed to extend from sea-level to about 17,000 feet. . . . So we went to sea-level and flew in and out of cloud between 50 and 100 feet.'

So bad was the weather that five of the Wellingtons from 149 Squadron turned back but Squadron Leader Harris pressed on regardless with his other two remaining Wellingtons piloted by Flying Officer Macrae and Flight Lieutenant Stewart. The five Blenheims of 139 Squadron also turned back because of poor visibility.

Before take-off all the pilots had been instructed to bomb only naval ships found clear of land. If any of the warships were tied up alongside in harbour, they were not to be attacked. Under no circumstances were bombs to be dropped on land where civilian casualties could result. These orders were very explicit and stemmed from the War Cabinet's insistence that Bomber Command should do nothing to provoke retaliation on British or French civilians.

President Roosevelt's appeal would be respected, the gloves would stay on. But to young men, ready, willing and able to demonstrate their prowess in battle, their orders seemed crazy. They had no way of understanding just how weak Bomber Command really was. The stage was being set for what would later become known as *La Drôle de Guerre*.

Detailed to lead 149 Squadron's eight aircraft that day was Squadron Leader Paul Harris. His second pilot was Pilot Officer Billy Brown, standing in for Pilot Officer Sandy Innes who was convalescing from an appendix operation. They had been with 149 for only a week having both just been posted from the crack 214 Squadron at Feltwell. What they found on arriving at Mildenhall gave rise to considerable misgiving. 149 Squadron was quite unprepared for war. This fact manifested itself only too soon as they ran towards their aircraft – they had no idea where Brunsbüttel was. No prior warning had been given of the target. No time had been allowed to study maps or prepare a plan of attack. No instructions had been issued to the captains other than the fact that there were two cruisers at the entrance to the Kiel Canal – 'go and take a crack at them.' After climbing aboard their aircraft they carried out the pre-flight checks only to find that their machine was unserviceable and so they had to hunt around for another. Flying Officer Bill Macrae, a Canadian, very nearly took-off without any bombs onboard; he just looked in the off chance and found none. On the way, Squadron Leader Harris ordered that the guns be tested, only to make the horrifying discovery that not one of them worked. He was flying to Germany in an aircraft that was completely defenceless. Not wanting to turn back on the first raid of the war he made the decision to press on regardless.

Typical of the lack of understanding which existed in the early days of the war is the personal recollection of the Brunsbüttel raid by Sergeant 'Bunny' Austin, the navigator in Paul Harris's Wellington.

> I recall vividly standing by for up to 24 hours or more in the crew room with the crew waiting to go somewhere, we knew not where but assumed it would be Germany. When the call did in fact come we all dashed out to the aeroplane. There was no briefing for crew members other than, I think, the captains, and when we got in the aeroplane and took-off I asked the captain, Paul Harris, where we were going, as navigator of the lead machine I would find it useful to know and after handing over to the second pilot, Pilot Officer Brown, he came back to the navigation table and said we were going to the Kiel Canal and I fortunately had all the available charts that one could have at that time in my navigation bag and taking it out we found the Kiel Canal or rather, we didn't find the Kiel Canal, it was an old Admiralty chart and it was labelled Kaiser Wilhelm Canal. I recall saying to Paul, 'Well, that's it', and he said, 'No, no, it's the Kiel Canal', and by some freak of fate a short distance off the Kaiser Wilhelm Canal there was a little tiny tributary marked Kiel Canal. Paul said, 'that's where we're going, that's where we're going'. So I then said, 'do we go straight there?' and he said, 'no, no, we must fox the enemy, we go up North East then across and then cut down', in other words make a deviation and we duly set course!

There was no sign of No. 9 Squadron, and after a couple of hours two of Harris's Wellingtons lost formation and returned to base, dropping their bombs in the sea. 149 Squadron's other three Wellingtons, led by F/Lt Duguid, got as far as Wangerooge then turned back because of the adverse weather. Bunny Austin goes on to say.

> I also remember on that trip that it was cloudy and on the second leg, which would have led us straight on into Denmark, if we had gone ahead, we lost one of the aeroplanes, by lost, I mean we lost sight of him, he didn't crash or anything, and in fact he didn't quite know what he was doing and he went on and was undoubtedly the crew which was later reported in the papers as having bombed Esbjerg in Denmark.

Meanwhile we proceeded, looking for warships at the entrance to the Kiel Canal.

Paul Harris and his crew didn't find the battleships *Scharnhorst* and *Gneisenau*. Suddenly their Wimpy shuddered; they had taken a direct hit by flak and the rear gun turret was damaged. Fortunately the gunner, Jimmy Mullineaux, had vacated it earlier because the guns were not working. The third aircraft was no longer in view having disappeared into the low cloud. Alone, with a damaged and defenceless aircraft, the Germans alerted and the weather poor, Paul Harris aimed his bombs at a bridge over the River Eider above Tönning and turned for home. He nursed L4302 the three hundred miles back and landed at Mildenhall six and a quarter hours after taking-off.

But No. 9 Squadron from Honington found Brunsbüttel, and the three aircraft led by F/Lt Grant flew into a hail of flak from the battleships' iron ring of anti-aircraft defences. On the approach of the bombers, *Luftwaffe* fighters from II/JG77 under the command of Oberstleutnant Schumacher took off from Nordholz near Cuxhaven. Feldwebel Hans Troitsch spotted S/Ldr Lamb's three Wellingtons flying low over the water. As he dived to the attack, two of the bombers turned and disappeared into low cloud. Troitsch pursued the remaining Wellington and shot it down in flames.* A second *Luftwaffe* pilot, Feldwebel Alfred Held, observed burning wreckage on the water and took it to be two twin-engined English bombers, (probably 107 Squadron Blenheims). While circling above this wreckage Held saw, far in the distance, a single Wimpy which he pursued, and after a short battle it crashed into the sea in flames. Meanwhile the Blenheims under F/Lt Doran at Wilhelmshaven were faring even worse. Flak brought down four and Leutnant Metz, another of Schumacher's pilots, shot down a fifth.† *Scharnhorst* and *Gneisenau* escaped unscathed, and *Admiral von Scheer* was hit by three bombs, none of which exploded. The only serious damage caused by the RAF that day occured when a stricken Blenheim crashed, either accidentally or as a last gallant attempt by its pilot, into the cruiser *Emden*, tearing a huge hole in the bows and inflicting the first casualties of the war on the German navy.‡

A week later the first decorations of the war were gazetted; to Flying Officer McPherson and Flight Lieutenant Doran, the DFC for their part in the Brunsbüttel and Wilhelmshaven raids.

The War Cabinet, however, was not unduly impressed with Bomber Command's performance on its first raid against the enemy, and decreed that in future bombers operating from home bases would confine their attacks to German naval ships at sea and not attempt to penetrate heavily defended naval bases. So the 'honour' of sinking the first capital ship of the war fell to Leutnant Schuhart commanding U-29 when his submarine torpedoed

* In April 1963, Generalmajor a. D. (Retired) Carl Schumacher said that he had always believed that Feldwebel Troitsch was the first to shoot down an RAF aircraft.

† The Air Ministry denied that any of these losses were due to fighter action, and attributed them all to flak.

‡ Eleven sailors killed and thirty injured.[1]

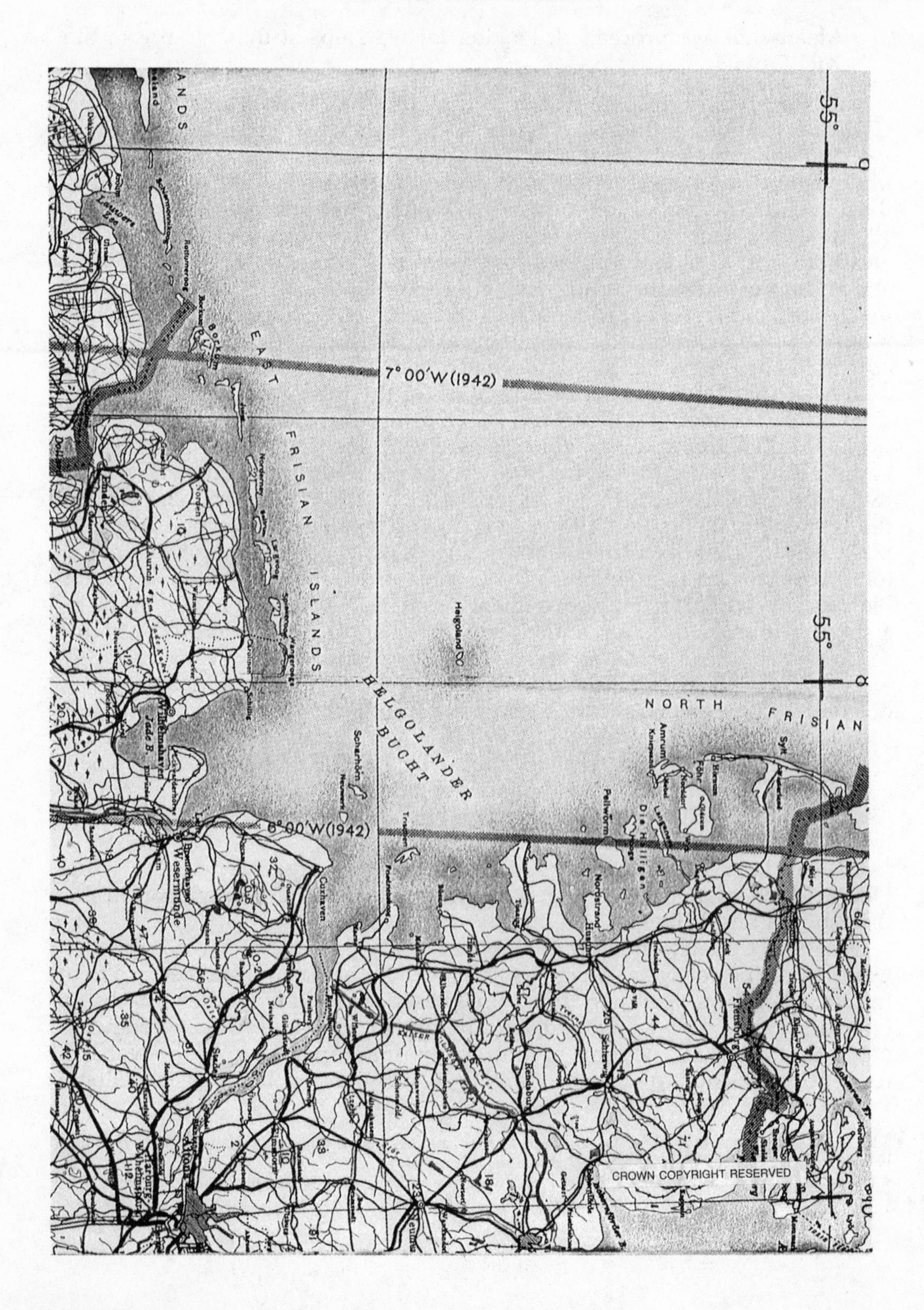

55°
7° 00'W (1942)
EAST
FRISIAN
ISLANDS
Helgoland
HELGOLANDER
BUCHT
NORTH
FRISIAN
6° 00'W (1942)
Wesermünde
Cuxhaven
Husum
Schleswig
Rendsburg
Altona
CROWN COPYRIGHT RESERVED

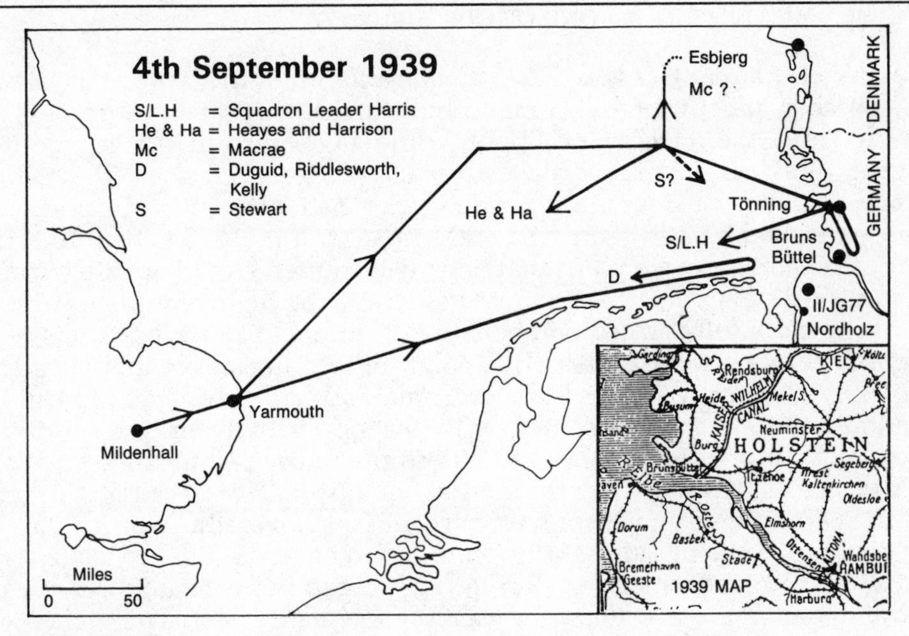


*No. 149 Squadron, Mildenhall*

| | |
|---|---|
| L4302 S/Ldr Harris | Dropped bombs on bridge over river Eider. |
| L4265 F/O Macrae | Dropped bombs on Brunsbüttel (?) |
| L4271 Sgt Heayes | Turned back, dropped bombs in sea. |
| L4229 F/Lt Stewart | Dropped bombs off Cuxhaven (?) |
| L4263 Sgt Harrison | Turned back, dropped bombs in sea. |
| L4272 F/Lt Duguid | Turned back, dropped bombs in sea. |
| L4374 F/O Riddlesworth | Turned back, dropped bombs in sea. |
| L4270 F/Sgt Kelly | Turned back, dropped bombs in sea. |

*No. 9 Squadron, Honington*

| | |
|---|---|
| Section No. 1 | Attacked by 9 Messerschmitt Bf 109E-1s. |
| L4320 S/Ldr Lamb* | Dropped bombs on merchantman (claimed a fighter). |
| L4268 F/Sgt Borley | Shot down. |
| L4275 F/Sgt Turner | Shot down |
| Section No. 4 | Encountered heavy A.A. fire from ship's defences. |
| L4278 F/Lt Grant | Claimed hits on a Battleship in harbour but German |
| L4287 Sgt Purdy | records mention no damage to either *Scharnhorst* or |
| L4262 Sgt Bowen | *Gneisenau*.. |

*Luftwaffe*

II/JG77 under Oberstleutnant Carl Schumacher at Nordholz (near Cuxhaven).

Feldwebel Alfred Held received the Iron Cross, Second Class, and his victory was widely proclaimed in the German and world press at the time and subsequently related in all historical accounts, as the first victory of a German fighter over a British bomber. Squadron Leader Lamb's Section was the only one that reported being attacked by fighters that day and Feldwebel Troitsch relates that he attacked a formation of THREE Wellingtons, one of which he shot down. Held attacked and shot down a SINGLE Wellington, which could only have been a survivor from Lamb's Section. It appears from this that Generalmajor Schumacher's assertion was correct and it was Troitsch and not Held who merited the laurels.[2]

* S/Ldr Lamb and his crew perished in a flying accident less than a month later (30.10.39).

and sank the aircraft carrier HMS *Courageous* on 17th September. By the 19th, Bomber and Coastal Command had carried out seven reconnaissance missions into the Heligoland Bight with single aircraft. Little could be achieved by these individual planes because wireless contact with base was proving a chancy business, and, even if they had succeeded in calling up a squadron of bombers, it would have taken several hours for them to arrive. In the meantime, any warships that had been spotted would be safely back in harbour. So a new policy was adopted whereby the Bight would be patrolled by nine or more fully armed bombers under orders to attack any units of the German fleet found in the area. This policy of reconnaissance in force started on 26th September. Whereas Bomber Command had an uneventful trip that day, the *Luftwaffe* was presented with the opportunity of a life time, an opportunity to put the Bomber *vs* Battleship controversy to the test.

A Dornier 18 flying boat of the coastal squadron 2/106 based at Nordeney was flying a long-range reconnaissance mission over the North Sea. The pilot could see little because of the heavy cloud cover. Suddenly his observer started; he had just seen a warship through a gap in the clouds. No, he was wrong; it was not one warship, it was a whole battle fleet. The pilot circled the gap in the clouds and counted four huge battleships and an aircraft carrier accompanied by cruisers and destroyers. At once the Do. 18 transmitted back this information. The time was 10.45 a.m. and the *Luftwaffe* had just found the British Home Fleet at sea and far from the safety of its base. Presented with this golden opportunity, nine He 111s of the 'Lion' Geschwader under the command of Captain Vetter and four of the new Ju 88s of the 'Eagle' Geschwader under the command of Leutnant Storp took off to do battle. Here was a chance in a million to cripple the Royal Navy, and only thirteen aircraft were sent to attack HMS *Nelson, Rodney, Hood, Renown* and the aircraft carrier *Ark Royal,* with its screen of cruisers and destroyers. Captain Vetter and Leutnant Storp did no better than Squadron Leader Harris, Squadron Leader Lamb and Flight Lieutenant Doran. One bomb from a Ju 88 hit HMS *Hood* but did not explode and bounced overboard. One bomb from another Ju 88 was seen to throw up a great fountain of water alongside the *Ark Royal,* but the pride of the Royal Navy sailed on and the chance of a lifetime was gone. Göring later claimed that the *Ark Royal* had been sunk, and dismissed as propaganda the British press photographs of her steaming into harbour.

Several days later, on 29th September, eleven Hampdens from No. 144 Squadron left Hemswell in two sections. One, consisting of five aircraft led by the Squadron CO, Wing Commander J. C. Cunningham, took off at 4.05 p.m. and was never seen again. The other, consisting of six aircraft led by Squadron Leader W. J. H. Lindley, found two German destroyers steaming at 20 knots in line astern and attacked from 300 feet, but the defensive screen was too effective and no damage was inflicted on the ships. Lindley's section got back safely but Cunningham's fell victim to Me 109s from II/JG 77. After that the theory of reconnaissance in force became less popular.

In both Britain and Germany disillusionment set in. The realities of modern warfare bore no relationship to the textbooks written by veterans of the 1914-18 War. Foul weather, poor navigation, inadequate training, wireless transmitters that froze up, guns that jammed, bombs that didn't explode – *that* was the reality. In modern jargon both adversaries were right at the bottom of the learning curve.

The next move was up to the German navy. In an incredible act of bravery, Leutnant Gunter Prien in U-47 sneaked past the defences into Scapa Flow, torpedoed and sank HMS *Royal Oak*, and then made good his escape. This attack led to increased surveillance of the east coast of Scotland by German reconnaissance aircraft. Next day, HMS *Hood* was spotted heading for the naval base at Rosyth in the Firth of Forth. Göring's Chief-of-Staff, Jeschonnek, gave orders for an attack to be made on the *Hood* and telephoned Captain Pohle at Westerland with a personal order from the Führer.

> Should the *Hood* already be in dock when KG 30 reaches the Firth of Forth, no attack is to be made. I make you personally responsible for acquainting every crew with this order. The Führer won't have a single civilian killed.

There we have it! *La Drôle de Guerre* – the Phoney War. Exactly the same orders that had been given to Harris, Lamb and Doran prior to the first British raid on Germany were now being issued to Pohle before the first German raid on Britain.

In Germany it was believed that Britain would soon 'see sense' and be prepared to sue for peace, or at least remain a supine observer cowed by the might of the invincible *Luftwaffe*, a *Luftwaffe* that had just been instrumental in subjugating Poland two weeks previously. The Führer considered it important not to antagonise the British populace at this stage of the game by bombing their cities, apart from which, the vast majority of his bombers were still tied up in Poland. Hence the very strict orders: 'The Führer won't have a single civilian killed.'

At any rate Captain Pohle, the Commanding Officer of I/KG30, had his orders. On the morning of 16th October, the *Luftwaffe* set-off for its first raid on the mainland of the United Kingdom. At 2.00 p.m. his squadron of nine Ju 88s flew over Edinburgh, and twelve thousand feet below lay the Firth of Forth spanned by its famous railway bridge. As German intelligence had told him that there were no Spitfires based in Scotland, his aircraft flew on in loose formation. HMS *Hood* had just arrived at Rosyth and was in the sea-lock, being readied for entry into the inner harbour. 'She was a sitting target but orders robbed us of our prize,' reported Pohle. Out in the roadstead lay the cruiser HMS *Southampton*. Through a hail of anti-aircraft fire Pohle dived his Ju 88 and released his 1,000 lb bomb. It went straight through three decks without exploding, came out of the side of the cruiser and sank an admiralty launch tied up alongside. 'Achtung! Achtung! Spitfire' was a cry later to become famous in the skies over Kent. German intelligence had got its facts wrong*; Spitfires thundered into Göring's new 'Wonder Bombers'. With smoke pouring from his port engine, Pohle turned seaward. Bullets slammed into his machine. He was a sitting duck. His radio-operator and rear-gunner were hit. The Spitfires came at him again. This time his observer was hit and his starboard engine packed up. Just before passing-out, Captain Pohle succeeded in ditching in the sea close to Grail. Five days later he regained consciousness in Port Edgar hospital, the sole survivor from his aircraft. In accord with the sentiment prevailing at that time, Flight Lieutenant George Pinkerton, a flight leader in 602 Squadron who had shot down the Ju 88, visited Helmut Pohle in hospital. Pinkerton's ground crew, Sergeant Harry Henderson and his comrades, carried the coffins of two dead members of Pohle's crew who were buried with full military honours in Portobello Cemetery, Edinburgh. The chivalry of World War I was still maintained by both sides during the early days of the war. The results of the attack had been minimal. The cruisers HMS *Southampton* and HMS *Edinburgh* together with the destroyer HMS *Mohawk* suffered only superficial damage. I/KG30 lost two aircraft, 4D+AK and 4D+DH. First Brunsbüttel and Wilhelmshaven now Rosyth, both were daylight raids on heavily defended naval bases. Bomber Command didn't get the message but the Royal Navy did. That very next day I/KG30 took off again under its new commander, Captain Doench. Their target was the British Home Fleet at Scapa Flow, but the birds had flown and were safely out of range in Loch Ewe on the West coast of Scotland. All that remained at Scapa Flow was the old depot ship HMS *Iron Duke*, whose sides were damaged by near misses. On the island of Hoy the first German bombs of the war fell on British soil.

October wore on into November with little activity from either the *Luftwaffe* or Bomber Command. By mid-November German aircraft had started sowing magnetic mines round the British coast. At sea, enemy U-boats were exacting a mounting toll on shipping, and the First Lord of the Admiralty was becoming increasingly restive. On the 17th, a reconnaissance plane patrolling the Wilhelmshaven area reported that it had spotted several warships exercising in the area. Because bombers could not reach the area before dusk, no action was taken. The First Lord of the Admiralty raged at such 'tepid indecision'. Things were truly grim. Shipping losses were mounting and the Germans were using magnetic mines to which we had no counter. Why, demanded Winston Churchill, did the RAF not venture to Wilhelmshaven? Bomber Command accordingly received instructions to mount 'a major operation with the object of destroying an enemy battle-cruiser or pocket-battleship'. This order removed the restriction on attacking enemy warships in the immediate vicinity of German naval bases. However, the 'greatest care' was still to be exercised to ensure that there would be no casualties to German civilians; 'no bombs are to be aimed at warships in dock or berthed alongside the quays.'

* No. 603 City of Edinburgh Squadron was based at Turnhouse and No. 602 City of Glasgow Squadron had just arrived on 13th of October at Drem near Haddington.

This was an echo of the Führer's order to Captain Pohle. Both sides were still intent on keeping the war within bounds.

At the same time as Winston Churchill was demanding a more aggressive policy from Bomber Command, a brand new Mk1A Wellington bomber was winging its way from the factory towards RAF Mildenhall. A few days previously it had been rolled onto the tarmac at Weybridge. At 4.30 p.m. on 16th November, Vickers chief test pilot Mutt Summers took it up and put it through its paces. After ten minutes it landed, had a few minor adjustments made, and took-off again. This time everything worked perfectly. The new Wimpy was taken on charge of No. 149 Squadron at Mildenhall on 20th November and given the Squadron letter R for Robert. As the large white letters OJ R were painted on the sides of its fuselage, Wellington N2980 was ready to go to war. It didn't have long to wait.

### *3rd DECEMBER 1939*

Bomber Command's response to Churchill was to mount a major raid on the German island fortress of Heligoland, two tiny rock outcrops in the German Bight, 75km north of Wilhelmshaven. Twenty-four of the RAF's latest Mk1A Wellingtons from 38, 115 and 149 Squadrons were detailed to attack any enemy naval vessels found in the area. The raid was led by the CO of 149 Squadron, Wing Commander R. Kellett, AFC. 149 Squadron provided twelve aircraft, grouped into four sections of three. Leading the attack, Kellett positioned his section well out in front. Following some distance behind and leading the remainder was Paul Harris with his section. Off to his right and behind flew the third section led by a young Canadian, Flight Lieutenant J. B. Stewart in a brand new Wimpy, OJ R. Directly behind Stewart flew the fourth section led by Flight Lieutenant A. G. Duguid.

Sitting next to Paul Harris was the second pilot, Pilot Officer Herome Alexander Innes, a handsome young Scot from Perth. The events of that day were later recorded in a little hardbacked notebook kept by P/O Innes.

> 3.12.39 The amazing has actually happened. We have been on a real live raid and what is more dropped our bombs with success and come away with no casualties except damage from AA fire and we went out 24 a/c 12 of ours and 12 of 38 Sq. up to a pt off Denmark and then S to Heligoland and then to Schillig Roads. Object to find and bomb any enemy warship – W/C Kellett leading and separated from us to reconnoitre Heligoland. Leaving Paul Harris and I to lead remainder. We were joined by rest of formation over Thetford where they were waiting – most impressive sight and awe inspiring seeing so many Wellingtons spoiling for a fight and without doubt the most efficient bombing plane in existence. The formation on these trips is amazing. No point in close up so we were spread back for several miles. I often wonder what the population think when we pass overhead heading for the North Sea. Anyhow when we got to the separation pt after a v. good trip north

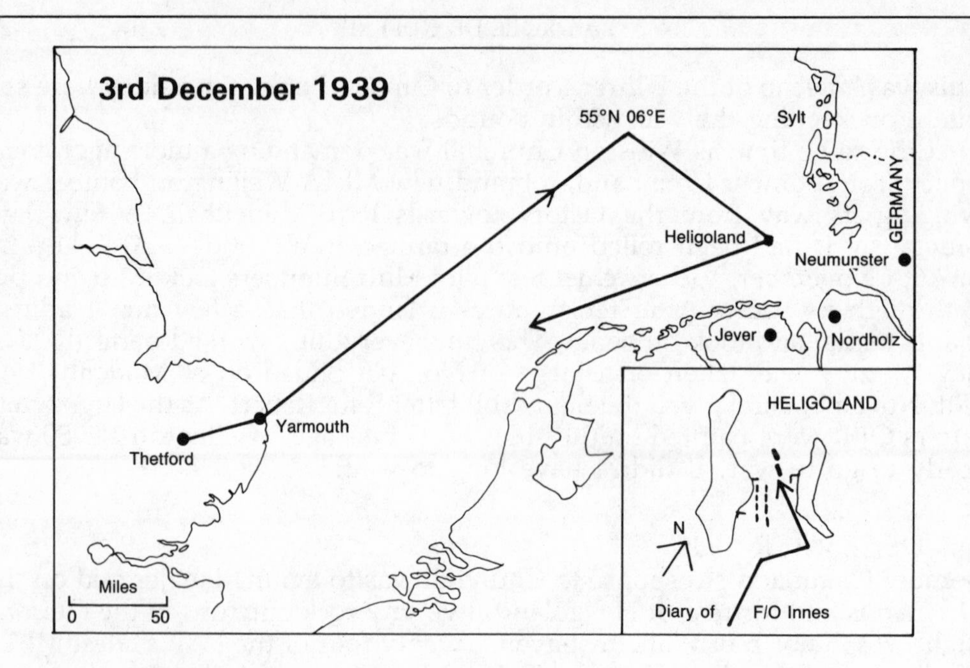


*No. 149 Squadron*

| | |
|---|---|
| N2960 W/Cdr Kellett, AFC | Bombed the two cruisers, all bombs missed. |
| N2892 F/O Turner | Bombed the two cruisers, all bombs missed. |
| N2946 F/Sgt Way | Bombed the two cruisers, all bombs missed. |
| N2893 S/Ldr Harris | Bombed the two cruisers, three hits claimed on one. |
| N2868 F/O Briden | |
| N2943 F/O Bulloch | Attacked by four ME109s, hits claimed on one. |
| N2980 F/Lt Stewart | Made a second attack on a ship outside the harbour. |
| N2945 Sgt Heayes | |
| N2867 F/O Smith | |
| N2984 F/Lt Duguid | Attack baulked by cloud. Returned with bombs on. |
| N2944 F/O Riddlesworth | Returned independently due to petrol running low. |
| N2894 F/Sgt Kelly | |

*Luftwaffe*

4 Me 109Ds of I/JG26 Jever led by Hauptmann Dickore intercepted.
1 Me 109 shot down by Cpl Copley (38 Sq.), Pilot Lt Günter Specht survived.*

| | |
|---|---|
| 4 Me 109Ds of 10(N) /JG26 Jever | Took-off too late |
| 4 Me 109Es of Jagd. Gruppe 101, Neumünster | to intercept the |
| 8 Me 109Es of II(J) /Tr.Gr.186, Nordholz | Wellingtons |
| 8 Me 110Cs of I/ZG26 Jever | Luftwaffe Report |
| | for 4th Dec. '39 |

* Günter Specht lost his left eye in this action but survived and went on to become one of the *Luftwaffe*'s top aces with at least 32 confirmed victories, 15 of which were American four-engined bombers. He was reported missing in action on the 1st January 1945 during 'Operation Bodenplatte'.

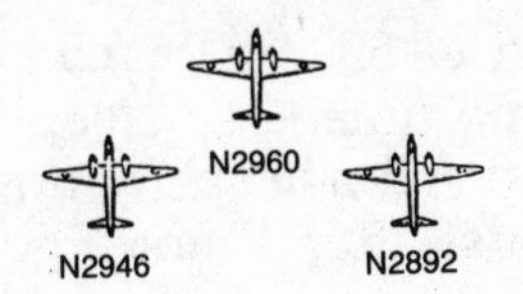


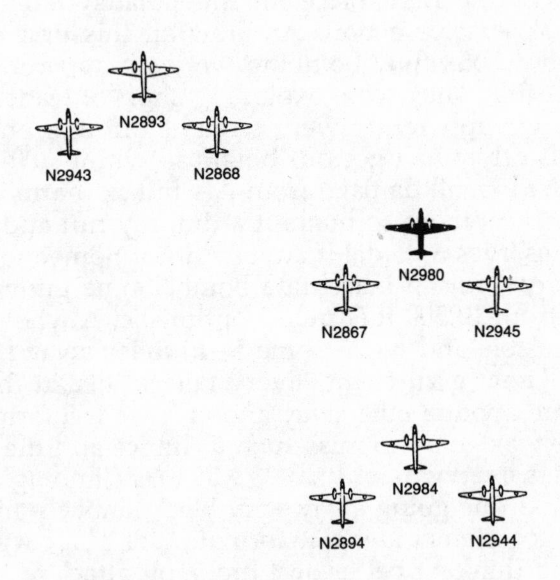


*149 Squadron, 3rd December 1939.*

grand weather 5/10 cloud. Threw out sea markers in case they were hit by bullets and flew on. Suddenly we saw Kellett's formation swing round and at same time got code signal saying that Cruisers were at Heligoland. We swung round after having passed within 2–3 miles of it. Amazing thing we were quite clear, no cloud yet no AA fire. Passing round W side we swung round and ran up to the North. Sure enough there in between the two islands were several ships. So I gave the usual orders for bombing. Amazing thing but it seemed exactly the same as bombing with practice bombs at Berners Heath. Apparently no ac ac fire which seemed odd – into cloud so had to go almost over target before release – I gave usual orders – left left, steady when S/L suggested altering course to avoid AA fire. So we turned right and then left and ran up and bombed. Not a good release for a bit to left of target but when they hit I saw first one bomb over ship by 20–30 yds then in quick succession the remaining three 500 SAP* fell amidship on the ship all three appeared to land at same time – so sleepy.

4.12.39 Dog tired yesterday and fell asleep writing it up. The bombs went off 3 in a bunch and one just after – not a good release – but as it turned out very fortunate for all three appeared to hit direct. Funny thing but I saw the last bomb strike and explode just before the first three – probably due to the three having to pierce the ship before exploding. I don't see how the ship could survive long after that. Unfortunately the clouds came up and though I took photos none of them showed the right place for immediately after release we turned off and took evasive action. Anyhow all this time while I was at the bomb window blissfully bombing we were apparently under the most intense AA fire. They were exploding short of leader and just ahead of us. In fact we apparently went straight through one burst during the run up. Also they had got our height to within 100–200 ft some of the squadron had small damage from AA but no harm. Stewart had cloud at the critical moment so made it a dummy run and came up a second time. He deserves a medal if anyone does. Someone says they blew up a AA battery with an inaccurate bomb. Some gunners even peppered the island from 10,500 ft (2 miles) optimistic. Anyhow we skidaddled as soon as possible and when some 5–10 miles away from island fighters appeared. Great excitement. Every tail gunner in the formation had a go. We were about a mile away and at least 4–5 formations between us but no one was going to miss such a chance and the first we have had, tracer bullets everywhere. I saw 3 Me 109s climbing to attack, then one attacking and one going away with black smoke pouring out so it may have been got. Remainder saw formation of 24 a/c with 4 guns apiece to the rear and thinking better of it broke off attack at least 600 yds away. We were very sick for we want to really test these a/c and turrets. After that there was no more excitement and we arrived home at 1410 after 5h 10m trip. Just late for lunch. Heard today that Marham Sq. saw a direct hit on cruiser – but still no photographs. When we got back, went immediately to Intelligence Officer where questioned, filled in forms, handed in logs etc. I was hauled off to Ops room, questioned by GC then put onto the phone and had to tell it all again to SASO. I couldn't tell much except that it was the largest ship there and I got it. Very tired that night and bed early.

5.12.39 I was thinking this evening on the dangers of aerial bombing. How one does not give a jot to the nature of a target (anyhow for high bombing). All you worry about is that it *is* the target. It might just as well be a mark on the ground. So there is a great danger of bombing targets involving immense loss of life and just because you can't see detail it doesn't worry you one bit. For instance there may have been 200–300

* Semi Armour Piercing.

> on that ship on Sunday and yet am I thinking about them? – No not a bit. War perhaps, but a most impersonal war.

An official source[3] states that the result of this raid was one minesweeper* sunk by a bomb which passed through the bottom of the vessel without exploding, some accidental damage on land to an anti-aircraft gun emplacement and one enemy fighter shot down. Not a single German, service or civilian, was killed in the attack, which a German report describes as 'cleverly delivered from the sun and executed with great certainty in avoiding the residential area of the island.'

Group Captain Harris and Wing Commander Austin both personally confirm that they hit a German warship that day. Bunny Austin relates:

> Again looking at my log-book I find that we did do another operation before the December 18th raid. This was against Heligoland over Heligoland on the third of December and again on this occasion Paul Harris was the skipper and Sandy Innes, Pilot Officer Innes was our second pilot. It was really a successful raid in the sense that the German ship the *Brummer* I think it was, was hit by a salvo of bombs and Sandy Innes did the bombing. I remember that I was a little upset on this particular occasion because Paul ruled that Sandy Innes should do the bombing if the ships were moving and I would do it if the ships were stationary. Before the arrival of Observers, NCO Observers, on the squadrons it had been the practice that the second pilot did the bombing and in all fairness Sandy Innes was a skilful bomb aimer. I think he would be the first to admit that he was extremely lucky, a salvo of bombs actually fell on the rear-end of the *Brummer*. In fact the bomb stick setting was not adjusted correctly and he'd actually salvoed the whole darned lot and he was lucky they hit. This raid led High Command up the garden path a little, although there was a fair amount of anti-aircraft fire we saw fighters but were certainly not seriously attacked and I don't think there were any losses at all, certainly not by our Squadron. Some people I think gained the impression that the Germans held-off because we were too formidable a target, wishful thinking I fear.

The war diary† of the Commander of North Sea Defence (BSN) on 3.12.1939, states that a minesweeper M1407‡ was sunk by a bomb which holed the forward section without exploding. No mention is made of any hits on a cruiser or on an *Artillerieschulschiffe* called '*Brummer*'.

During the action, Squadron Leader Harris's No. 3 aircraft (to the left and behind) became detached from his section and was set upon by four Me 109s. Three did not come any closer than 600 yards but the fourth ventured into

* German Situation Report West No. 104, 4th December 1939, states: 'A lugger was sunk by an unexploded bomb'.

† Bundesarchiv – Militärarchiv: Ref. No. RM61 II/v./M/149/35064.

‡ A converted trawler, formerly called the *JOHANN SCHULTE*

range and was fired at by the ventral and rear gun-turrets. The Me 109 was observed to fall away to one side emitting black smoke but later righted itself before it reached the water and flew off. In the first section, flak damaged Kellett's No. 2 and No. 3 aircraft but did not prevent them from reaching home. Leading Aircraftman J. Copley, in the rear turret of a 38 Squadron Wimpy, first learned of a hostile presence when an armour piercing bullet lodged in the quick release box of his parachute harness. He was credited with shooting down a Messerschmitt that ventured too close and was later awarded the DFM. By accident, a Wellington from 115 Squadron released over land a bomb that had been 'hung-up' in its bomb-bay. By good fortune it hit a military target, an anti-aircraft gun emplacement, the first British bomb of the war to land on German soil. All twenty-four Wellingtons headed for home – four stragglers bringing up the rear.

Back at Mildenhall, Wing Commander Kellett turned to Paul Harris as they strolled away from their aircraft and asked, 'Did I lead all right?' to which Paul Harris replied, 'Go a little slower next time.'

*14th DECEMBER 1939*

In the North Sea, His Majesty's Submarine *Salmon* had torpedoed the German cruisers *Nürnberg* and *Leipzig* the previous day and they were now limping back under their own steam to the safety of Wilhelmshaven.

At this period of the war, Coastal Command had the right to order sweeps as required and now called up Bomber Command to go and finish them off. A large force of Hampdens and Wellingtons were brought to 'stand-by'. The Hampdens took off at dawn on the morning of the 14th but found nothing and returned. Just before 11.45 a.m., twelve Wellingtons from 99 Squadron under the command of Wing Commander J. F. Griffiths, flying in the leading aircraft piloted by Squadron Leader McKee, took off from Newmarket. The weather was bad. As they passed over Yarmouth at 1,000 feet the aircraft were flying just below 10/10 cloud. Proceeding out over the sea, the weather deteriorated. Approaching the Dutch coast just before 1.00 p.m. the squadron had to descend to 600 feet because of low cloud and they flew on through drizzle and fine rain. Experience on 4th September and 3rd December indicated that the fighter defences of North-West Germany were weak and apparently half-hearted. The twelve aircraft were formed up into four sections of three, as 149 Squadron had been on the previous Heligoland raid. Terschilling was sighted at 1.05 p.m., and the formation turned slightly northwards as though heading for Heligoland to put the flak-ships off the scent. They were thought to have been the early warning source on Kellett's raid. Actually the Germans had been using a form of early-warning radar called 'Freya' which had given the defences eight minutes warning of the attack. When they reached the map reference 54°N 07°30'E the squadron swung round in the direction of the Schillig Roads. By now the weather had deteriorated to such an extent that they were flying at only 200 feet above the waves and just below the cloud base. The Wimpys were armed with three 500 lb SAP bombs that had to be dropped from at least two thousand feet to enable them to penetrate armoured decks, and Griffiths had been ordered not to drop his bombs unless he could see his target from that height. At 2.15 p.m., the island of Wangerooge was sighted about two miles dead ahead. The bombers then turned due east and flew parallel to the coast until they spotted a submarine on the surface. The submarine fired a red-ball signal cartridge. In response, Griffiths fired two red signal cartridges on the off-chance that it might be the required recognition signal. The submarine promptly crash-dived. The course was then altered to a north-easterly heading and at 2.25 p.m. two cruisers were observed steaming due south about a mile away. The heading was changed to north to enable Griffiths to fly parallel with the ships so that he could examine them for torpedo damage inflicted by HM Submarine *Salmon* the previous day. One of the cruisers was the *Nürnberg* doing about ten knots, but they passed one another too quickly for any damage assessment to be made. To give himself enough time to prepare for an attack, Griffiths continued to head north then turned in a wide arc to port until his squadron pointed southwards on the same heading as the cruisers. At 2.29 p.m., three escorting destroyers appeared dead ahead. They opened fire immediately on the Wellingtons as they flew overhead at a height of only 200 feet. Five minutes later the two cruisers came into view putting up a fierce barrage of flak from main and secondary armament along with pom-pom fire. Prudently the Wellingtons skirted the cruisers and, knowing that they could not attack with their 500 lb SAP bombs from such a low level, decided to call it a day. The aircraft turned westward towards home and, as the island of Wangerooge loomed up out of the mist half a mile ahead, three tiny specks were observed climbing towards the formation.

Harry von Bülow's Messerschmitts were now stationed on Wangerooge and his new Bf109E-1s were more potent than the Bf109Ds that had intercepted Kellett eleven days earlier. The Messerschmitts formed up in line astern from below and attacked the right-hand aircraft in the last section. Sergeant Brace's aircraft was hit and fell away in flames towards the sea. On his left, Flying Officer Cooper was seen to be in trouble. His undercarriage came down and he broke away from the formation and disappeared into the clouds, heading south towards the German coast. The rear and under turrets of the two rearmost sections blazed away at the attackers. One of the Messerschmitt 109s spiralled down trailing black smoke and was seen by several observers to crash into the sea. From above and behind the leading aircraft of Squadron Leader McKee, a Me 110 dived into the attack and opened fire at a range of 250 yards. In the rear turret, Corporal Bickerstaff aimed his two Brownings and fired directly into the cockpit. Tracers were seen to drill into the fuselage at the pilot's position and emerge out of the other side. The German aircraft burst into flames and was last seen diving towards the sea where it was claimed to have been seen hitting the water. Directly behind the first section, Flight Lieutenant Brough fought-off another Me 110 which was also claimed to have crashed into the sea. Meanwhile in the leading section,

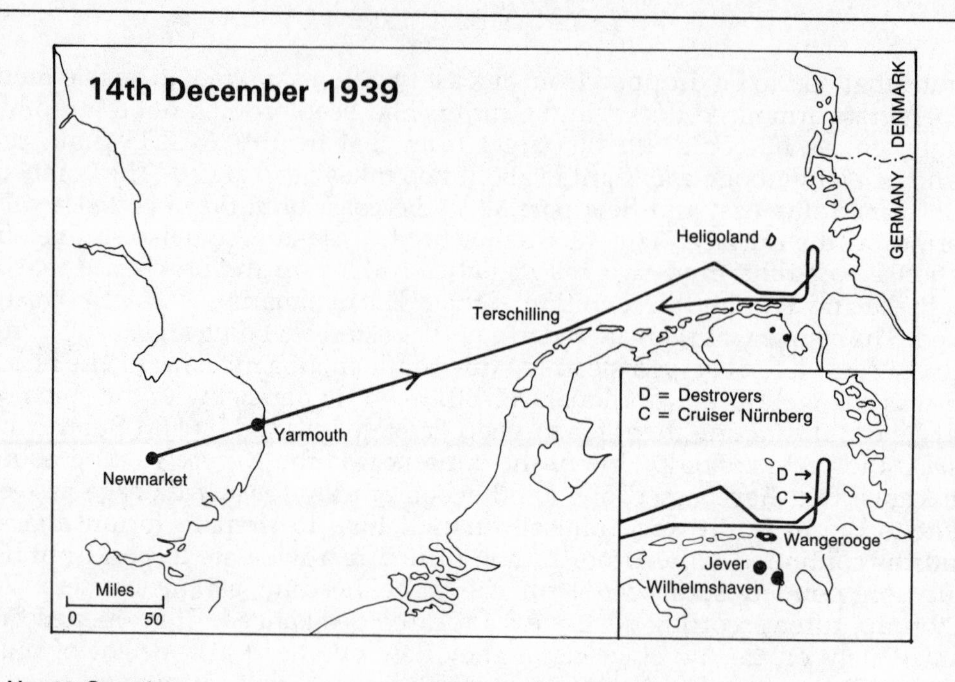


*No. 99 Squadron*

| | |
|---|---|
| N2958 S/Ldr McKee | Claimed a fighter shot down by Cpl Bickerstaff. |
| N2887 F/O Dyer | |
| N2870 P/O Lewis | Collided with N2911 and crashed into the sea. |
| N2913 F/Lt Brough | |
| N2886 F/Sgt Healey | Shot down in flames |
| N2911 F/Sgt Downey | Collided with N2870 and crashed into the sea. |
| N2912 S/Ldr Catt | |
| N2914 F/O Smith | |
| N2999 F/Sgt Williams | |
| N2957 F/Lt Hetherington | Crash landed at Newmarket, three killed including captain. |
| N2986 Sgt Brace | Shot down in flames. Possibly shot down a Me109. |
| N2956 F/O Cooper | Last seen heading for German coast with undercarriage down. |

*Luftwaffe*[4]

II/JG77: 3 Squadrons of Me109E-1s based at Jever.

Staffel 4.

| | |
|---|---|
| Oberleutnant Henz | Claimed one Wellington. |
| Feldwebel Sawallisch | Claimed two Wellingtons. |
| Leutnant Demer | Claimed one Wellington |
| Leutnant Brankmeier | Shot down and killed (possibly by N2986). |

I/ZG26: 1 'Schwarm' (4 aircraft) of Me11OCs at Jever.

Staffel 2.

| | |
|---|---|
| Captain Restemeier (CO) | Claimed one Wellington. His fighter was badly damaged and the pilot was wounded in the head. |
| Hauptgefreiter Schulze | Claimed one Wellington. |

Note: Most history books assert that the RAF first encountered Göring's new Me110 'Destroyers' during the Battle of Heligoland Bight on the 18th of December 1939. In fact, Restemeier's 'Schwarm' of Me110s attacked 99 Squadron on the 14th of December 1939. Two days later, 2/ZG26 was transferred from Jever to Crailsheim (Würzburg area) and was replaced by twenty-three Bf110s of I/ZG76.

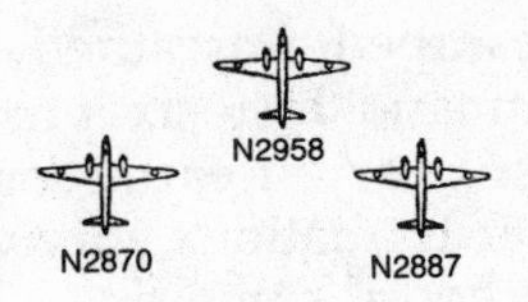


N2913
N2911
N2886

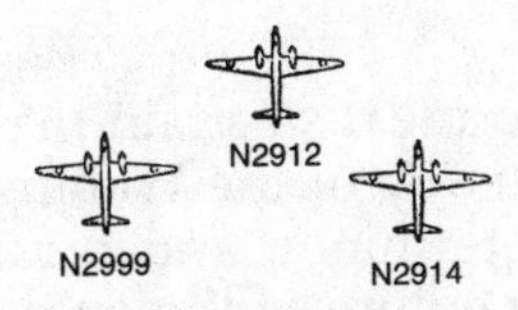


N2957
N2956
N2986

*99 Squadron, 14th December 1939.*

Pilot Officer Lewis's Wellington was observed to falter and turn towards the rear where he collided with the Wellington flown by Flight Sergeant Downey. Both aircraft crashed in the sea. Another Wellington, flown by Flight Sergeant Healey, was seen to be on fire and it heeled over to show the geodetic members on the underside of the aircraft well exposed. Crews in the third section could see four blazing wrecks on the water and at first assumed they were twin-engined Messerschmitt 110s until it was realised that six of the Wellingtons had vanished from the formation. The blazing twin-engined wrecks were Wellingtons, not 110s. Later a Wellington reappeared out of the clouds once they were well on the way home. It was Flight Lieutenant Hetherington, the leader of the ill-fated rear section. The last attack occurred as the now much-depleted formation crossed the Dutch frontier just after 3.00 p.m. Arriving back at Newmarket, six of the Wellingtons landed safely but Hetherington's aircraft had been badly damaged and crashed in a field just off the racecourse killing the pilot and two of his crew.

Yet again the German navy had escaped unscathed. For the price of one fighter shot down, Bomber Command lost six precious Wellingtons and five-and-a-half irreplaceable crews. How on earth could the concept of daylight raids by self-defending bomber formations survive in the face of a loss rate of fifty per cent? The official report[5] came out with this surprising comment:

> After careful analysis of individual reports by all members of crews, it seems almost possible to assume that none of our aircraft were brought down by fire from the Messerschmitts.

Jackie Baldwin who was the cheerful and popular AOC of No.3 Group got it just about correct when he referred to the events of the 14th thus: 'I place it somewhat on a par with the Charge of the Light Brigade.' Air Commodore Norman Bottomley, Bomber Command's Senior Air Staff Officer and the future Deputy Chief of Air Staff from 1941, wrote in his covering letter[5]:

> *Formation Flying*
> It is now by no means certain that enemy fighters did in fact succeed in shooting down any of the Wellingtons. Considering that enemy aircraft made most determined and continuous attacks for 26 minutes on the formation, the failure of the enemy must be ascribed to good formation flying. The maintenance of tight, unshaken formation in the face of the most powerful enemy action is the test of bomber force fighting efficiency and morale. In our Service it is the equivalent of the old 'Thin Red Line' or the 'Shoulder to Shoulder' of Cromwell's Ironsides.

Down at the sharp end, Sandy Innes jotted down some comments in his little notebook.

> 14.12.39 The other side of war with a vengeance tonight – aircraft lost – left right and centre. First of all Jimmy Carter and Forbes Irving came over from Methwold and told us they had lost a plane last night – straight in while night flying. No apparent reason. Three dead. And then tonight came news of 99 and the result of their Sweep in the Heligoland Bight. Clouds 900 feet so too low to bomb though they saw some cruisers. However they came round again in hopes but no good and the fighters came in, Me 110 and 109 Seven attacks delivered, so Germans must have got over their shocks at the dustbins.* We got 3 of them maybe 4 and they got one of ours down. Another one hit which collided, both being lost. Two missing on way back and one went in near Newmarket – total 6 aircraft and about 5½ crews. What a shambles in practically every case it was the unarmoured port wing which caught alight. Why in heavens name they didn't bung on armour there as well beats me.

* dustbins: the name given to the Mk 1A Wellington's ventral (underneath) gun turret.

With six aircraft lost out of a force of twelve, the part played by the German fighter defences should have been the subject of the closest scrutiny. Comments in Bottomley's letter[5] such as '. . . it is remarkable that our casualties were so light' and 'Had it not been for good leadership, losses from enemy aircraft might have been heavy' do not seem to tally with the facts.

1. The surviving Wellingtons (including Hetherington's) were found to be full of *bullet* holes.
2. The report[5] clearly states: 'Enemy fighters were difficult to see when below near the sea, owing to the overcast sky, poor visibility and the effective camouflaging of the upper surfaces of the aircraft'.
3. At least three Wellingtons were *seen* to have been brought down by the action of enemy fighters. (Sandy Innes's diary)

So the myth of the Wellington's invulnerability to fighter attack when flying in 'tight, unshaken formations' was to be upheld – for another four days anyhow:

> It may be argued that Wellington formations are quite capable of defending themselves successfully against fighter attack. That is certainly true . . .[5]

The culprit on the 14th was decreed as flak. Henceforth, daylight raids on heavily defended targets would take place from heights out of range of anti-aircraft guns.

Across the North Sea, the *Luftwaffe* report was more precise. *Lagebericht** West No. 115, *Luftwaffe* HQ, 15th December 1939 states:

> German pilots registered 5 kills, plus one probable but unconfirmed kill. One German fighter shot down.

The German naval flak gunners did not submit one single claim for an aircraft shot down.

> At 3 p.m. on the afternoon of 17th December, Baldwin telephoned on the scrambler to Air Commodore Bottomley at Bomber Command HQ at High Wycombe, to urge a further operation against the German fleet.
>
> The Group Commander pointed out the importance of seizing the very first suitable day in view of the few such occasions which were likely to present themselves under winter conditions. He stated that from the point of view of preparation, the details of the plan had been thoroughly considered by all concerned, and he was satisfied that if Monday 18th December were given as zero day, there would be no undue haste in planning and preparation right down to the crews engaged.
>
> Air Chief Marshal Sir Edgar Ludlow-Hewitt, C-in-C Bomber Command, concurred. He approved Baldwin's proposal to mount a new

* Situation Report.

attack on the German fleet at Wilhelmshaven on the 18th, subject only to a proviso that the Wellingtons bomb from at least 10,000 feet, which should take them above effective flak. Group Captain Goodwin, SASO at 3 Group HQ, drafted orders for the operation to be carried out by twenty-four Wellingtons. Nine aircraft would come from 149 Squadron at Mildenhall, including that of the formation leader, Wing Commander Richard Kellett, who had also led the 3rd December sweep; nine would come from 9 Squadron at Honington; the remaining six from 37 Squadron at Feltwell. 'Task: to attack enemy warships in the Schillig Roads or Wilhelmshaven', began the Operation Order. 'Great care is to be taken that no bombs fall on shore, and no merchant ships are to be attacked. Formations shall not loiter in the target area, and all aircraft are to complete bombing as soon as possible after the sighting signal has been made.'

'Not only did I have all the leaders into the Operations Room the night before the mission went out,' wrote Baldwin to Ludlow-Hewitt a few days later, 'but I personally explained to each of them my ideas on formation flying and what I meant by mutual assistance, and they all professed that they agreed and understood.'

Late in the afternoon of Sunday the 17th, the order went out to the squadrons taking part in the operation to stand-by at two hours notice for take-off from 0730 hours on the morning of the 18th. Pilots and observers were briefed by squadron and station commanders. Before dawn on the 18th, a Whitley of 4 Group, from 78 Squadron at Dishforth in Yorkshire, flew out across the North Sea, approaching the island of Heligoland at 0800 in patchy cloud, ideal cover for a daylight bomber operation. The crew signalled their weather report, and turned homewards towards England. 3 Group HQ passed the final readiness order to the Wellington squadrons: take-off would be at 0930; squadrons would take up formation over King's Lynn before crossing the North Sea. The attack on Wilhelmshaven was on.[6]

The first full-scale fleet engagement of World War II was less than six hours away. Over that self-same little bit of North Sea where the *Arethusa* had chased the *Stettin* and *Frauenlob* a quarter of a century before, a fleet of Messerschmitts would shortly tear into a fleet of Wellington bombers. In this forthcoming battle, the Royal Air Force would be the first to learn that daylight raids over heavily defended targets were untenable and seek safety in the hours of darkness.

It was not until December (1939) that the Wellingtons were again involved in serious encounter with the German air defences and, from the point of view of the effect which they had upon subsequent operations, the three actions which were fought on 3rd, 14th and 18th December were among the most important of the war.[7]

# 4

## *No. 149 (East India) Squadron – Mildenhall*

'F for Freddie' was a very famous film star in 1941. Those of us who were around at the time will have no difficulty in remembering the name of the picture that featured this celebrity. If, as is more likely, that era is familiar only through the pages of history books or post-war films, then 'F for Freddie' was a Wellington bomber of No. 149 Squadron based at Mildenhall. The name of the film was *Target for Tonight* and it was made at a time when the morale of the nation was at a very low ebb. We stood alone. Poland, Norway, Denmark, Holland, Belgium and France had all fallen under the heel of the Nazi jackboot. Only the Battle of Britain had saved us from a similar fate. Huge areas of London, Coventry, Clydebank and many other cities lay in ruins. Over four million tons of our shipping had been sent to the bottom between June 1940 and March 1941. We dearly wanted to know that we could 'give it' as well as 'take it'.

Along to our local cinema came *Target for Tonight*. There, we were treated to the spectacle of a 'typical' RAF raid on an enemy rail junction and secret fuel dump. Our spirits soared as 'F for Freddie' dived through a hail of tracer shells and flak to drop its bombs – bang on target. We thrilled as the young bomb aimer pressed the 'tit' and reported 'bombs gone'. But it was all pure hokum. There is no record of 'F for Freddie' ever having been used operationally. In a secret report to the Air Ministry on 18th August 1941 it was revealed that Bomber Command was lucky to get one bomb in ten within *five miles* of its target. Fortunately for national morale, the Butt Report and its scandalous findings were kept secret. Every night as we gathered round the wireless to listen to Alvar Liddell, Bruce Belfrage, or John Snagge read the nine o'clock news, names like Mannheim, Gelsenkirchen, Frankfurt, Hamburg, Cologne, Essen and Dortmund became synonymous with our growing determination to repay Hitler for the havoc he had wrought. Satisfaction at hearing the marshalling yards at Hamm had been bombed (yet again) was always tinged with apprehension as we waited to hear the price that had been paid. The news that 'One of our aircraft is missing' always brought forth a sigh and a shake of the head; secretly we hoped it was not 'F for Freddie'. Hokum perhaps, but in 1941 'Target for Tonight' was immensely popular and just what the doctor ordered. So what if 'F for Freddie' never fired a shot in anger? It was worth its weight in gold. No. 149 Squadron probably did more for the war effort with that one film than all the bombs it had dropped on Germany up till then. Though only acting in the film, the pilot of 'F for Freddie', Group Captain P. C. Pickard, DSO DFC, later played the role of real life hero when he led his Mosquito squadron in the legendary attack on Amiens prison in 1944. Sadly he did not survive the attack.

It is not surprising that No. 149 Squadron should have been chosen to lift the nation's spirits in 1941. The squadron had played a prominent role in a much earlier propaganda film made during the early days of the Phoney War. This film was called *The Lion has Wings*, and starred Ralph Richardson and Merle Oberon. Films made during the war portraying the exploits of Bomber Command are very few and far between. After the war, cinema audiences were deluged with celluloid re-runs of the stiff-upper-lip exploits of the RAF and the rather less formal missions of the USAAF. Without doubt the most famous of all these post-war films was *The Dam Busters*. Made with the benefit of hindsight it provides a realistic insight into the workings of Bomber Command in 1943. By then the threads were beginning to be pulled together. Experienced aircrews, radio-navigation, four-engined heavyweight bombers, all combined to fulfil Lord Trenchard's vision of the RAF as a powerful strategic weapon of war. Over four years the RAF matured into a dedicated, highly professional and, above all, lethal organisation. How different things were in 1939. *The Lion has Wings* grants us a rare glimpse into the past. It allows us to see the RAF as it was in the beginning. Present-day audiences, conditioned by slick camera work and spectacular special effects, would find it more than a little hammy if not downright hilarious in places. The important thing is not to look at the actors but at the faces of the airmen, young, eager and – dare one say it – naïve. These were faces that belonged on the school rugby pitch or bending over the oars as Oxford and Cambridge pulled for the finishing line. Paul Harris is there, laughing and joking with his comrades as they stand by their Wimpys in mock readiness to take off and teach the jolly old Hun a lesson. Less than a month after the film was released in November, those same young innocent faces climbed aboard their aircraft in earnest and headed out over the North Sea towards Wilhelmshaven where the jolly old Hun shot them out of the sky.

Number 149, along with 9, 37, 38, 99 and 115, made up the operational squadrons of No. 3 Bomber Group together with 214 and 215 squadrons in reserve. Formed initially as a night bomber group equipped with Handley Page Heyfords, Handley Page Harrows and Fairey Hendons, there had been no requirement and hence no training for formation flying. By the summer of 1939 the group had been re-equipped with the Vickers Wellington Mk1, and its role suddenly switched to that of day bombing in preparation for carrying out the Ruhr Plan.

That summer of 1939 saw Europe having a fit of the jitters. To counter the massive propaganda the Germans were giving their *Luftwaffe*, the Air Ministry instructed No. 3 Group to lay on a series of formation flights over Europe for the purpose of 'Showing the Flag' and helping to bolster French morale. Selected squadrons did three flights to Marseilles and one to Bordeaux, flew over Paris on Bastille Day and put in an appearance at the XXVth International Aviation Exhibition in Brussels where the RAF pilots warily exchanged chivalrous compliments with their *Luftwaffe* counterparts. The results of this flag-waving exercise were most revealing. Out of all the squadrons that took part, only two could fly in perfect formation, No. 9 and No. 214. All the others gave the impression of competing in a race with some squadrons scattered all over the sky and showing little semblance of any formation at all. The problem stemmed from the fact that every squadron had its own ideas and whimsies about formation flying. Every squadron acted independently and subscribed to one of two schools of thought. The first held that a formation of bombers should fly as tightly together as possible thereby forfeiting individual manoeuvrability but gaining the advantage of mutual supportive cross-fire from the power operated turrets of the nearby aircraft. Number 214 Squadron belonged to this school of thought. The alternative school felt that bomber formations should only be held together loosely thereby retaining the manoeuvrability of individual aircraft albeit at the expense of mutual support. (Apart from this it took a great deal of skill and concentration to hold a group of bombers in tight formation.) One of the few joint exercises with Fighter Command did nothing to convince the 'loose formation' school of the immense superiority in speed and manoeuvrability of modern fighters.

Another problem confronting the group was that many of their Squadron COs were of 1914–18 vintage and did no flying whatever. As a consequence they had no experience or knowledge of modern, fast, well-armed bombers or how to deploy them. The lessons of the formation flights over France were ignored.

On 28th August 1939 one of the Flight Commanders who had led No. 214 Squadron to Marseilles and Bordeaux in July was posted from 214 reserve squadron at Feltwell to be Flight Commander of 'B' Flight in 149 operational squadron at Mildenhall. His name was Squadron Leader Paul Harris. He had had five years experience of flying in Egypt, Palestine and the Sudan and was a firm believer in the tight formation theory. As was customary in those days he requested that his crew be transferred with him, and his navigator, Bunny Austin, has this to say.

> Paul himself was a highly respected Flight Commander. He was rather more serious perhaps than most officers at that time perhaps because, at 32, he was a little older than the average. He commanded considerable respect from all because of his ability and his modest manner. He was a stickler for discipline and insisted that the crew practised at all times their safety procedures. An interesting side light on that, rather typical of Paul, he was larger than the average and with his Irvin flying jacket on had the greatest difficulty in getting through the escape hatch which

> was underneath the Wellington. We had a special drill for this, I recall it vividly. The drill was that the rest of the crew went first then Paul would leave the controls, get down into the escape hatch and I would put both feet firmly on his shoulders and I would push him through the escape hatch and I would then follow.

Peacetime drills and exercises suddenly became for real at 11 a.m. hours on 3rd September 1939. Britain declared war on Germany.

At 5 p.m., No. 149 Squadron received orders to send twelve aircraft to attack part of the German fleet reported in the North Sea. An hour-and-a-half later three Wellingtons of 'A' Flight led by Squadron Leader H. I. Dabinett took off to commence the operation. Ten minutes later the remaining nine Wellingtons from 'A' Flight had their take off cancelled on orders from Group Headquarters. For three-and-a-half hours Squadron Leader Dabinett and his three aircraft searched for the elusive German fleet but could not find it because of adverse weather conditions and approaching darkness. Dabinett, Turner and Way dropped their bombs in the sea and headed home for Mildenhall. Next day, 4th September, the two battle cruisers were reported at Brunsbüttel and it was the turn of 'B' Flight under the command of Squadron Leader Harris.

Of 149 Squadron's eight aircraft that headed out over the North Sea towards Brunsbüttel on that first raid, five turned back early having lost formation in low cloud, leaving their Flight Commander and two others to press on to the target. In the event, the Vickers gun-turrets proved useless because the sights did not follow the guns and the ammunition belts were forever getting stuck in the ducts. Flight Lieutenant Stewart's Wimpy developed a leak in a fuel tank and had to make a forced landing at Honington. Valuable lessons had been learned. Better gun-turrets, stricter discipline and self-sealing fuel tanks were top of the priority list. In the three months' lull between 4th September and 3rd December two of the problems were put right. The Mk1s were replaced by Mk1As and the squadron got a new Commanding Officer. Nothing was done about the vulnerable fuel tanks. During the lull, 149 Squadron practised formation flying. Squadron Leader Harris was a fully qualified flying instructor with eight years' flying experience behind him, five having been spent operationally in the Middle East. Promoted to Squadron Leader in Flying Training Command in February 1939, he had to leave because there was no appointment for him. Had he not left the Command before the outbreak of war he would probably never have got out, as flying instructors were 'frozen' because they were needed so desperately. A firm believer in the 'tight formation' philosophy, he set about ensuring that all *his* aircraft could defend themselves. Another problem that occupied his mind was bombing accuracy. At the time, the *Luftwaffe* Ju87B-1 'Stukas' were enjoying tremendous success as high-accuracy dive bombers, and this, thought Paul Harris, was the way to sink a battleship. The story is taken up by his navigator, Bunny Austin.

> Paul was particularly keen that we should improve our bombing and our gunnery and on every conceivable occasion he could, we went to Berners Heath, the local range, and practised. Paul had a lot of courage and obviously a lot of conviction that the Wellington was a magnificent aeroplane which indeed it was. He certainly believed that it could operate as a dive bomber and on one particular occasion over Berners Heath in that September, in fact I see from my Log Book that it was 21st September, we were practising high altitude dive bombing which he, on each dive, made steeper and steeper. My job was to stand in the Astrodome and watch the aeroplane to see that we were not losing any fabric from the wings as we got steeper and steeper. On the final dive, a tremendous sheet of fabric on our top main plane burst out and we had to limp back to Mildenhall with both wings severely damaged. I think Paul lost some of his enthusiasm thereafter for high altitude dive bombing.

As the Mk1s were put out to grass, they were replaced by the very latest Mark 1As having new turrets produced by Frazer-Nash, and in this respect 149 Squadron was particularly fortunate. Archie Frazer-Nash frequently drove up in his Bentley and climbed aboard Paul Harris's new Mk1A to be taken up to test the three turrets and their Browning machine-guns. Occasionally Archie Frazer-Nash's partner, Captain E. G. Thompson, would go up as well and do a bit of experimenting. Many of the bugs were ironed out on these flights and AC1 Doxsey in the front turret, AC1 Mullineaux in the rear turret and Sergeant Austin in the ventral turret picked up a lot of valuable experience on how to operate and look after their defensive armament. The retractable ventral turret was intended as defence for the underside of the aircraft. Capable of rotating a full 360° when lowered, it could also fire two degrees above the horizontal when trained aft, very useful in backing up the rear gunner against attacks from astern. Unfortunately it knocked 15 knots off the aircraft's speed just when it was needed most and demanded additional power from the engines when it could be least afforded.

After three months of comparative inactivity pressure started to build up for some kind of response from Bomber Command to Churchill's call for action. As November drew to its close, the first indication that something was afoot became apparent when 149 Squadron got a new Commanding Officer, Wing Commander Kellett, AFC. Richard Kellett was very well known in aviation circles, having won the World Long Distance record with the RAF Long-Range Development Flight in 1938. This feat had been a great boost for British aviation in what were otherwise pretty depressing times. On 5th November 1938, Squadron Leader Kellett led a flight of three Vickers Wellesley monoplanes from Ismailia in Egypt to Darwin in Australia, non-stop. Adverse winds caused one Wellesley, piloted by Flight Lieutenant H. A. V. Hogan, to land at Koepang in Timor to refuel. The two remaining Wellesleys, piloted by Sqn Leader Kellett and Flight Lieutenant A. N. Combe, reached Darwin on 7th November having flown 7,162 miles in just over 48 hours. In 1938 this was an incredible feat.

Wing Commander Kellett had scarcely settled into his new command when he received orders on 2nd December to prepare his squadron (together with 38 and 115 squadrons) for a major raid on the German island fortress of Heligoland. Winston Churchill's call for more vigorous action was to be answered and next day the weather promised well. The outcome of that raid gave much encouragement to Bomber Command and appeared to vindicate their policy of self-defending formations tackling heavily defended targets in daylight. The few German fighters that had turned up seemed unable to shoot down any of the bombers. Were enemy fighters impotent against power-operated turrets in tightly packed formation? Was this proof of one of the cornerstones of Bomber Command policy: 'The bomber will always get through'? That day everything certainly seemed to point to those conclusions.

Exactly a week after getting back safely from Heligoland Paul Harris took charge of 'R for Robert'. This was the same aircraft in which Flight Lieutenant Stewart had so bravely turned back for a second try at the German cruisers on the 3rd. Training was resumed in their new aircraft, and that day they took off with Pilot Officer Swift as second pilot to practise formation flying, air firing and high-level bombing. They did the same again three days later, this time with Pilot Officer Innes as second pilot and practising low-level bombing. The mood changed abruptly however when the news of 99's heavy losses filtered through on the night of the 14th. They now perceived that the events on the 3rd at Heligoland had been a fluke. Next time they might not be so lucky. Sandy Innes jotted down his thoughts in his little notebook.

> 15.12.39 Naval Officers arriving to stay here. There is a really big push coming off shortly. An auspicious moment to think of it after Thursdays effort. However given reasonable conditions it shouldn't be too bad. Apparently only five people know what it is. I would like to know but could guess pretty well I think.

On the morning of the 17th, Paul Harris opened his Sunday newspaper over breakfast to reveal the headlines:

> THE KING HONOURS GRAF SPEE VICTORS
>
> Commodore Harwood, leader of the attack on the German pocket battleship *Admiral Graf Spee,* Knighted and promoted Rear-Admiral. Captains of the cruisers, *Achilles, Ajax, Exeter* – Companions of the Order of the Bath.

After breakfast Paul Harris and his crew climbed aboard 'R for Robert' and took off to do some more training in formation flying and high-level bombing. After landing, Sandy Innes opened his notebook and wrote one line:

> 17.12.39 Tomorrow's the day – Stand by from 7 a.m. Soon know now.

That evening, Wing Commander Kellett and Squadron Leader Harris were summoned to Group Headquarters along with the Squadron Commanders and Section Leaders of 9 and 37 Squadrons for a briefing. In the words of a later 3 Group report: 'He (the Group Commander) stated that from the point of view of preparation, the details of the plan had been thoroughly considered by all concerned. . . .'*

Richard Kellett, the officer detailed to lead the raid, was a newcomer to 149 Squadron. He had never flown with 9 or 37 Squadrons before as a group. He had never had a chance to practise formation flying or bombing with the other two squadrons he was to lead. He had never been given the opportunity to discuss or formulate any kind of plan for bombing or fighting, whether as a group or by squadrons or by flights. Neither had he been given time to discuss the tactics to be followed in the event of fighter attacks. In short, he was not given the chance to impose his will on what was otherwise an incoherent assortment of squadrons. In particular, one of the squadrons he was to lead had never faced the enemy before, and had a non-flying Commanding Officer who believed in the 'loose formation' theory and intended experimenting with a new kind of formation – flying stepped down in pairs – on their first-ever encounter with the enemy. As Paul Harris later said, 'Group Headquarters laid on no Group formation training – a fatal error.'

As it transpired, two chance remarks were to prevent the forthcoming raid from degenerating into a total massacre. After the 3rd December raid Kellett had asked if he had led all right, to which Paul Harris had replied, 'Go a little slower next time.'

At the briefing on the evening of 17th December, Paul Harris was told that Flight Lieutenant Peter Grant would be flying with him with three of No. 9 Squadron's aircraft. This was the first time they had ever flown together and Paul Harris's parting words to Peter Grant were, 'Stay close to me whatever happens.'

* Comment by Group Captain Paul Harris – 'What utter rubbish.'

*No. 149 (East India) Squadron*

Badge: A horseshoe and a flash of lightning interlaced.

Motto: *Fortis nocte* ('Strong by night')

Authority: King George VI, February 1938.

The horseshoe is indicative of good fortune in the First World War when the squadron flew extensive operations with the loss of only one pilot and observer. A further reason for the horseshoe is that much of the squadron's work was in connection with the cavalry. The flash of lightning is symbolic of the speed with which work was done during a comparatively brief history.

*No. 9 Squadron*

Badge: A bat.

Motto: *Per noctem volamus* ('Throughout the night we fly')

Authority: King Edward VIII, November 1936.

Unofficial World War II name: 'Ipswich's "own" squadron'.

*No. 37 Squadron*

Badge: A hawk hooded, belled and jessed, wings elevated and addorsed.

Motto: 'Wise without eyes'

Authority: King George VI, April 1943.

This badge is indicative of the duties of blind flying.

# 5

## *The Battle of Heligoland Bight*

It was the season of 'Peace on Earth, Good Will Toward Men'. Christmas Eve was less than a week away. It was also the coldest winter on record for half a century. At Boulogne the Channel froze. In places the ground temperature dropped to forty below and tins of anti-freeze solidified. That morning of the eighteenth of December 1939, *The Times* headlined: *GRAF SPEE* SCUTTLED WITHOUT A FIGHT.

At Mildenhall the weather was overcast, mainly cloudy with visibility between two and four miles. In accordance with Group Operations Order B. 60 dated 17th December 1939, Wellington bomber N2960 took off at 9.27 a.m., with W/Cdr Richard Kellett AFC at the controls. Next was N2892 piloted by F/O F. W. S. Turner, followed by N2962 flown by F/O J. H. C. Speirs.

Waiting his turn at the head of the runway sat Paul Harris at the controls of N2980. The windsock indicated a 10–20 mph wind from the east north east. As he sat there with his hand on the throttles his mind flashed back to the time almost twenty-five years before when, as a small boy of eight, he had been walking down a country lane near Oxford one day in 1915. Suddenly, over the hedge flew an aeroplane – narrowly missing the little lad as he gazed up in open-mouthed wonder. At that instant he knew what he wanted to be more than anything else in the world – an aeroplane pilot. As soon as he was the right age he applied to Cranwell but his mathematics let him down. Reluctantly he chose the Law as his profession and qualified as a Solicitor in 1930 but his heart just wasn't in it. In the summer of 1931 he tried the RAF again. This time fortune smiled on him and he was accepted for a Short Service Commission. Starting at No. 2 Flying Training School at Digby in December of that year he was already a fortnight over the top age limit, but Europe was unsettled and the RAF desperately needed good pilots. At the Commissioning Board his keenness carried the day and a blind eye was turned on the fact that he was over age.

In a Wellington the second pilot sat on a folding seat to the right of the pilot. P/O Herome Alexander Innes came from a service family. His father had been the Commanding Officer of the 2nd Battalion of the Black Watch. The army though was not for Sandy because he had always longed to be a pilot. Upon leaving school (Rugby) he joined the General Accident, Fire and Life

Assurance Company Limited but slowly came to the conclusion that office life did not suit his temperament. He was the outdoor type and loved a day on the hill with his shotgun and his dog Astra or driving his little MG round the Perthshire countryside or better still, skiing in the Alps. Towering above all, however, was his passion to fly. In 1938 he joined the Royal Air Force. From Peterborough he was posted to Stradishall and thence to No. 214 Squadron at Feltwell. There he joined Paul Harris's crew flying Handley Page Harrow bombers. As it became more obvious that war was on the way, crews were transferred from the highly trained and disciplined 214 Squadron to less well prepared operational squadrons. Along with the rest of Paul Harris's crew he was posted to No. 149 Squadron at Mildenhall – 'to hot up the squadron's formation flying and prepare it for battle.'

The wireless operator sat in a tiny compartment directly behind the pilot. AC1 'Jock' Watson was a very quiet pleasant young chap, never known to flap and too self-effacing to catch the eye, but his skill as a wireless operator was quite exceptional. One of Paul Harris's original crew from 214, he rarely engaged in social mixing but had an affinity for a pint of good beer.

The navigator sat in his own little cubicle behind the wireless operator. He also doubled as the gunner in the ventral turret and occasionally as bomb aimer. Sgt Austin was never referred to as anything other than 'Bunny' (after the pre-war tennis champion 'Bunny' Austin). His father was a Warrant Officer in the RAF and his son decided to carry on the tradition, joining as a wireless operator/mechanic apprentice in 1932. On passing out in 1935 he was posted to No. 16 Squadron where, to his delight, he became an air-gunner almost immediately. His one aim was to fly and his sights were set on becoming an air-observer. After a tour of duty with No. 36 Squadron in Singapore he returned to Britain where he eventually joined Paul Harris's crew in 214 Squadron, transferring to 149 Squadron three days before the Germans invaded Poland.

The tail gunner sat in isolation at the rear of the aircraft. Politely referred to as 'Tail-End-Charlie', his was the loneliest job of all without even a parachute for company. AC1 Jimmy Mullineaux had falsified his age to join the RAF. On leaving school he started work in a Birmingham factory only to find that he wasn't happy there. He left to get a job in another factory but once again left after a short stay. A third try at factory life convinced him that he was not cut out for that kind of life so, unbeknown to his parents, he joined the RAF in 1937. There he was truly happy.

The front gun turret was manned by AC1 Doxsey. He was very young and was the only one who had not transferred from 214 Squadron as part of the original crew. All gunners were volunteer ground crew and no special emphasis was placed on their training. There were no Gunnery Leaders then and the only training they got amounted to what they picked up on training flights or actual missions. Very occasionally they were allowed to fire 200 rounds on training flights, but otherwise they spent their time attending to their ground duties.

'R for Robert' was clear for take-off. Paul dragged his thoughts back to the matter in hand and eased the throttle levers gently forward. The two Pegasus XVIII engines responded and N2980 turned into the wind and gathered speed down the runway. By the time the wheels had cleared the ground and been retracted into their housing in the engine nacelles, N2943 with F/O H. L. Bulloch at the controls was lined up at the head of the runway. Behind him waited F/O M. F. Briden in N2961. The remaining three Wellingtons, N2984 piloted by F/Lt A. G. Duguid, N2866 piloted by F/O A. F. Riddlesworth and N2894 piloted by F/Sgt Kelly, followed three minutes later. No. 149 Squadron was airborne and circled over Mildenhall aerodrome as it waited for the rest of the formation.

At Honington, twelve miles away, the scene was repeated exactly as No. 9 Squadron's nine aircraft took off. The two squadrons joined up over Mildenhall and set course for King's Lynn. Feltwell's six Wellingtons were late. They missed the rendezvous and caught up with the main formation about an hour later, a hundred miles out over the North Sea. The course set from the Wash was 040° True, as far as Latitude 55° North. The plan was to avoid the concentration of flak ships around the Frisian Islands, thought to have been the source of early warning on previous raids. As they climbed steadily to 14,000 feet, Paul observed with some concern that the broken cloud over England was gradually thinning out. By the time 37 Squadron caught up, the cloud had disappeared completely and left them in a bright, crystal clear sky. Looking out of his cockpit Paul estimated that he could see as far as fifty miles – not a good omen, for German fighters would have no trouble in spotting them. Sgt Hough, in the lead aircraft, completed his calculations and informed his pilot, W/Cdr Kellett, that they had reached their first turning point. The compass was set to a new heading of 091° True. As they droned steadily eastwards at a speed of one hundred and forty miles an hour, Jimmy tried traversing his turret and noticed how sluggish it had become. The hydraulic oil was thickening up in the freezing temperature. It was one of the coldest winters on record and everyone onboard 'R for Robert' was becoming acutely aware of the numbing December chill. Bunny hugged his Irvin jacket tight about him as the icy draughts spilled in through the turret gaps and blew relentlessly down the unheated fuselage.

It was just coming up for noon when Paul glanced out of his cockpit and saw two Wellingtons peel away from Kellett's formation and head for home. F/Lt Duguid, leading the second vic in the first formation, was having trouble maintaining the revs on his starboard engine. With his speed dropping he could no longer hold position so he ordered Sgt Murdoch to send a signal by Aldis lamp to his No. 2 and No. 3. Off on his starboard side, F/O Riddlesworth dutifully obeyed and closed up on Kellett. F/Sgt Kelly could not have noticed Duguid's signal because he too broke away from the formation and followed the ailing Wimpy down and on to the heading for the homeward journey. N2984 and N2894 arrived back at Mildenhall a little before

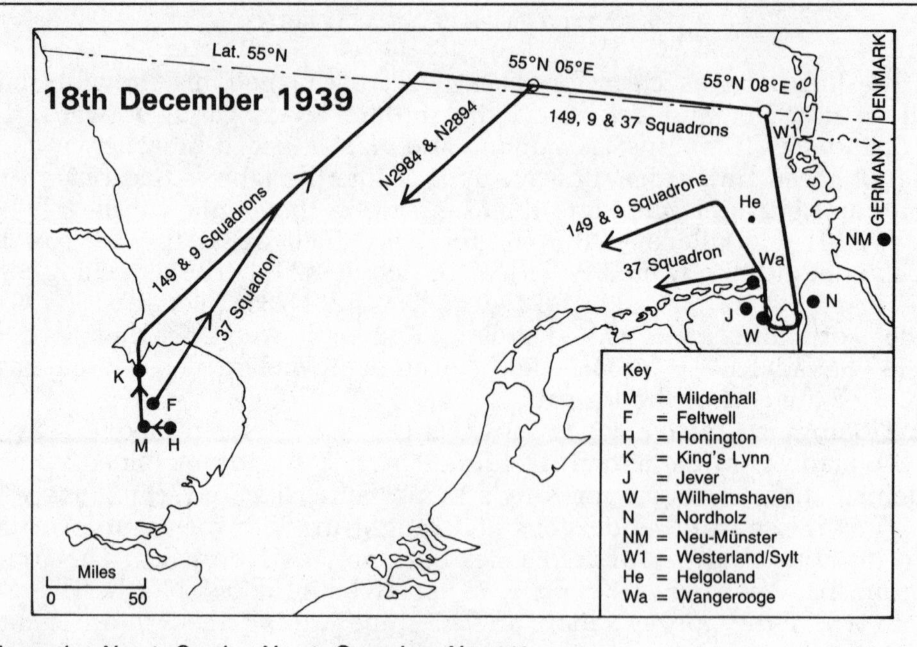


*Formation No. 1, Section No. 1. Squadron No. 149*

| | |
|---|---|
| N2960 W/C Kellett | Landed Mildenhall 1600 hrs. |
| N2892 F/O Turner | Landed Mildenhall 1610 hrs. |
| N2962 F/O Speirs | Shot down, no survivors. |

*Formation No. 1, Section No. 2. Squadron No. 149*

| | |
|---|---|
| N2984 F/Lt Duguid | Returned Mildenhall early. Reported engine trouble. |
| N2866 F/O Riddlesworth | Landed Mildenhall 1600 hrs. |
| N2894 F/Sgt Kelly | Returned Mildenhall early. Accompanied N2984 back. |

*Formation No. 2, Section No. 1. Squadron No. 149* (+ 500 ft on Formation No. 1)

| | |
|---|---|
| N2980 S/Ldr Harris | Landed Coltishall 1600 hrs. |
| N2943 F/O Bulloch | Landed Mildenhall 1600 hrs. |
| N2961 F/O Briden | Ditched near Cromer Knoll, no survivors. |

*Formation No. 2, Section No. 2. Squadron No. 9* (+ 500 ft on Formation No. 1)

| | |
|---|---|
| N2964 F/Lt Grant | Landed Honington 1600 hrs. |
| N2981 Sgt Purdy | Landed Honington 1600 hrs. |
| N2983 Sgt Ramshaw | Ditched 100 miles from the Wash, 4 survivors. |

*Formation No. 3, Section No. 1. Squadron No. 9* (+ 500 ft on Formation No. 1)

| | |
|---|---|
| N2872 S/Ldr Guthrie | Shot down, no survivors. |
| N2871 F/O Macrae | Landed North Coates Fitties, 1600 hrs. |
| N2873 Sgt Petts | Landed Sutton Bridge, 1600 hrs. |

*Formation No. 3, Section No. 2. Squadron No. 9* (+ 500 ft on Formation No. 1)

| | |
|---|---|
| N2941 F/O Allison | Shot down, no survivors. |
| N2940 P/O Lines | Shot down, no survivors. |
| N2939 F/O Challes | Shot down, no survivors. |

*Formation No. 4, In pairs, stepped down, Squadron No. 37* (+ 1000 ft on Formation No. 1)

| | |
|---|---|
| N2904 S/Ldr Hue-Williams | Shot down, no survivors. |
| N2903 F/O Lemon | Landed Feltwell, 1540 hrs. |
| N2888 F/O Wimberley | Shot down, 1 survivor. |
| N2889 F/O Lewis | Shot down, no survivors. |
| N2935 F/O Thompson | Shot down, no survivors. |
| N2936 Sgt Ruse | Shot down on the island of Borkum, 3 survivors. |

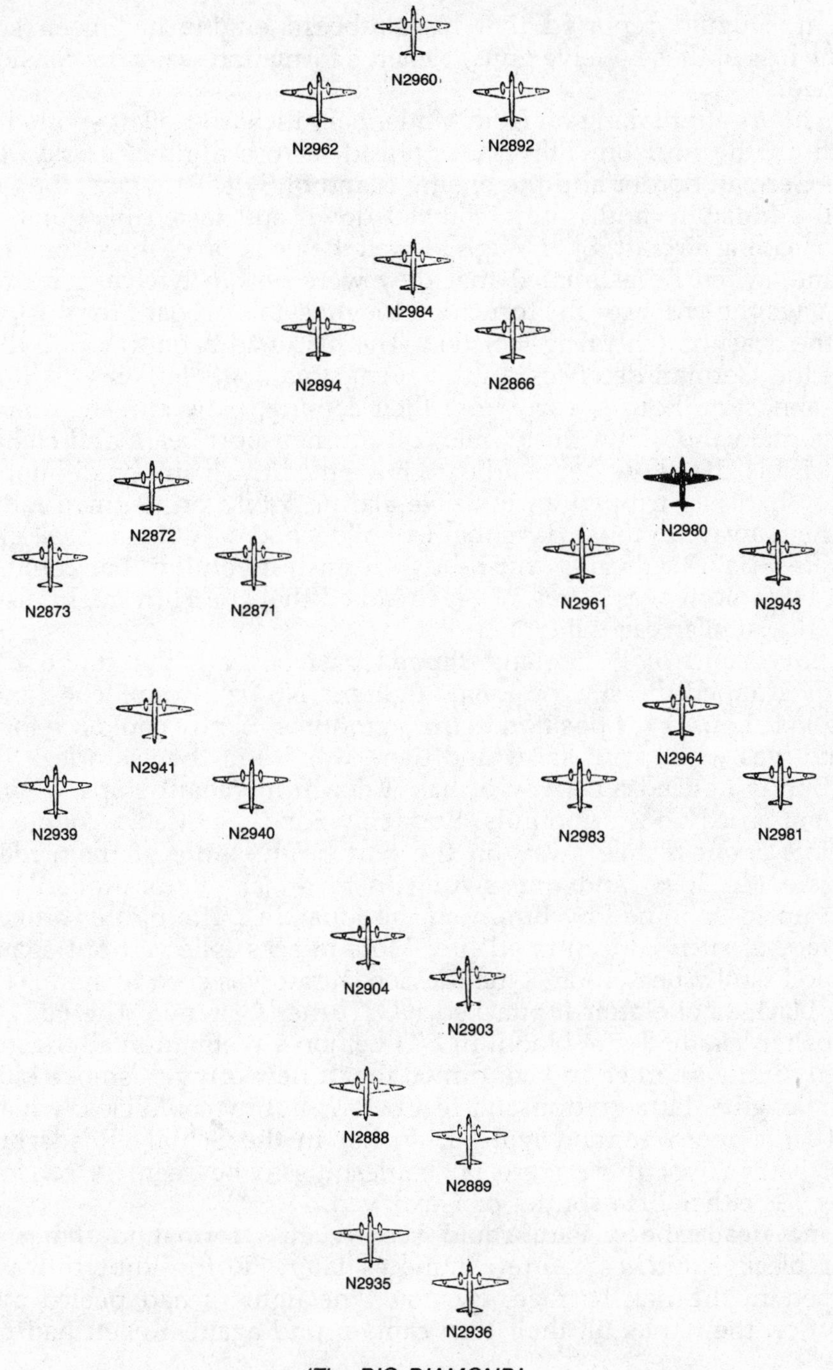


*'The BIG DIAMOND'*
*149 Squadron, 9 Squadron and 37 Squadron, 18th December 1939*
*Time 11.30 hrs; Position 55°N; 4°30'E; Height 14,000 feet*

1.30 p.m. Duguid reported that his starboard engine had been surging. With the loss of these twelve guns, Kellett's formation was now considerably weakened.

Three hours after taking off from Mildenhall, Richard Kellett spotted a hazy smudge on the horizon. Fifty miles ahead, across a gin-clear sky, lay the Danish-German border and the enemy island of Sylt. Paul gave the order to lower the 'dustbin' and Bunny climbed down and tested his guns.

In the leading aircraft, Sgt Hough plotted the position of the second turning point and, when he estimated that they were within twelve miles of Sylt, Kellett gave the order for the formation to wheel to starboard for the long run down the coast of Schleswig-Holstein. The plan had been to nip in the back door of the German defences. In the event, this dog's leg was to afford the enemy almost an hour's warning of their coming. Now cruising due south, with the mainland about thirty miles off on their port beam and Heligoland clearly visible ahead on their starboard bow, the British airmen did not realise that they had just tripped an invisible alarm. A blip on German radar had given them away. In those days the RAF pilots had only the faintest glimmer that there was a frightfully 'hush-hush' British invention that could detect aircraft by radio waves. They never dreamed that the Hun might also have perfected a similar capability.*

The tiny island of Heligoland slipped past beneath the starboard wing as Sandy scanned the sky for enemy fighters. No flak from Heligoland, that was a good sign. At his position in the astrodome, Sandy could see for miles. The land was white with snow and there was ice in the estuaries. Beneath them, Bunny noticed a convoy of half a dozen merchant ships, a tempting target, but strictly out of bounds. Suddenly Sandy spotted a couple of tiny black dots about a mile away on the port beam. More of them followed, they were Me 109s, and one swung in to attack 'R for Robert'. Jimmy opened up to be joined by Bunny in the 'dustbin'. The fighter broke away in the face of such concentrated fire. More attacks followed but again they were successfully beaten-off. One Messerschmitt was seen to spiral seaward trailing black smoke after it attacked F/O Turner's aircraft. The tail gunner, AC1 Coalter, claimed first blood. In F/O Lemon's Wellington all the gunners reported hitting another and confirmed that it flew off with smoke billowing from the engine. Fifteen thousand feet below, Bunny could clearly make out several large merchantmen lying at anchor in the Schillig Roads but that was all battleships; there were no battleships to be seen. A convoy was heading for either Brunsbüttel or Cuxhaven.

Looking dead ahead Paul could see Kellett's formation flying into a wall of black splotches. A few minutes later, 'R for Robert' was itself enveloped in the flak barrage. By now, the fighters had peeled away to hang-off on the flanks till their turn came round again. Kellett had made a

* The *Oslo Report*, which confirmed the existence of 50 cm radar at Wilhelmshaven, was not received in London until early November 1939.

feint towards Bremerhaven and, as the bombers crossed the coast just to the west of Cuxhaven, another convoy of merchant ships could be seen heading up the river Weser towards Bremerhaven. The leading aircraft was carrying a Royal Navy observer, Lieutenant Commander Rotherham, to help identify German battleships. He spotted a very large passenger liner with two funnels, tied up in harbour, which he took to be the *Bremen*. Off to starboard could be seen the great naval base of Wilhelmshaven, but they were too far away to make out anything clearly. As the bombers passed to the south of Bremerhaven, it became obvious that there were no major naval targets at Brunsbüttel, in the Schillig Roads or in the Jade Busen. Kellett ordered a signal to be sent, a series of dashes followed by the letter W. Their target would be Wilhelmshaven but they needed to fly over it to get a closer look. The whole formation turned to starboard and headed west across the Jade. Just to the south of Wilhelmshaven, Kellett wheeled again in another arc to the north on a course set to bring them directly over Bau Haven. As a result of this manoeuvre, the formation out on the port side of the 'Big Diamond' had to open-up to full throttle in an effort to keep up. The two Wellingtons on the outside of this formation were struggling and Sgt Petts made repeated calls to his leader, S/Ldr Guthrie, to slow down – but got no reply. By now, the flak had really thickened up as the battleships in the harbour joined in. The flak was accurate for height but trailed behind the bombers. Over the intercom Jimmy kept up a running commentary. On several occasions he exclaimed excitedly, 'Hurry up Sir, hurry up, it's catching up on us.' Sandy watched fascinated as the jet-black splodges suddenly appeared and immediately expanded and there was a bump as if it was too close. As he looked back, Sandy could see all the bursts hanging about in the sky and it reminded him of coming out of a large wood and seeing all the tree tops on the sky line. For ten minutes they flew straight and level over Wilhelmshaven. In the harbours and docks below him Sandy could make out three* large warships and four destroyers. The order was given to open bomb doors. In the leading aircraft, W/Cdr Kellett had an agonising decision to make. There beneath him lay the pride of the German Navy, the battleships *Scharnhorst* and *Gneisenau*.

> A pocket battleship, then thought to be a cruiser, and a battleship, were then noticed in the inner harbour. The position of the target was not clear until the visual signal for attack commencing (diving 1,000 feet) had been made. As it was then realised that there was risk of dropping bombs on land, particularly from that direction, no bombs were dropped.[1]

W/Cdr Kellett's orders were quite specific: 'Great care is to be taken that no bombs fall on shore, and no merchant ships to be attacked.'

* Aerial photographs later revealed a fourth large warship in the harbour.

From their vantage point, fifteen thousand feet up in the cloudless sky, it was painfully obvious that there were no enemy battleships 'clear of land' at the expected anchorages at the mouth of the Elbe or in the Schillig Roads. Their prey was safely tied up alongside the quays and jetties in Bau Haven. Since it would have been impossible to aim bombs at the battleships without killing civilians on shore, Kellett had no alternative but to abandon his mission.

Looking down from the cockpit of 'R for Robert' Paul spotted four big ships anchored in the middle of the outer harbour. They looked like merchantmen but intense anti-aircraft fire arched skyward from their decks. Paul reasoned that they had to be fleet auxiliaries, and therefore legitimate targets. He gave the order to P/O Innes to attack them. In great haste, Sandy took aim and pressed the bomb release. Following his leader's example, another aircraft in Harris's section dropped its bombs on the four ships. A total of six 500 lb SAP bombs, dropped in haste in the middle of the harbour, was all there was to show for the RAF's first major attack on the German mainland. The results were not observed.

Paul was not the only one to drop aimed bombs that day. Sgt Herbie Ruse was concentrating on keeping formation with F/O Thompson. Number 37 Squadron was trying out a new kind of formation, flying stepped down in pairs, rather than the conventional vics of the other squadrons. Herbie Ruse was flying behind and below Thompson and as they cleared Wilhelmshaven Herbie saw his leader open his bomb doors, apparently on his own initiative, as they approached a German vessel lying in the Schillig Roads. The navigator, Sgt May, shouted up, 'He's going for that ship! He's going to overshoot!' Recalling the punishment meted out to S/Ldr Glencross of 214 Squadron, Ruse shouted back, 'Are you sure it's naval?' Weeks before, Glencross had been taken off flying duties and given a desk job because he had had the temerity to drop bombs on a German minesweeper that had fired on him, without first making absolutely certain it was a *naval* vessel. The Wellington in front of him released its bombs. Sgt May pressed his own bomb release. N2936 lifted as the weight of the bombs vanished. He watched three fountains shoot up into the air followed seconds later by his own three as the sticks splashed harmlessly into the sea.

The lead Wellington was just clearing the flak barrage as Kellett looked back at the disarray behind him. His own four and Paul Harris's six were still flying in tight formation, but off to port No. 9 Squadron's six had opened out and S/Ldr Guthrie was some distance ahead of his formation. Bringing up the rear, No. 37 Squadron was straggling and S/Ldr Hue-Williams was racing ahead to try and catch up with the leaders. Approaching Wilhelmshaven his No. 2, F/O Lemon, had made a spectacular departure from the formation. The story is taken up by 'Cheese' Lemon:

> At about this time P/O Paul Templeman who was sitting in the second pilot's seat, made ready to return to the bomb aimer's position for the

> run-up on the target. On getting down from his seat he inadvertently caught his parachute harness on the flap lever, and the lever was placed in the full-flap position. Before the hydraulics could work, the main power unit had to be turned on, therefore no power had gone to the flaps, and they remained up, and I was not aware the lever was in the down position. However, as we approached the target the main hydraulic power was turned on to put the bomb doors down. This activated the flaps at the same time, causing the aircraft to climb rapidly and lose forward speed. As we were experiencing heavy flak at the time I assumed that we had received a direct hit. By the time I had located the problem, 37 Sqn was a considerable distance ahead of me. I followed in their wake and at the target area jettisoned my bombs in the bay, as no target was available. It was obvious by now that all hope of catching up the squadron had gone. I pulled the revs and the throttle levers back, stuck the nose in an almost vertical position and headed for the deck. We cleared the heavy flak but ran into intense light flak as our height decreased. The loop* and the aerials were torn off. The vibration and noise were nerve-racking. Our only chance was to hug the sea and get there before the fighters came in. We streamed out towards the Frisian Isles but ran into flak from the island defences and shipping. This, in actual fact, was I believe our salvation as the fighters stayed clear of the area. Just after clearing the islands the rear gunner spotted two Me 109s coming in for a rear attack. I shoved the nose down another fifty feet and we really were on the deck. The rear gunner's voice came through and said one of the Me 109s had hit the sea with his wing and cartwheeled straight in. After a while the other aircraft abandoned the attack.

Meanwhile, back at 10,000 feet, Kellett's bombers proceeded on their northerly heading towards the open sea. Miraculously, not one of the Wellingtons was hit as they flew on, enveloped in flak. They sailed through to emerge out the other side, unscathed. The time was coming up for half past one, an hour after they first tripped the alarm. The fighters were patiently waiting for the flak to subside. When it did, they fell on the pride of RAF Bomber Command like a ton of bricks.

Earlier that same day, around the time that W/Cdr Kellett was setting-off for Wilhelmshaven, Oberstleutnant Carl Schumacher was chatting to his adjutant, Leutnant Miller-Trimbusch. 'Splendid weather for fighters,' he remarked as he studied the sky over the German Bight. The day had dawned cold but sunny. The early morning mists over the East Frisian Islands had evaporated to reveal a sky of purest blue satin, clear to the horizon in all directions. 'The Tommies are not such fools – they won't come today,' dutifully replied Miller-Trimbusch as he surveyed a cloudless sky that was indeed ideal for their fighters. Schumacher nodded his agreement. A month before,

* Radio Direction Finding loop, located in front of the astrodome.

Geschwaderkommodore Schumacher had been appointed to command the new *Luftwaffe* Group JG1 set up to defend the North Sea area. At the outbreak of war he had been in command of the fighter Wing II/JG77. Now, he was responsible for the whole Air Force Group controlled from Jever, just a few kilometres to the west of Wilhelmshaven. He was feeling good, for not only was it a perfect day for his fighters but he had at last received the reinforcements he had been asking for since Heligoland had been attacked by British bombers a couple of weeks before. The previous day the long-range fighter Gruppe I/ZG76 had arrived from Bonninghardt after a distinguished record in Poland. Equipped with the latest twin-engined Messerschmitt Bf110-C fighters, I/ZG76 was a potent addition to his armoury. Under his command he now had between eighty and one hundred single and twin-engined fighters, all ready to go at a moment's notice. Miller-Trimbusch's words: 'The Tommies are not such fools – they won't come today,' hung in the cold frosty air as, a couple of hundred miles to the west, Kellett's captains set their compasses on the heading that would fly them into history.

The German fighter defences under Oberstleutnant Schumacher consisted of the following units.

II/JG77 under Major von Bülow-Bothkamp on the island of Wangerooge;
III/JG77 under Captain Seliger at Nordholz near Cuxhaven;*
Jagdgruppe 101 under Major Reichardt, one squadron at Westerland on Sylt;
Jagdgruppe 101 under Major Reichardt, two squadrons at Neumünster;
10(N)/JG26 (Nightfighters) under Staffelkapitän Steinhoff at Jever;
I/ZG76 under Captain Reinecke at Jever.

II/JG77; III/JG77; Jagdgruppe 101 and 10(N) JG26 were equipped with the Messerschmitt 109. I/ZG76 was equipped with the Messerschmitt 110.

The second squadron of Zerstörergeschwader 76 (i.e. 2/ZG76) was commanded by Staffelkapitän Wolfgang Falck. This officer had been one of those trained at Lipetsk, the *Luftwaffe*'s secret base near Moscow in the early thirties. He had become well known and liked in pre-war aviation circles. Indeed, such was his reputation that the prestigious magazine *The Aeroplane* published an article about him early in 1940 entitled 'Memories of Peace'.†

To acquaint themselves with their surroundings and get used to flying out over the sea, Wolfgang Falck and his 'Lady Bug' squadron were exercising in the clear blue skies close by the island of Borkum. Hidden among the sand-dunes on the island of Wangerooge, eighty kilometres to the east, Leutnant Hermann Diehl of LN-Vers, Regiment 3, was spending his lunch hour demonstrating the usefulness of his new 'Freya' radar to a naval officer who was visiting his experimental installation. Diehl was using Falck's flight of Messerschmitt Bf110s as a demonstration of how he could detect intruding

* Formerly II(J)/Tr. Gr. 186 for the aircraft carrier 'GRAF ZEPPELIN' which was never completed.
† See Appendix A.

aircraft that came within range of his equipment. After a while he swung the 'Freya' radar beam northwards towards Heligoland. Suddenly he spotted a large echo coming from the direction of Sylt. Diehl knew that there were no German aircraft reported in that area, and so he immediately picked up his phone which had a direct line to the Geschwader HQ in Jever. It was lunchtime and Hermann Diehl received short shrift from the other end of the line. 'Tommies approaching in weather like this? You're plotting seagulls or there's interference on your set,'[2] came the sceptical reply. Shades of Pearl Harbor! There had been no alarms from the naval radar on Heligoland or any of the patrol boats up there. In desperation, Diehl rang up the local commanding officer of II/JG77 fighter group based close by on Wangerooge. Harry von Bülow was however at that moment at the Geschwader HQ in Jever. Nobody wanted to know. Twenty minutes later, the naval radar on Heligoland (also a 'Freya' set) reported intruding aircraft as well. But still the fighters were not scrambled. The report had first to go through the naval exchange at Wilhelmshaven and all the 'official channels' before it reached Geschwader HQ at Jever.

While the German radar was every bit as efficient as its British counterpart, the problem lay in communications. Arguments still persisted between the *Luftwaffe* and the *Kriegsmarine* about precisely who was responsible for each sector, and considerable overlap existed between the fighters and the flak ships. The British had succeeded in marrying their radar chain to an efficient fighter control organisation. No such union existed between the *Luftwaffe* and its long range electronic eyes. The report from the Heligoland radar was only hesitatingly passed through the naval HQ exchange to the *Luftwaffe* at Jever, thus confirming Hermann Diehl's original alert. Twenty-two Wellington bombers cruised majestically down the coast of Schleswig-Holstein as the *Luftwaffe* struggled to overcome their simple disbelief that the Royal Air Force could flaunt itself before them 'on a brilliant day that promised only a massacre'. Fifty-seven doomed men among the hundred and twenty in the British formation were granted an hour's extra life because the Germans couldn't believe Bomber Command would be so foolish. Only when observers on Heligoland spotted the bombers through binoculars did the *Luftwaffe* finally grasp the fact that they were under attack. The naval observers sent a signal saying that forty-four bombers were heading for Wilhelmshaven – precisely double Kellett's numbers. This is more likely to have been an error of duplication in transmission rather than a mistake in addition. Belatedly the order went out from Jever for the fighters to scramble.

First off the ground were six Messerschmitt Bf109D-1s of 10(N)/JG26, a nightfighter squadron based at Jever. Their commanding officer was Staffelkapitän 'Mäcki' Steinhoff. One of his fighters took up position on a course parallel to the bombers about a mile away on their port beam, and radioed their course, height and airspeed back to base. One or two of the other Me 109s launched probing attacks against the intruders but were beaten off by the concentrated fire from the turrets. But Steinhoff's pilots did not have long to press home their attacks. At 1.10 p.m. the bombers crossed the mudflats of Wurst, to the west of Cuxhaven. The flak units 214 (Cuxhaven), 244 and 264 (Wesermunde) opened up. The fighters broke away and circled out of range of the flak as Kellett made his turns westward over the *Jade Busen* and again northward for Wilhelmshaven. By now the flak had intensified, being joined by the flak units 212, 222, 252, 262 and 272, ringing the city. From the dockyards, the battleships *Scharnhorst* and *Gneisenau* opened up, together with all the other naval ships in the harbour.

Far away to the west, Feldwebel Walz was humming quietly to himself as he relaxed in the radio operator's position of the Me 110. It was a glorious day. The sun shone through the cockpit canopy and, as he gazed back, he could make out the island of Borkum between the 110's twin tails. They were on a familiarisation flight 'to get acquainted with the sea, the coast and the islands'. Suddenly his radio crackled into life. British bombers were over Wilhelmshaven and they had been ordered to intercept them. Walz immediately informed his pilot, Staffelkapitän Falck, and the starboard wing dipped as the fighter banked steeply on to a heading of 110 degrees. Far on the horizon, Falck could make out the tiny black dots of a flak barrage as he and his Rottenflieger, Unteroffizier Fresia, raced for the fray. At last, Diehl's 'seagulls' had been recognised for what they really were and the *Luftwaffe* was belatedly getting its act together.

'The sepia shades of Camels and Archie' still coloured the perceptions of the airmen from Mildenhall, Honington and Feltwell. Many had joined up at a time when Harrow, Heyford and Hendon bombers were looked upon in the RAF as the very latest thing and the biplane fighter was their only adversary. Lumbering northwards at less than two hundred miles an hour, the crews could clearly see fighters taking off from a well-camouflaged aerodrome at Schillig Point. These were not the sedate biplanes they were accustomed to, but modern 350 mph, cannon-armed, monoplane fighters. The *Luftwaffe* pilots that were racing to get airborne down the runways at Jever, Wangerooge and Neumünster had learned many valuable lessons from the previous encounters with the Wellingtons. They knew that the twin-guns at the rear made stern attacks dangerous, but they now also knew that the turrets could not traverse to a full right-angle with the fuselage. This meant that their targets had a blind spot on the beam. JG1's squadron commanders urged their fighter pilots to knock-out the rear turrets at long range with their 20 mm cannon, where the Wellington's 0.303s were useless, and then close in for the kill. The biggest bonus, however, was the fact that, if they managed to get hits on the bomber's wings, there was a good chance of the aircraft exploding in a great ball of fire.

Through a criminal omission on the part of the Air Ministry, the aircraft lacked self-sealing tanks. If hit in a fuel tank, especially that in the port wing, a Wellington could be transformed within seconds into a flying bonfire. Even if the tanks did not ignite, rapid loss of fuel would almost certainly bring down a crippled aircraft on a long run home.

Perhaps it was just as well that it was not generally appreciated by those who flew in Wellington bombers during those early days that this was the case. Had they known that the port wing tanks did not even have the benefit of armour plating they might have been more apprehensive as the flak barrage lifted and the fighters pounced.

First blood was credited to Unteroffizier Heilmayr in an Me 109E-1 from II/JG77 at 1.30 p.m. Immediately afterwards, 'Mäcki' Steinhoff, who was the CO of 10(N)/JG26, reported attacking a Wellington and watching it spiral downwards in flames into the sea.

Racing towards the Schillig Roads from his exercise grounds close by Borkum, Wolfgang Falck spotted a close formation of Wellingtons twelve miles south-west of Heligoland at 11,000 feet. Number 9 Squadron, out on the left flank of the big diamond, had been left behind as the bombers wheeled northwards for Wilhelmshaven over the Jade Busen. S/Ldr Guthrie's six aircraft were separated from the main formation and flying flat-out to try and catch up. Falck and his Rottenflieger, Fresia, swung in behind the bombers and Falck went for the Wellington on the right and Fresia for the one on the left. After two attempts, Falck saw the bomber disintegrate in mid-air. Fresia's victim dropped away with its port engine in flames. From Guthrie's original formation of six aircraft, only two made it back home. The captains of these two survivors reported that they had observed one aircraft in F/O Allison's section catch fire and explode in mid-air while another went down with its port engine on fire. P/O Lines was flying No. 2 position in Allison's section and F/O Challes was flying the No. 3 position. After his initial success, Falck turned his attention to the lead Wellington in the first section, but this time he did not get things all his own way. The rear-gunner got in a long burst on the attacking Messerschmitt 110 and Falck's starboard engine jerked to a standstill. With petrol streaming from his holed wing-tanks and clouds of smoke billowing from the cockpit, Falck broke-off his attack to try and nurse his stricken fighter back to Jever. Unhappily, his victim had also succumbed to cannon and machine-gun fire and the blazing Wimpy flew headlong into the sea. In their reports, both Petts and Macrae described how their leader, S/Ldr Guthrie, was last seen about twenty miles from the Schillig Roads being attacked by an Me 110 which he shot down in flames. Unteroffizier Fresia's second victim was F/O Allison. Meanwhile, Wolfgang Falck was struggling to see where he was going. The ammunition in the fuselage was in flames and his cockpit was full of dense smoke. He opened the cabin window to clear the smoke and peered out searching for Jever. Shortly, his port engine packed up as well and he knew he could never reach his home base without power. He fired off all his ammunition and dumped his remaining fuel to lighten the aircraft and see if it would glide as far as Wangerooge. Fortunately, the wind was in his favour. With a great rush, the ground rose up to meet him and he quickly activated the compressed-air pump to lower his undercarriage. Falck made a skilful dead-stick landing and his machine rolled to a stop just short of the control tower. Feldwebel Walz climbed out of the rear compartment to join his pilot on the ground. The 'Lady Bug' on the fuselage had done its job well and brought them both safely back.

Bill Macrae, 'a wild, brave, passionately alcoholic Canadian short-service officer', was flying No. 2 to S/Ldr Guthrie. The fierce little Canadian cursed his gunner as he kicked and banked the Wellington under attack and heard no sound of answering fire from his own rear turret. 'I'm trying, skip, but my fingers are too stiff to get the guns to bear!' shouted the frozen, desperate gunner who was wounded moments later. Fabric was flapping from great gashes torn in the wings and fuselage, and fuel leaked from the tanks. Around him, No. 9 Squadron was disintegrating. Off on his port beam, Sgt Petts was desperately making repeated calls to his leader to slow down. Despite opening up to full-boost, Petts was getting left further and further behind. As the fighters closed in for the kill, he decided that he would never catch up with Guthrie, and so he pushed the nose of his Wimpy down and dived as fast as he could towards sea level in an effort to shake off his pursuers. Levelling-off just above the water he suddenly remembered a drill he had practised during co-operation exercises with Fighter Command. When the Messerschmitts came in to the attack he slammed his throttles shut and, as the Wimpy lost speed, the fighters overshot and Robertson in the rear turret held his fingers on the triggers. On one occasion when an Me 110 closed on the Wellington due to this unexpected drop in speed, Robertson was treated to the spectacle of the German rear-gunner putting his fingers to his nose in a rude gesture before opening fire on the bomber. The gunner in the 'dustbin' was badly wounded in the thigh, and Ginger Heathcote, the second pilot, scrambled down the fuselage and dragged Bob Kemp up out of his turret and helped him on to the rest bunk. Heathcote then scrambled forward to help Balch, who had been hit in the foot, out of the front turret. In the rear turret, Robertson emptied his guns into an Me 110 and heard the hammers click dead. He was out of ammunition, and just at that moment there were no more Messerschmitts to be seen. With two wounded gunners and with his rudder controls partly jammed, Sgt Petts nursed N2873 the two hundred miles to the English coast to land at Sutton Bridge in Lincolnshire. Macrae later made an emergency landing at the coastal aerodrome of North Coates Fitties. Petts and Macrae were the only two from No. 9 Squadron's port formation in the big diamond to make it back.

'R for Robert' was leading the starboard formation in the big diamond. At the briefing the previous evening, Paul Harris had been told that three aircraft from No. 9 Squadron, under the command of F/Lt Grant, would be flying in his formation. Fair-haired and elegant, Peter Grant was almost a Hollywood caricature of the sporting young English public-school boy. After the briefing, Paul strolled across to Peter and said, 'Stay close to me whatever happens,' and fortunately that is precisely what he did. Harris's six Wimpys stuck together like a rolled-up hedgehog, guns bristling all round. The Messerschmitts could not penetrate the wall of lead. Their cannons however outranged the Wimpy's Brownings, and from a safe distance they hammered fire into the tightly-knit bunch of bombers. Looking out of his cockpit, Peter Grant was dismayed to see petrol pouring from one of his wing tanks. Quickly he switched on the pumps to transfer fuel from the holed tank to the ones that seemed intact. He later remarked, 'There was absolutely nothing we could do except sit there being picked-off one by one.' On his port side he noticed that Sgt Ramshaw was losing fuel from several punctures in his tanks. Later he learned that Ramshaw's turrets had jammed and the rear-gunner had been mortally wounded. Defenceless, N2983 dropped beneath the formation and limped homeward under the shelter of their guns.

Paul had little time to heed all the commotion going on around him. His eyes were firmly glued on Kellett as he struggled to hold N2980 in tight formation on his leader's vic. Bunny was manning the 'dustbin'. He vividly recalls sitting there watching holes suddenly appear in the fabric, as if by magic, and bits of geodetic disintegrate in front of his eyes while at the same time feeling quite helpless to do anything about it. At the astrodome, Sandy was calling out the attacks as they developed. The elevator was hit and badly damaged, the wings and fuselage were holed repeatedly, and the torn and tattered fabric flapped in the slipstream as the fighters pressed home their attacks. Off on his port bow, Paul watched fascinated as an Me 109 swung in to attack Kellett's weakened formation. His leader had only four aircraft since the premature departure of Duguid and Kelly. The fighter broke away and came round again. Three times it tried to mount a beam attack and three times it missed. Oberleutnant Fuhrmann eventually got fed up with the difficult deflection shooting and, throwing caution to the winds, tried an attack from dead astern. This was precisely what the tail-gunners had been trained for – mutual supporting fire. All the tail-gunners in Kellett's vic ripped into him. Spuming smoke, Fuhrmann's fighter curled away seaward. The pilot managed to pull his machine out of its steep dive to make a perfect ditching, amid a cloud of spray, a couple of hundred metres from the island of Spiekeroog. Observers on the shore watched as the pilot clambered out of his cockpit onto the wing and jumped into the sea just as his fighter sank. He struggled desperately to swim to the shore but his heavy flying gear soaked up the icy water. Those standing on the beach watched helplessly as Johann Fuhrmann drowned a couple of hundred metres from safety.

Suddenly a twin-engined fighter streaked across N2980's path, intent on attacking Kellett's four Wimpys. Paul recalled the event 'just as if it were yesterday. The fellow shot straight across my bows blotting out the sun, jolly nearly rammed him. Young Doxsey let fly with a long burst but the so-'n-so got Speirs, went up in a great huge ball of flame.' F/O Speirs was flying No. 3 in the lead formation when the Messerschmitt's fire lanced into his fuselage. There was an explosion to the rear of the cockpit, close to the wing root. Almost certainly the fighter had hit a high-pressure oxygen bottle. The bomber was immediately engulfed in flames. N2962 fell away from the formation to plunge into the sea ten thousand feet below. There were no parachutes.

Still the fighters came on. At one point Paul was alerted by a voice on the intercom from the front turret shouting, 'I'm hit, I'm hit,' but at the height of the battle there was nothing he could do about it. He watched out of the cockpit as Riddlesworth, the remaining pilot from Duguid's vic, closed up to take Speirs's place behind Kellett. Over the intercom came a report from Sandy that F/O Briden had been hit and was spuming fuel out of his wing tanks. The surviving nine Wellingtons from Kellett, Harris and Grant's three vics drew closer together as they battled their way through this hornets' nest. Aided by disciplined and determined formation-flying, they pressed resolutely onward till they were out of range of the fighters.

Some distance behind the leader's formation straggled No. 37 Squadron. They had opened out in the barrage over Wilhelmshaven and were dangerously spread out as they emerged from the flak. Their leader, S/Ldr Hue-Williams, was observed by Peter Grant racing far ahead of his formation in an attempt to catch up with the leaders. He had just succeeded in doing so when an Me 110, piloted by Oberleutnant Gordon Gollob, made a dive across his stern and raked the bomber with cannon and machine gun fire. Peter Grant watched as Hue-Williams dived towards the sea with his starboard wing well on fire. Captain Reinecke, the CO of I/ZG76, later noted in his report: 'The Wellington is very inflammable and burns readily.'[3]

No. 37 Squadron's experiment with the 'stepped down in pairs' formation can be considered a failure by results. 'Cheese' Lemon, flying No. 2 to Hue-Williams, had previously departed the formation over Wilhelmshaven in a spectacular dive to sea level after inadvertently applying full-flap. 'Christ, we've lost everything now. We're on our own,' thought Greaves, the front gunner. At that moment the rear gunner, Corporal Kidd, shouted: '109s!' Lemon clung desperately to the waves as the gunner called out the attacks. 'They're coming in . . . now . . . left! Now, right, right! He's overshooting.' They were hit repeatedly in the fuselage, the Wellington still streaking along with the spray breaking on the perspex of the front turret where Greaves tried in vain to bring his guns to bear. 'If we go down now, we've had it,' he thought, struck by the ghastly vision of the aircraft plunging unhesitatingly to the bottom of the sea if Lemon lost control for a moment. The observer in the astrodome was commenting on the German attacks. Suddenly, as one of the fighters closed again, there was a cry of choked astonishment from the rear turret: 'Christ! He's gone straight in!'. Leutnant Roman Stiegler of II/JG77 was in hot pursuit of 'Cheese' Lemon's Wellington as it skimmed across the water when suddenly he found himself just a few feet above the waves. His wing tip touched the surface and his Me 109 cartwheeled and disappeared in a cloud of spray. Stiegler's wing man thought better of it and broke away. They were alone. There was an outburst of nervous hilarity on the intercom about the German's collision with the North Sea. Then Lemon cut in: 'Come on, cut the chatter, we've got to get home.'

Silent, exhausted by fear, they settled down for the long run back to Feltwell, flying all the way almost at sea level. In the front turret, Greaves swore he could taste the salt. At 3.40 p.m., N2903 landed back at Feltwell. After a half-hearted debriefing, they waited for the next Feltwell aircraft to return, yet by evening none had come.

After dropping his bombs over the Schillig Roads, Herbie Ruse, who was No. 37 Squadron's 'Tail-end-Charlie', was concentrating on holding formation on his leader. Herbie's only concern was to keep station on Thompson, to bomb when he did, to change course when he did. At the briefing the previous evening he had been surprised to learn that they were to bomb above 10,000 feet, for he could never remember any crew scoring hits in bombing practice on a target as small as a ship from that height. On exercises they had trained to attack in succession in pairs, making a series of runs over the target to judge their own errors. Before take-off that morning, it had been pre-arranged that, when a German Naval vessel was sighted, the leader's pair would attack on the original course, the second pair would move out to port then attack and bomb from that quarter whilst the third pair, Thompson and Ruse, would move out to starboard and attack from there. This scheme was devised by the pilots of 37 Squadron themselves after several training sessions with fighter squadrons. It was to have been just as they practised in training but without the refinement of going round again to judge their errors. Now, however, their leader, Hue-Williams, was a mile or so ahead going flat-out to try and catch up on Kellett, and 'Cheese' had made his unexpected and spectacular departure from the formation over Wilhelmshaven. According to plan, Wimberley and Lewis broke away to port and Thompson put his nose down and dived steeply to starboard followed closely by Herbie who watched his airspeed indicator going 'literally off the clock'. Just at that moment Herbie spotted a German fighter underneath them 'climbing like a lift'. In November they had carried out fighter affiliation exercises with Spitfires from Tangmere, and the fighter pilots had reported that they could have wiped out 37 Squadron in ten minutes. Then, nobody believed them. Tangmere could save its line-shoots for the *Luftwaffe*; Wellington bombers could take care of themselves. Now, it wasn't the friendly Spitfires that were climbing to make a mock attack but Messerschmitts, and the Tangmere boys were about to be proved dead right.

Oberleutnant Helmut Lent had just landed at Jever after an observation patrol along the coast. No sooner had he finished refuelling than he impatiently opened the throttles of his Me 110 and started to taxi towards the runway. Paul Mahle, his armourer, had just finished changing a drum of 20 mm ammunition and clung desperately to the wing as they bumped along the ground. As the Me 110 gathered speed, Mahle slid off the wing and hurled himself to the side to avoid being struck by the tailplane.

Herbie Ruse's Wellington was by now racing downwards at an incredible 300 mph, shaking in every rivet. Harry Jones in the rear turret was irrelevantly startled to see red roofs on the coast to port of them. 'The roofs can't be red!' he muttered. 'Those are German houses, we have red roofs in England.'

Down the runway at Jever, Lent's fighter gathered speed. The joystick was eased back and it climbed swiftly to do battle. The visibility was so good that Lent could see fighters buzzing round the Wellingtons. 'Ah, that will be von Bülow's crowd,' he thought as he headed for the fray. Just at that moment he spotted a couple of Wellingtons sneaking off westwards in an effort to make a low-level escape over the sandbanks. He banked steeply and fell in behind the rear one. Harry Jones watched as the 110 streaked towards him at a closing speed of more than a hundred miles an hour. 'My God, isn't it small,' he thought, as so many thousands of air-gunners would think in their turn, in the next five years as the slim silhouette of the fighter swung in, guns winking. The first attack came on the Wellington's blind spot on the beam. With all guns blazing, the 110 streaked past but such deflection-shooting was not easy and the stream of bullets seemed to have no effect. Lent swung round again but this time came in dead astern. At six hundred yards Harry squeezed the triggers. His guns fired a single round and stopped. They were frozen up. He tried to traverse the turret. It was jammed by the cold. Lent thought he had knocked out the rear turret as there was no answering fire. Harry was still wrestling with his guns when the 110 came round again. There was a violent explosion in the turret and a savage pain in his ankle and back. 'Skip, I've been hit!' he called down the intercom. 'Can you do anything back there? No? Then for God's sake get out of the turret,' answered Ruse. Harry dragged himself up the fuselage towards the rest-bed, half-conscious, with his back scored by one bullet, his ankle shattered by a second. Tom Holley, the observer, was manning the 'dustbin' and struggled to bring it to bear as the Messerschmitt raked the Wellington yet again. Morphia in hand, Fred Taylor, the wireless operator, bent over Harry Jones, trying to lift his wounded leg onto the rest-bed. A burst of machine-gun fire smashed through the port side of the fuselage, shattering Taylor's head and back. Harry had persuaded the quiet northern boy to put aside his wartime scruples and get married only a few weeks before. Taylor collapsed on him, dying. The next burst caught Tom Holley as he struggled to pull himself up out of the 'dustbin' turret, now jammed and useless. Hit in the face and side, Holley fell dead, draped half-in, half-out of his gun-turret. By now N2936 was gushing a trail of dense black smoke and was clearly doomed. Helmut Lent broke away and set off in pursuit of Thompson's Wellington. When he caught up with it he attacked from astern once again. Later, when filling in his combat report, he wrote: 'Both the enemy's engines began burning brightly. As the plane hit the water the impact broke it apart and it sank.' Out of the side window, Harry Jones glimpsed Thompson's Wellington with its tail shot to pieces. Its rear gun-turret had simply disappeared and with it Harry's friend, Len Stock, a little instrument repairer from North London. It crashed into the sea beyond Borkum and the waves closed over the last resting place of N2935 as the body of Sgt Tilley, its observer, floated to the surface, to be recovered later by the Germans.

Herbie Ruse could smell the cordite from the explosions in the fuselage as he laboured to keep N2936 in the air, his revolution-counter gone mad and his propellers in coarse pitch. Calmly he wound back the actuating wheel controlling the aircraft's trim so that if he himself was hit and fell from the controls, the Wellington should automatically seek to recover from the dive. Then the elevator controls collapsed and he knew his aircraft was finished. Beside him Tom May fought to help pull back the control column. Harry Jones, lying on the rest bunk, was astounded to see a burst of fire tear up the floor between May's legs as he stood straddled in the cockpit. May was hit only once, slightly wounded in the buttock. They saw the sand dunes of an island rushing up to meet them. It was Borkum, just a few miles east of neutral Dutch waters. With a grinding, wrenching, protracted shriek of metal and a whirlwind of sparks from the frozen ground beneath, Herbie brought the Wellington to rest. There were a few seconds of merciful silence. May jettisoned the canopy and jumped down. Ruse was about to follow when he heard Jones's painful cry: 'I'm trapped!' As flames began to seep up the fuselage, Herbie hoisted Harry off the floor. 'My God, you're heavy, Jonah,' he complained. Then he half-dragged, half-carried the gunner out of the wrecked aircraft. The three men lay silent, exhausted and in pain, behind a dune in the sandy, frozen waste as their aircraft burned. At last a German patrol arrived to greet them with the time-honoured cliché: 'For you the war is over.'

Wimberley and Lewis had likewise broken away westwards over the Schillig Roads. Oberstleutnant Carl Schumacher, the Geschwader commander, dispatched Lewis over the island of Wangerooge. For several days afterwards the wreck of N2889 could be seen sticking up out of the mud-flats off Spiekeroog. Only the body of the tail gunner, A/C Geddes, was recovered.

'Pete' Wimberley battled his way westward through a succession of attacks but finally he too could no longer keep his battered and beaten-up aircraft in the air. He was forced to ditch in the sea close to the island of Borkum. Shortly, a German patrol boat arrived and picked Wimberley out of the water. He was the only survivor from N2888. In his book, *'Angriffshone 4000'*, Cajus Bekker affirms that Helmut Lent 'brought down a third Wellington which had already been shot up. This plunged into the sea fifteen miles north west of Borkum'. It could only have been N2888. Because he had simply delivered the *coup de grâce*, Lent was credited with only his previous two kills. So, for five of No. 37 Squadron's six Wellingtons, their first encounter with the *Luftwaffe* had also been their last. As Wimberley's Wimpy crashed into the sea at 1.45 p.m., the rear formation of the big diamond ceased to exist.

Out over the sea, having passed directly over a flak ship ten miles south west of Heligoland, Kellett's tightly knit band fought doggedly for its life. It is a measure of the fierceness of the struggle that continued for almost half an hour that, from those that survived, No. 149 Squadron was credited with six kills, three possibles and five doubtfuls. No. 9 Squadron claimed five kills, two possibles and five doubtfuls. No. 37 Squadron's lone survivor was credited with two doubtfuls.

Quite suddenly things quietened down. Paul looked at his watch and noted that it was just after 1.50 p.m. At the astrodome, Sandy, scanning the skies for fighters, found to his immense relief that they were on their own. Behind, Peter Grant glanced up for a moment and 'quite suddenly, there were just a few Wellingtons flying alone in a clear sky'. Schumacher's fighters had reached the limit of their endurance. Sandy glanced around again to make sure and spotted Briden just behind, staggering resolutely onward in his badly shot-up machine, petrol streaming from his riddled tanks. Ramshaw was still tucked underneath but he too was losing fuel fast. In 'R for Robert' there was subdued elation at their timely deliverance but little outward sign of celebration as they relaxed, all utterly exhausted by their exertions. 'Everyone pouring with sweat and throats so dry we could only croak,' wrote Sandy in his little notebook next morning. Just at that, a very stern captain's voice came over the intercom: 'Navigator, remove the body from the front turret and attend to him.' Bunny Austin extricated himself from the 'dustbin' and made his way forward to help young Doxsey out of the front gun-turret and back to the rest bed. Bunny enquired, 'What's wrong boy? Where are you hit?' 'It's my flying boot, I'm hit in my foot,' came the reply. On examination it was found that the bullet had taken the sole clean off young Doxsey's flying boot. The lad was greatly concerned, not because he had been hit but because he might be asked to pay for a new pair. At that, the tension evaporated completely. Paul put his hand into the depths of his flying jacket and produced a flask of rum. He handed it round. 'We had one damn good swig and it put new life into us,' wrote Sandy later. Over the intercom came a request for help from Jimmy Mullineaux. Thinking he had been wounded, Paul ordered Sandy to pass the rum down to the rear gunner. Opening the turret doors, Jimmy shouted to Sandy to give him a hand reloading the guns but Sandy didn't seem to understand. He passed the rum flask into the outstretched hand of the gunner who grasped it and closed the turret doors. The rum flask was not seen again until they all climbed down at Coltishall aerodrome, two hours later. Paul shook it but there wasn't a drop left. Jimmy smiled sheepishly.

> The route out was almost due north to north-west about 20 miles west of Heligoland, for as long as the attacks continued. As soon as they were abandoned, a course was set about west for the base. There were then only 10 aircraft in the formation, two of these gradually dropping back.[4]

In his report, Richard Kellett also went on to say: 'The enemy pressed home their attacks in a splendid manner,' striking a curiously gallant note in describing an ill-matched slaughter.

The battle over, JG1's initial tally of downed British bombers stood at thirty eight. Their 'bag' is listed in Table 1. Clearly this initial claim was grossly exaggerated. In reality, Bomber Command lost ten aircraft in the actual battle while two later ditched in the sea on their way home and three made emergency landings back in Britain. The losses that day are given in Table 2.

The large discrepancy is hard to explain. It is important to stress that German fighter pilots were not permitted to make unsubstantiated claims. Their reporting procedure was very rigid and had to be strictly adhered to. Before any claim could be confirmed it had to pass through many bureaucratic channels. Questions such as type of aircraft, nationality, exact position, altitude and time of engagement had to be meticulously answered. The fighter pilot had to complete a combat report that described in detail how the engagement progressed until the final kill. If possible, witnesses on the ground had to be found to corroborate the claim. On top of all that, another fighter pilot had to be cited as a witness and testify in writing that he had observed the combat and could vouch for the fact that the enemy aircraft had crashed. To back up their claim of thirty-eight aircraft shot down, the *Luftwaffe* insisted that there had been a force of forty-four Wellingtons (later increased by the German High Command to a force of fifty-two Wellingtons). A couple of hours later, the initial score was modified by XI Air Administrative Region in Hamburg to thirty-four bombers destroyed. Months later, once all the reports had been carefully sifted and analysed, the Reich Air Ministry in Berlin issued a statement confirming twenty-seven of the claims. This was still more than double the true figure and five more than Kellett's entire force. For many years, even long after the war, German historians have disputed the official British figures in the belief that they had been originally issued to conceal the enormity of the disaster. Careful examination of the Operations Record Books of all squadrons equipped with Wellingtons at that time reveal no deception. Obituaries from the Commonwealth War Graves Commission record the identity of all service personnel who died during the war and have no known grave, as would be the case for aircraft shot down over the sea. None of the airmen reported missing on that day belonged to any squadron other than 149, 9 and 37. Reference to other RAF squadrons operating twin-engined bombers indicate no other type of bomber being involved. Finally, personal discussions with Air Commodore Kellett, Group Captain Harris and Wing Commander Austin confirm *without a shadow of doubt* that only twenty-two Wellingtons took on the might of the *Luftwaffe* that day.

The Germans were not alone, however, in over-estimating their score. British newspapers headlined the fact that twelve enemy fighters had been destroyed and no fewer than six of them were Göring's new and much vaunted Messerschmitt Bf110s. In reality, no Me 110 was reported missing. JG1 confirmed the loss of two Me 109s and a further one written-off after crash-landing. Two 109s and two 110s were very severely damaged, while seven 110s and one 109 suffered slight damage. In all, the *Luftwaffe* put up twenty-five 109s and nineteen 110s. Forty-four fighters against twenty-two bombers gave odds of exactly two to one. It is significant that the surviving British aircrews estimated that there had been between sixty and eighty fighters in the sky over the Heligoland Bight. This over-estimation of aircraft numbers engaged in combat would crop up many times in later conflicts as the war progressed.

*Table 1*

| | | | | |
|---|---|---|---|---|
| 1 | 14h 30 | Uffz Heilmayr | II./JG 77 | 30 km SSW Helgoland |
| 2 | 14h 30 | Stfk J. Steinhoff | 10. (N)/JG 26 | 30 km SSW Helgoland |
| 3 | 14h 30 | Fw W. Szuggar | 10. (N)/JG 26 | 30 km SSW Helgoland |
| 4 | 14h 30 | Uffz Niemeyer | II./JG 77 | NNW Wangerooge |
| 5 | 14h 30 | Uffz Niemeyer | II./JG 77 | NNW Wangerooge |
| 6 | 14h 30 | Oblt Henz | II./JG 77 | NNW Wangerooge |
| 7 | 14h 30 | Lt Schirmböck | II./JG 77 | NNW Wangerooge |
| 8 | 14h 35 | Obstlt Schumacher | Stab/JG 1 | N Spiekeroog |
| 9 | 14h 35 | Stfk J. Steinhoff | 10.(N)/JG 26 | 35 km SSW Helgoland |
| 10 | 14h 35 | Uffz Gerhardt | 10.(N)/JG 26 | 35 km SSW Helgoland |
| 11 | 14h 35 | Uffz Wilke | 10.(N)/JG 26 | 35 km SSW Helgoland |
| 12 | 14h 35 | Uffz Portz | 10.(N)/JG 26 | 35 km SSW Helgoland |
| 13 | 14h 35 | Stfk W. Falck | I./ZG 76 | 20 km SW Helgoland |
| 14 | 14h 35 | Uffz Fresia | I./ZG 76 | 20 km SW Helgoland |
| 15 | 14h 40 | Fw Gröning | I./ZG 76 | E Langeoog |
| 16 | 14h 42 | Lt H. Lent | I./ZG 76 | 5 km N Borkum |
| 17 | 14h 45 | Stfk W. Falck | I./ZG 76 | 20 km SW Helgoland |
| 18 | 14h 45 | Uffz Fresia | I./ZG 76 | 20 km SW Helgoland |
| 19 | 14h 45 | Oblt Jäger | I./ZG 76 | NW Borkum |
| 20 | 14h 45 | Oblt G. Gollob | I./ZG 76 | NW Langeoog |
| 21 | 14h 45 | Ofw Fleischmann | I./ZG 76 | NW Spiekeroog |
| 22 | 14h 50 | Oblt D. Robitzsch | JGr. 101 | SW Helgoland |
| 23 | 14h 50 | Oblt R. Kaldrack | JGr. 101 | SW Helgoland |
| 24 | 14h 50 | Oblt Poitner | II./JG 77 | NW Norderney |
| 25 | 14h 50 | Fw Troitzsch | II./JG 77 | NW Norderney |
| 26 | 14h 50 | Fw Troitzsch | II./JG 77 | NW Norderney |
| 27 | 14h 50 | Oblt Lang | II./JG 77 | NW Norderney |
| 28 | 14h 50 | Oblt Peters | II./JG 77 | NW Norderney |
| 29 | 14h 50 | Lt Schmidt | II./JG 77 | NW Norderney |
| 30 | 14h 50 | Oblt Jung | II./JG 77 | NW Norderney |
| 31 | 14h 50 | Ofw Droste | II./JG 77 | NW Norderney |
| 32 | 14h 50 | Uffz Holck | II./JG 77 | NW Norderney |
| 33 | 14h 50 | Lt H. Lent | I./ZG 76 | 10 km WNW Borkum |
| 34 | 15h 00 | Oblt Gresens | I./ZG 76 | 25 km NW Borkum |
| 35 | 15h 00 | Lt Graeff | I./ZG 76 | 25 km WNW Borkum |
| 36 | 15h 00 | Uffz Kalinowski | I./ZG 76 | 25 km WNW Borkum |
| 37 | 15h 00 | Lt Uellenbeck | I./ZG 76 | 50 km N Ameland |
| 38 | 15h 5 | Lt Uellenbeck | I./ZG 76 | 50 km N Ameland |

| Totals: | | |
|---|---|---|
| | Stab/JG 1 = | 1 |
| | 10.(N)/JG 26 = | 6 |
| | JGr. 101 = | 2 |
| | II./JG 77 = | 14 |
| | I/ZG 76 = | 15 |
| | | 38 |

*Les Aiglons, Combats Aeriens de la Drôle de Guerre* by C. J. Ehrengardt; C. F. Shores; H. Weisse; J. Foreman. Published by Charles Lavauzelle, Paris-Limoges, 1983. Page 91.

*Table 2* (See Appendix B)

| Aircraft | Captain | Squadron | Credited to: |
|---|---|---|---|
| N2962 | F/O Speirs | 149 | Ofw Fleischmann or Fw. Grönning |
| N2872 | S/Ldr Guthrie | 9 | Stfk Falck |
| N2939 | P/O Lines | 9 | Stfk Falck |
| N2941 | F/O Allison | 9 | Uffz Fresia |
| N2940 | F/O Challes | 9 | Uffz Fresia |
| N2904 | S/Ldr Hue-Williams | 37 | Oblt Gollob |
| N2935 | F/O Thompson | 37 | Lt Lent |
| N2936 | Sgt Ruse | 37 | Lt Lent |
| N2888 | F/O Wimberley | 37 | Lt Lent (Coup de Grâce) |
| N2889 | F/O Lewis | 37 | Obstlt Schumacher |
| Me 109D | Oblt Fuhrmann | 10(N)/JG 26 | N2866 F/O Riddlesworth (+ Turner & Speirs?) |
| Me 109E | Lt Stiegler | 6/JG 77 | N2903 F/O Lemon |

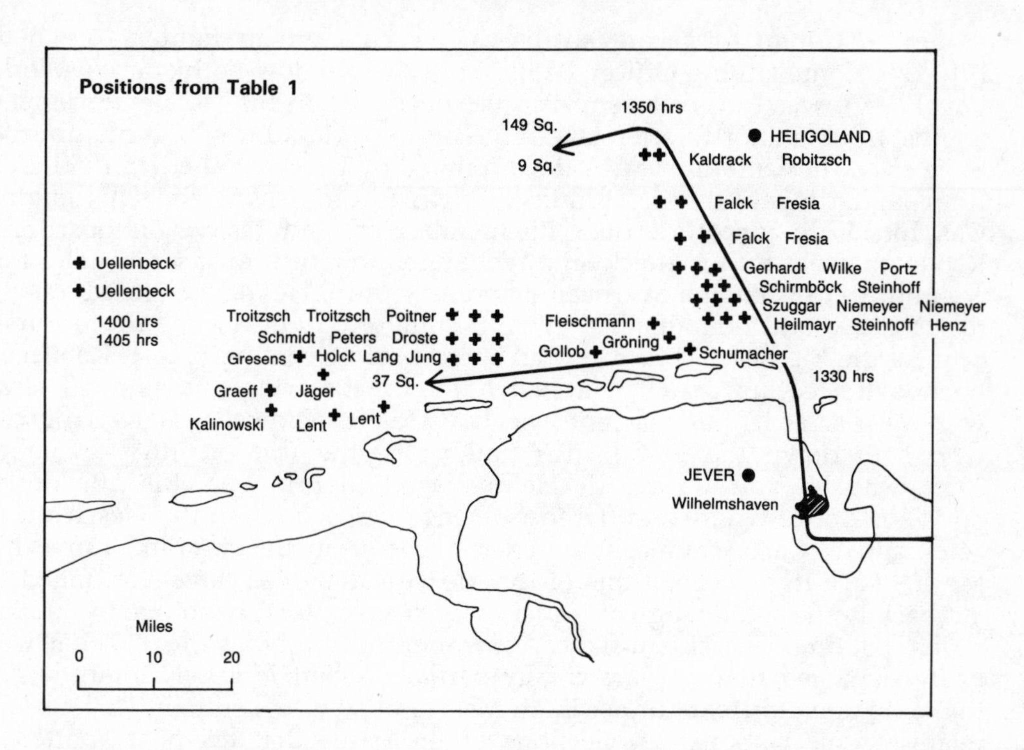
Positions from Table 1
1350 hrs
149 Sq.
9 Sq.
HELIGOLAND
Kaldrack Robitzsch
Falck Fresia
Falck Fresia
Gerhardt Wilke Portz
Schirmböck Steinhoff
Szuggar Niemeyer Niemeyer
Heilmayr Steinhoff Henz
Uellenbeck
Uellenbeck
1400 hrs
1405 hrs
Troitzsch Troitzsch Poitner
Schmidt Peters Droste
Gresens Holck Lang Jung
Fleischmann
Gröning
Gollob
Schumacher
37 Sq.
1330 hrs
Graeff Jäger
Kalinowski Lent Lent
JEVER
Wilhelmshaven
Miles
0 10 20

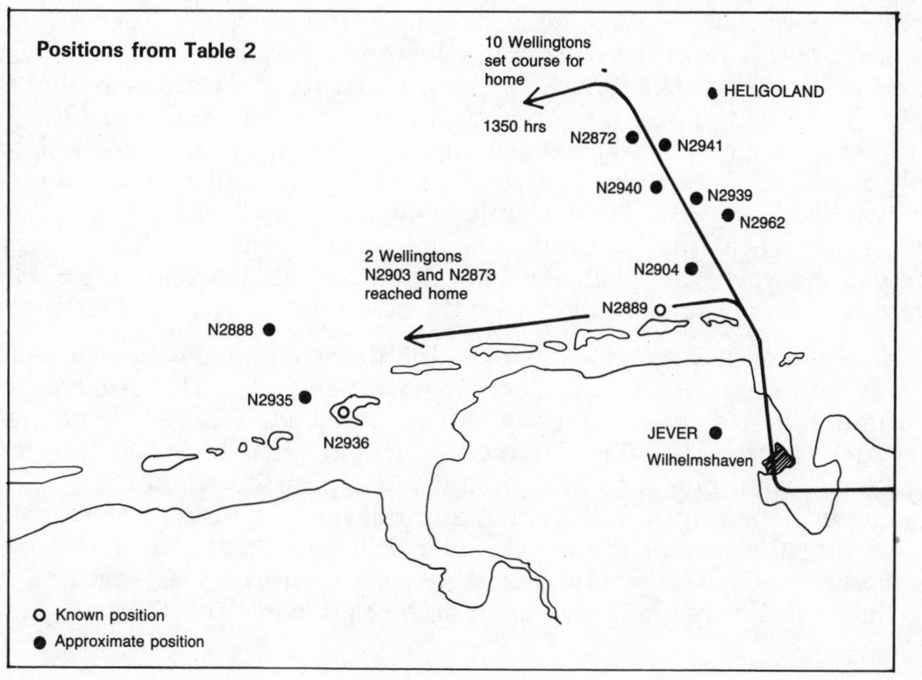
Positions from Table 2
10 Wellingtons
set course for
home
1350 hrs
HELIGOLAND
N2872
N2941
N2940
N2939
N2962
2 Wellingtons
N2903 and N2873
reached home
N2904
N2889
N2888
N2935
N2936
JEVER
Wilhelmshaven
Known position
Approximate position

Bomber Command's true score was seven German fighters downed. II/JG77's Commanding Officer, Major Harry von Bülow-Bothkamp (a World War I Ace), was forced to return to base early when his Me 109 developed engine trouble shortly after take-off. The two Me 109s of Fuhrmann and Stiegler crashed into the sea. A third, piloted by Leutnant Dietrich Robitzsch from Jagdgruppe 101 at Neumünster, was forced down when his engine was hit. With glycol all over his windscreen and his vision obscured, Robitzsch broke off his attack on a Wellington to return to base. Just short of Neumünster his engine overheated and seized up. He forced-landed among the trenches and dugouts of a troop-training ground. The right tyre burst, causing the Me 109 to slew round in a circle before coming to rest. Robitzsch opened the cockpit hatch, climbed out onto the wing and jumped clear without a scratch. His machine was a write-off. Feldwebel Hans Troitsch, who shot down the first British bomber of the war on 4th September 1939, was hit and wounded. He managed to bring his Me 109 down on Wangerooge where it suffered extensive damage. Even the Geschwader commander, Carl Schumacher, had to retire from the fray and nurse his Me 109 back to Jever. Not one of the Me 110s deployed, however, failed to get back home. Wolfgang Falck just made it back to Wangerooge by dint of skilful piloting. The circumstances surrounding the other Me 110 that was badly damaged that day are totally baffling. Oberfeldwebel Dombrowski, the radio operator/rear gunner in an Me 110 piloted by Leutnant Uellenbeck, relates in his personal recollections of the battle that his pilot spotted a flight of *three* Vickers Wellingtons 'flying extremely low'. The position of the encounter is recorded as having taken place fifty km north of the Dutch island of Ameland. The time was 2.00 p.m. (GMT).* At precisely that time, Kellett's surviving force of ten bombers was more than a hundred km away to the east, flying above 10,000 feet and, by then, clear of attacking fighters. Only one of No. 37 Squadron's aircraft survived past the island of Borkum and that was F/O Lemon. His last encounter with the *Luftwaffe* was observing Roman Stiegler cartwheel into the drink. The only other Wellington that sought the safety of the waves and made it past Borkum was No. 9 Squadron's Sgt Petts. There is a strange similarity between the accounts of Petts and Dombrowski.

> We met each stern attack with a drill that we had agreed as a result of experience gained in fighter co-operation exercises. The usual sequence ran: 'There's one coming in, he's coming in. Get ready, get ready. Back, back.' Throttles slammed shut and pitch levers to full coarse. Bursts from our guns and enemy tracer past the windows. 'OK, he's gone.' Open up to full throttle and full revs. . . . I do remember quite clearly the end of the attacks: the drill had proceeded as before but Robertson's 'Get ready, get ready; Back, Back,' was followed by a jubilant 'I've got him, I've got him, he's gone in!' The 110 had of course

* 3.00 p.m. (15h 00) German time.

> been obliged to get down to our level just above the water for his stern attack and there was no height in which to recover any loss of control. Robertson's next comment was, 'The other one's gone home, he's had enough!'
>
> 400 m . . . 300 m . . . the Wellington turns towards us. Our bullets miss. Another try. The two enemy aircraft have separated and their defensive fire is not concentrated. Nevertheless, three further attacks are unsuccessful – taking quite a toll on our nerves! The pilot must be an old hand at this game. Every time we open fire he turns towards us and our shots pass over him.

Sgt Petts was flying 'just above the water', and Oberfeldwebel Dombrowski confirms that 'they are flying extremely low', when referring to the Wellingtons engaged by Leutnant Uellenbeck and his Rottenflieger.

Throttles wide open and heading due west from Wangerooge, Sgt Petts would certainly have managed to reach Ameland by 2 p.m. The question is where Dombrowski's other two Wellingtons came from. Likewise, where did the Me 110 spring from that Sergeant Robertson jubilantly claimed had 'gone in'?

Question marks notwithstanding, somebody shot thirty-three bullet holes in Uellenbeck's fighter, wounded the pilot and rear gunner and forced them to break off their attacks. But by 2 p.m. there simply weren't enough Wellingtons left for Uellenbeck to claim one, let alone two, victories. Kellett reported that he counted ten Wellingtons in his formation after the battle. This means that F/O Macrae must have caught up with and joined the nine survivors from Kellett's and Harris's formations. This only leaves one Wellington that could have been in the right place at the right time to shoot down Uellenbeck, and that was N2873 piloted by Sergeant Petts.

By dint of careful scrutiny of all the available records and reports on the action*, it is possible to account for the ten Wimpys shot down and allocate them to just seven of the *Luftwaffe* fighter pilots. Apart from Falck, Fresia and Gollob, there were only two other Me 110s of I/ZG76 that reported their position as being anywhere within twenty-five km of Kellett's main formation. All the other Me 110s reported their engagements as having taken place in the vicinity of Borkum, over eighty km away. In Uellenbeck's case, the distance was over one hundred and twenty km. Paul Harris confirmed that F/O Speirs was shot down by an Me 110, and the only two candidates left are Oberfeldwebel Fleischmann or Feldwebel Gröning. What happened to the other seventeen official German claims will probably remain a mystery.

The Geschwader commander, Carl Schumacher, had been forced to retire early from the battle because of damage to his Me 109E-1. On returning to fighter HQ at Jever he was presented with reports coming in thick and fast

* See Appendix B.

from his fighter squadrons. None it seemed had returned empty-handed, except III/JG77 at Nordholz. From Captain Seliger there were no reports of any victories. How could that be? Then his adjutant owned up. In all the excitement, the headquarters staff had clean forgotten all about the Gruppe at Nordholz. They had never been sent the order to scramble. Next day, at a briefing for the international press in Berlin, Schumacher was quoted as saying that things had all gone according to plan; he had even been able to hold squadrons 'in reserve'. That sounded so much better.

Shortly after 3.00 p.m. (German time), the last fighter returned to base and the *Luftwaffe* was able to take stock of the day's events. By chance, Generalleutnant Wolff, who was in charge of XI Air Administrative Region, happened to be visiting the island of Borkum that day. He watched Herbie Ruse crash-land his Wimpy. Afterwards he examined the wreckage carefully and made a surprising discovery. Straight away he made for Jever where he took Carl Schumacher aside. 'We examined the wreck minutely and believe you me, Schumacher, there wasn't a single bomb on board,' he confided. Added to this, the information extracted from the surviving British pilots, Wimberley and Ruse, had the Germans completely mystified. Not only had the British dropped no bombs on Wilhelmshaven but it now appeared that they hadn't been carrying any in the first place. The explanation offered by the two British pilots seemed to confirm that the RAF had taken leave of its senses.

'No attack was ever intended'; 'The Wellingtons were only on a navigation training exercise'; 'It was a training flight for new pilots and navigators'; 'Instead of bombs, the aircraft had been carrying extra trainees' – thus affirmed Wimberley and Ruse. To this day, all the German accounts of the battle seek to comprehend why Bomber Command should have been so foolhardy. Lengthy explanations have been proffered to account for the large discrepancy in numbers and the seemingly irrational behaviour of the British. The explanation is quite simple. The Germans miscounted and the British pilots lied to their captors.

When I put the question to Paul Harris he laughed aloud and, with a grin from ear to ear, he said, 'Well old chap, it's like this. Wimberley and Ruse told them a great big fib, didn't they, and the Jerries swallowed it, hook, line and sinker.'

The Germans did concede, however, that the British had put up a good fight and the Geschwaderkommodore noted in his report the 'tight formation and excellent rear-gunners of the Wellington bombers'.

While Schumacher and Wolff were scratching their heads over the seemingly eccentric behaviour of the 'Tommies', Richard Kellett was shepherding the remnants of his battered little flock homeward. Paul Harris handed round his precious rum flask as he assessed the situation.

> Flying number three on my port side was F/O Michael Briden with his second pilot Billy Brown. As soon as we were clear of the fighters I was

able to take stock of my flight. All seemed OK, except one, poor Briden; I could see petrol streaming from his port tank. Our tanks were not self-sealing. He called me up on the R/T to say that he was running short of petrol and could they take the shortest possible route home. Sandy looked back and confirmed that there was a plume of gas spraying out of Briden's port wing. Finally, some fifty miles off our coast his engines failed. I followed him down and he ditched successfully. I got a DF fix on him and I did a run over the aircraft low down and released my dinghy which was situated at the rear of the starboard engine nacelle. I did this in case his had failed. The aircraft was still floating. However, it was not intended that the dinghy should be released in the air, only after ditching; so, to my horror, it stuck on my tailplane and for a moment I thought I was going to join Briden. However, apart from severe vibration all was well so, having done all I could, I tottered home and landed at the first aerodrome I could find. N2980 was but little damaged; it had acquitted itself well but poor Briden and Brown were not found, the whole crew was lost. I fear their dinghy must have been holed by a bullet, and the sea was cold.

Bunny Austin vividly remembers the battle and the return journey home.

During the raid itself, the most striking thing was, perhaps a little in retrospect, the vision of sitting there in the turret watching one's own aircraft being shot out of the sky and being quite helpless to do anything about it. There is no doubt as Paul says, the losses in the other squadrons were due very largely to loose flying and, if you have to fly in daylight at that sort of height with very poor armament you must make the most of it and keep tight formation. The 0.303 inch gun turrets were pretty useless against 20 mm cannon. The German fighters should in fact have done probably better than they did. On the way back we formated later on Briden. We kept with him because he was losing fuel from his wing tanks and it was clear that he was in difficulty. Ultimately he ditched about thirty miles off Cromer. He made a very good ditching and all his crew got out into the dinghy. It was at this time that Paul decided that the thing to do would be to drop our dinghy to give them an additional dinghy in the sea. There was some protest because they were not designed to be loosened in the air and there was always the risk that it would catch around ones own tailplane. Indeed this is what happened. We circled and tried to get a fix. Jock Watson transmitted the position and we then flew as accurate a course as we could back to the English coast. I kept the most careful navigation fix that I could bearing in mind that in those days we were entirely without radar and working almost solely on dead reckoning navigation.

From Cromer and Sheringham the lifeboats put out and headed at full speed for the position given by Jock Watson to join a destroyer, a high speed

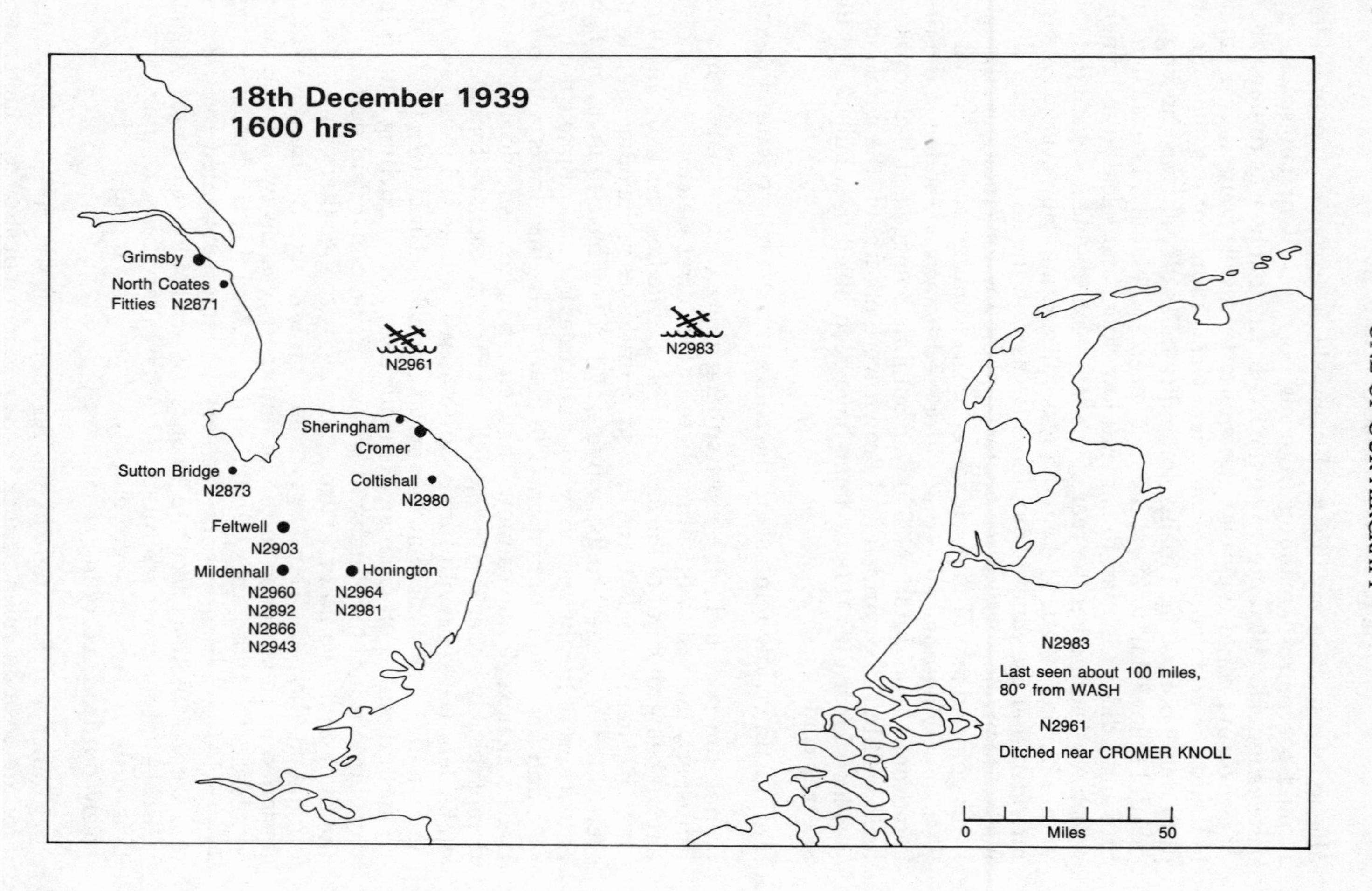
18th December 1939
1600 hrs
Grimsby
North Coates
Fitties N2871
N2961
N2983
Sheringham
Cromer
Sutton Bridge
N2873
Coltishall
N2980
Feltwell
N2903
Mildenhall
N2960
N2892
N2866
N2943
Honington
N2964
N2981
N2983
Last seen about 100 miles,
80° from WASH
N2961
Ditched near CROMER KNOLL
0
Miles
50

launch and another lifeboat in the search, but the North Sea in December was just as implacable a foe as the *Luftwaffe*. They had been warned in training that they might expect to survive for fifteen minutes under such conditions. Michael Briden and his crew were never seen again.

No. 9 Squadron's N2983 was more fortunate. Sergeant Ramshaw spotted a trawler about a hundred miles out from the Wash and ditched as close to it as he could. Less than fifteen minutes later the 'ERILLAS', skippered by S. Sinclair, reached the scene and rescued the survivors. The rear gunner, LAC Lilley, had been killed during the battle but the other four crew members were hauled from their dinghy and that night were safely in Grimsby Hospital. Ironically, on the same day that Briden and Ramshaw ditched in the North Sea due to lack of fuel from their holed tanks, the Air Ministry in London issued an order that Bomber Command should desist from further attacks in the Heligoland Bight area until Wellington bombers had been fitted with armour plating on *all* their fuel tanks.

With the dinghy stuck firmly on the tailplane, the elevator holed and ready to break at any moment, the fuel tanks dangerously low and the starboard engine feathered to cut down the awful juddering on the controls, N2980 sought a safe haven. The first available aerodrome was Coltishall close by Norwich. Having spent over six-and-a-half hours in the air and endured the undivided attention of the *Luftwaffe* during the biggest air battle of the war to date, they were met by a highly irate engineering superintendent who roared up in his big car and greeted them with the words: 'You can't land here, this airfield is not completed.' As Bunny Austin said, 'I won't give you the words that were used back to him.' Sandy commandeered a push-bike and headed for the nearest phone to inform Operations of Briden's predicament: 'Had awful trouble getting on for some fool of a girl in the exchange was behaving with bureaucratic efficiency in spite of it being a priority call. Ticked me off for my language and said she would report me just because I said: "for Christ's sake get a bloody move on".'

After the little misunderstanding with the site engineer had been amicably settled, Mr Bowles ran them the fifty miles back to Mildenhall in his big Rover, 'which was a damned good show,' noted Sandy.

Meanwhile, the rest of No. 149 Squadron were landing at Mildenhall. Kellett, Turner, Riddlesworth and Bulloch all touched down safely. Apart from a collection of assorted bullet holes and the odd chunk of missing geodetics they had all survived the battle virtually unscathed. Likewise, Grant and Purdy returned to Honington with only superficial damage. Had the Air Ministry fitted self sealing tanks and armour plating to the port wing, then Briden and Ramshaw would undoubtedly have made it back as well. Grant told his tale to the CO and the Adjutant in the Officers' mess, then went exhausted to bed. An officer who put his head into the mess a little later found it deserted but for the CO, who sat bowed and old, alone by the fireplace. Macrae forced-landed at North Coates Fitties in an aircraft that had been shot to pieces. By chance, Sandy Innes happened to see the aircraft some days later: 'Flew photographer up to Northcoates in Magister. Coldest trip I remember. Below freezing and landed in a snow storm. At Northcoates is Macrae's Wellington where he forced-landed after Mondays affair. God knows how he got back and how no one was hit. Plane was riddled with bullets and they had even gone through armour plating. Three petrol tanks at least were holed. Rear turret was riddled.' Petts could not make it back to Honington either and burst a tyre on landing at Sutton Bridge. N2873's starboard wing had been on fire but the armour plating had kept the fire away from the fuel tanks. The starboard side of the fuselage had more holes in it than a sieve. Lemon was the only survivor from No. 37 Squadron to make it back to Feltwell. N2903 landed safe and sound.

That night there was a party at the 'Bird in Hand'. Paul Harris's wife, Kit, had pints of beer all lined up along the bar and, as Sandy later noted, 'I can't remember anything being so good as my first pint of beer that night and did I need it.' As they drank their pints, they listened to 'Lord Haw-Haw' on the wireless telling them that the *Luftwaffe* had just shot down thirty-eight of their twenty-two Wimpys. That raised a great laugh.

Next day, both sides were hailing the 'Battle of Heligoland Bight' as a major victory. The Germans had a special reason for going to town on the story. In his *Berlin Diary* William L. Shirer relates:

> Berlin, December 18.
>
> The populace is still a little bit puzzled about how the big victory of the *Graf Spee* suddenly ended by the pocket-battleship scuttling itself off Montevideo yesterday afternoon. But Goebbels and Göring have pulled a neat one to make them forget it as soon as possible. The attention of the German people tomorrow morning will be concentrated by the press and radio on something else, an alleged victory – this time in the air – off Heligoland. An official statement which the papers and radio have been told to bang for all it's worth says that thirty-four out of forty-four British bombers were shot down this afternoon north of Heligoland. A very *timely* victory. We had just left the evening press conference after firing embarrassing questions about the *Graf Spee* and were putting on our overcoats downstairs when Dr Boehmer rushed in breathlessly and said he had some big news and would we please return upstairs to the conference room. Then he read us in breathless tones the communiqué about the thirty-four British planes being shot down. Suspect it is eyewash.

Oberstleutnant Carl Schumacher, Staffelkapitän 'Mäcki' Steinhoff, Staffelkapitän Wolfgang Falck, Oberleutnant Pointner, Leutnant Lent, Oberfeldwebel Fleischmann and Unteroffizier Niemeyer were summoned to Berlin to be interviewed by the German and international press on the events of the 18th of December. Over the Christmas and New Year period, newspapers round the world regaled their readers with the heroic exploits of the Royal Air Force or the *Luftwaffe* depending on their particular sympathies.

'WILL ANOTHER FILM BE MADE?' trumpeted *Der Angriff*.

*The Lion has Wings*. A film bearing this title was made using mock-ups and models and all that sort of paraphernalia – when English politicians dreamed up the first successful attacks on Kiel and Wilhelmshaven. And British cinema audiences will soon be able to see the lion rampant stretching its wings on the screen.

Outside, in the cold light of day, the old lion was already looking rather toothless. But today, if they wish to make another film – this time about the 18th of December operation, they will not have any difficulty thinking of a title. 'The wings the lion once had' is all they need to call it.

*Der Angriff*, 19th December 1939.

The Germans were not alone however in embellishing the facts. That following Thursday, newspaper reporters descended on Mildenhall, as Sandy recorded in his little notebook.

The press came down to take our photos going off on the raid and returning, exactly three days late but that didn't worry them. So we all had to get into our full flying kit, Mae Wests, parachutes, etc., and perform the most ridiculous antics – very nearly running to our planes. Then pictures of the Wellingtons flying and crews getting out. The mere fact that some of those were never on the raid is nothing of course to them. Then finally they picked on me to pose for them and God was that a performance. . . . And finally my photo in the papers. Splashed all over. Enormous affair in the Scotsman – and in the Sunday Graphic – I will never be able to live that down!

'HEROES OF THE BIGHT' HOME: NAZI ACES ROUTED: RAF ROUT NAZI SUPER-FIGHTERS: RAF GETS BEST OF BIGGEST AIR BATTLE OF THE WAR – 12 NAZI PLANES SHOT DOWN: SEVEN OF OUR MACHINES WERE LAST NIGHT UNACCOUNTED FOR.

These were but a few of the front page headlines that filled the papers over that festive season. As morale boosters they were just what the doctor ordered but as a true record of the events that day, they painted a picture viewed through rose-coloured spectacles. The Air Ministry indulged in a little verbal subterfuge to conceal the truth about the British losses but Sandy Innes had his suspicions.

We lost 10 a/c over Wilhelmshaven and two came down near England and one crew was saved. Air Ministry said that '7 of our a/c are not accounted for' because three were seen going towards Germany under some control but no power. So only 7 are unaccounted for. True of course, but it is juggling with the truth which is a pity and tends to sap confidence in the veracity of our reports. However its a damn good show that we got so many of them!

Slaughter of these proportions at this still squeamish moment of the war provoked an unprecedented upheaval and *post mortem* at 3 Group and at Bomber Command. Ludlow-Hewitt, a C-in-C already well known for his sensitivity to casualties, flew in person to Norfolk to hear first-hand accounts of the operation. Group Captain Hugh Pughe-Lloyd, a 3 Group staff officer who had commanded No. 9 Squadron until a few weeks before, said in one of a mass of reports inspired by the disaster, 'I dislike the course taken to the target. On this occasion we made land-fall near the German-Danish frontier and ran the whole way down it, giving the enemy all the warning he can get.' This was almost the only instance of open criticism of the planning of the operation.

Most senior officers studied the events of 18th December and drew much more hopeful and face-saving conclusions. They readily accepted that the Wellingtons had to be provided with beam guns and self-sealing tanks. But, granted these measures, it seemed to them that the elements of Kellett's formation which had stuck rigidly together as ordered had fared astonishingly well. Only one of Kellett's own section of four aircraft had been lost, and an impressive list of enemy fighters destroyed had been accepted. Of the six aircraft on the starboard side, all would have survived the battle had they been fitted with self-sealing tanks.

Why therefore had the port and rear sections of the formation fared so badly? Air Vice-Marshal Baldwin's report[5] to Ludlow-Hewitt contained no breath of criticism of the strategic and tactical concepts underlying the operation.

> I am afraid [he wrote firmly on 23rd December] there is no doubt that the heavy casualties experienced by 9 and 37 Squadrons were due to poor leadership and consequent poor formation flying. Squadron-Leader Guthrie is reported as being almost a mile ahead of his formation. For some unknown reason Hue-Williams, who, I thought, was a very sound leader, appears to have done the same thing. . . . I have not by any means given up hope of being able to drive home the lessons learnt. . . . I have already taken steps to prevent a repetition, but I was allowing a certain period to elapse before pinning results on to individual actions, although instances of bad leadership have already been pointed out to all units.

In his reply to Baldwin's letter of 19th December 1939, Ludlow-Hewitt acknowledged the importance of good formation flying.[6]

> I do not think you can do more than get your unit and flight commanders together and rub into them the vital importance of good formation flying. The maintenance of tight unshaken formations in the face of the most powerful enemy action is the test of bomber-force fighting efficiency and morale. It is the Air Force equivalent of the old 'thin red line' in the Army, or if you like, of the Greek phalanx or of Cromwell's Ironsides,

> and it is that aspect which should be brought home to all captains of aircraft. The great and unforgiveable crime is for the leader of the formation to fly away from his followers.

In truth, the blame for the heavy losses cannot be laid at the door of the 'captains of aircraft'. Guthrie and Hue-Williams had never faced the enemy before and paid the ultimate price for their inexperience; Kellett, Harris and Grant had, and survived. There had been no prior planning or liaison between the participating squadrons. The ultimate blame must rest squarely on 3 Group Headquarters. As Paul Harris points out, 'There is no doubt that the other two Squadrons (9 and 37) left us because they were untrained. One cannot blame them for this because we had been given no previous opportunity to fly together. Group Headquarters laid on no Group formation training – a fatal error.'

In conclusion, 3 Group's summary of the lessons to be derived from the events of 18th December stated, 'There is every reason to believe that a very close formation of six Wellington aircraft will emerge from a long and heavy attack by enemy fighters with very few, if any, casualties to its own aircraft.' 3 Group's operational instruction No. 21 of 23 December 1939 stated: 'With the intention of combining useful training and operations, sweeps will continue to be carried out . . . If enemy aircraft are encountered, gunners will be able to practise shooting at real targets instead of drogues. . . .' 'The gist of all these comments seemed to display a surviving if somewhat chastened confidence in the principle of the self-defending formation.'[7]

Some senior RAF officers still persisted with the notion that self-defending bomber formations could take care of themselves. Air Commodore Norman Bottomley issued a tactical memorandum on the 29th December 1939 in which he continued to refer to the 'inviolability of a tight bomber formation,' and he put the losses of the 14th and 18th down to straggling.

> Even more instructive was the difference in tone between what Sir Edgar Ludlow-Hewitt said in December 1939 to his Group Commander, Air Vice-Marshal Baldwin, and what he said in January 1940 to the Air Staff. On the former occasion most of his remarks were concerned with the need for better formation flying, better gunnery and greater crew efficiency as the means of successful daylight bombing. On the latter occasion he pointed to the December actions as strong evidence against carrying out the Ruhr plan. In fact, the actions in December 1939 were taken as a powerful warning of the superiority of the day-fighter over the day-bomber, and the series of formation attacks was not continued after 18th December.[8]

Cajus Bekker[9] considers that the British decision to abandon daylight raids after the 18th December 'was to have a decisive influence on the future conduct of the war'.

JG1's summary of the lessons learned on 18th December was altogether more realistic and their report concluded:

> The British seemed to regard a tightly closed formation as the best method of defence, but the greater speed of the Me 109 and Me 110 enabled them to select their position of attack. Rigid retention of course and formation considerably facilitated the attack. . . . It was criminal folly on the part of the enemy to fly at 4,000 to 5,000 metres in a cloudless sky with perfect visibility. . . . After such losses it is assumed that the enemy will not give the Geschwader any more opportunities of practice-shooting at Wellingtons.

Having found that the crashed Wellington on Borkum had no bombs on board and believing the stories told by Wimberley and Ruse, the Germans reached the logical conclusion that the British had been indulging in some form of suicidal exercise, which was indeed not far from the truth.

Paul Harris was now in no doubt as to where he stood on that issue. 'After 18th December I hoisted the warning flag and let it be known that I would not go on any more raids unless they were competently led, and I named only two people I would follow, one of whom was of course Kellett.'

Richard Kellett was later accused by the survivors of the other squadrons of flying too fast for them to keep up. This is totally refuted by Paul Harris. Indeed it had never been intended that the four formations of the big diamond should stick rigidly together. This is clear from the conclusions drawn from the operation.[10]

> THE SIZE OF FORMATIONS
>
> 6. Although 24 aircraft were sent out on the reconnaissance on the 18th December, this formation was not necessarily meant to keep any particular disposition except for convenience in approaching the target area and bearing in mind that the formations should not be in line astern, or all at one height. The instructions issued on the evening of 17th December, during the conference held at Headquarters and attended by leaders, were that, whilst the four formations of six aircraft should proceed in company, each one was a self-contained unit for defensive purposes.
>
> 7. It has always been considered that a formation greater than 12 aircraft is unwieldy and therefore unmanageable by one leader, and that the largest possible defensive formation where mutual support is possible is probably one of six aircraft.
>
> 8. The only object therefore in sending more than 6 or 12 aircraft on any operation is in order to achieve concentration in time over the target area, and thus split the defences. Unless leaders of formations will understand this principle and not endeavour to follow the leader of the whole formation to the detriment of their followers' station-keeping, the formation is bound to suffer.

Sadly, S/Ldr Guthrie and S/Ldr Hue-Williams seem to have failed to take those instructions on board and suffered the consequences. S/Ldr Paul Harris kept his head and his formation of six Wimpys survived the battle intact. W/Cdr Richard Kellett lost only one aircraft, and that might have survived if his formation had had the extra twelve guns that turned back early.

A couple of days after the raid, Air Chief-Marshal Sir Edgar Ludlow-Hewitt, C-in-C Bomber Command, arrived at Mildenhall with his retinue, to hear the story first hand. Paul Harris well remembers the occasion.

> A few days later the C-in-C Bomber Command Ludlow-Hewitt, came to see our squadron in person. This was quite an occasion. Our AOC, Baldwin, the Station Commander, Franky Coleman, Kellett, and others all crowded into Kellett's office while Ludlow-Hewitt, surrounded by a galaxy of Staff Officers, asked questions. Star turn, Aircraftsman first-class, Jimmy Mullineaux, was brought in so that the C-in-C, Ludlow-Hewitt, could talk to this hero, which indeed he was (I was very proud of him), but after a time it was all too much for him; the eminent 'Brass Hats,' the questioning and the Braid so affected him that my highly strung, modest, little Jimmy suddenly said, full of courtesy and respect to the last, 'May I faint please,' which he promptly did, into the arms of Sandy Innes, who carried him out. He was but an AC1 and very young, one of the first DFMs of the War.

Ludlow-Hewitt later put his finger on the problem when he said, 'All our previous experience had indicated that the fighter defences of north-west Germany were weak and apparently half-hearted. The tremendous opposition encountered on the 14th and 18th did, therefore, come as a surprise to us, and there is no doubt in my mind that it was due to strong reinforcements by crack squadrons from elsewhere.'[11] How right he was.

The day before the battle, I/ZG76 arrived at Jever. Their Me 110s probably accounted for eight of the ten Wellingtons shot down. Two of the pilots, Lent and Gollob, went on to become top Aces with 260 victories between them. Of the fighter pilots who took part in the action, eight later won the Knight's Cross of the Iron Cross; four added the Oakleaves, three the Swords, and two the Diamonds, to their Ritterkreuz. 'Mäcki' Steinhoff achieved the incredible total of 176 victories (six in the jet-propelled Me 262). Surprisingly enough, the official British history of the battle states: 'There was nothing to suggest that any 'crack' squadrons had been brought into the area before the engagement.'[12] With a combined total of approximately *five hundred* confirmed victories when the war ended, Schumacher's pilots that day can only be described as 'crack'. Kellett on the other hand referred to his pilots and crews with typical service understatement: the RAF raiders are described by their leader as 'just a normal team'. The Germans, he says, 'were worthy opponents'. But to have fought their way through the combined strength of *four Luftwaffe* fighter squadrons, *in daylight*, Kellett and his crews were every bit as 'crack' as their adversaries.

Notwithstanding JG1's actual score of twelve bombers shot down, it had not been altogether an impressive performance by the German fighter pilots. Even after their belated interception, they made repeated ineffectual long-range attacks. Had they then possessed the experience they went on to gain over the fields of Kent and on the Russian Front, it would have been remarkable if any of Kellett's Wimpys had survived at all. Nevertheless, twelve Wellingtons lost out of a force of twenty-two was a disaster on a scale hitherto unprecedented. A fifty per cent loss was ten times the casualty rate which Bomber Command could ever hope to sustain. 'From 18th December onward we tacitly abandoned the belief that our Wellingtons and Hampdens could operate by day in the face of German fighter opposition.'[13] 3 Group's Wimpys were sent off to be fitted with armour-plating in their port wings and *French* self-sealing coverings for their petrol tanks.

The Battle of Heligoland Bight was Bomber Command's rude awakening to the facts of life as they pertain to modern technological warfare. Kellett's casualties were just twelve of the 8,325 aircraft they lost, and the 57 men who died that day would be followed by more than 55,500 as the war pursued its relentless course. Few of those who survived that raid on Wilhelmshaven lived to enjoy the celebrations on VE Day*.

Wing Commander Kellett was shot down in a Wellington bomber during a combined operation to take Tobruk early in 1942. He was captured by the Germans and spent the remainder of the war as a PoW, eventually landing up at the famous Stalag Luft III of *Wooden Horse* and *Great Escape* fame. He was repatriated after Germany was defeated in 1945. He died on 3rd January 1990.

Flying Officer Turner was the captain of Halifax KK645 of No. 76 Squadron which was reported missing from operations against Hanover on the night of 22/23 September 1943.

Flying Officer Riddlesworth was killed in a flying accident on the 25th February 1941 when Wellington L4276, of No. 11 OTU, crashed.

Flying Officer Bulloch was killed two weeks later while leading a flight of three Wellingtons on a daylight armed reconnaissance sweep into the German Bight on 2nd January 1940.

Flight Lieutenant Grant was sent off to give a lecture to a Bomber Command gunnery school on the realities of facing fighter attacks in daylight. On his return he was severely reprimanded for having given 'an unpatriotic talk likely to cause dismay and demoralisation'. He retired from the RAF in 1945 as a Wing Commander.

Sergeant Ramshaw retired from the RAF in December 1966 as a Wing Commander. He died in May 1972.

Of Sergeant Purdy we can find no trace.

Flying Officer Lemon was shot down by night fighters whilst attacking Duisburg on the night of 25/26th July 1942. His Wellington bomber caught fire and he and his crew were forced to bale out over Holland. He was captured and spent the rest of the war as a PoW. After repatriation he later

* VE Day – Victory in Europe Day, Tuesday, 8th May 1945.

commanded No. 53 Squadron during the whole of the Berlin Airlift.

Sergeant Petts was commissioned in November 1941 and took part in the first two 1,000 bomber raids on Cologne and Essen. He was awarded the DFC and Bar in 1944, having taken part in over one hundred missions. He survived the war and died in 1969.

Flying Officer Macrae, that 'wild, brave, passionately alcoholic Canadian', died most pathetically. He collected his Distinguished Flying Cross from the King at Buckingham Palace on the 5th March 1940. After a celebration party with his crew, he took off from Weybridge to fly home to Norfolk, and crashed.

Sergeant 'Herbie' Ruse spent the next six years as a Prisoner of War in the company of Tom May, 'Jonah' Jones and Pete Wimberley. They were the only survivors from the aircraft that were shot down during the battle.

Sergeant Holley, Sergeant Tilley, Corporal Taylor and A/C Geddes were all buried with full military honours in the cemetery on Borkum.

As for the crew of old 'R for Robert', they collected no fewer than three medals that day. Paul Harris and Sandy Innes each received the DFC while Jimmy Mullineaux was awarded one of the first DFMs of the war.

Squadron Leader Harris was hospitalised with a bad case of pneumonia shortly after the raid and did not fly again until 5th March 1940. He was promoted to Commanding Officer No. 7 Squadron with the task of re-forming with Stirling bombers. Later, he was given a mobile Wellington Wing in the Western Desert which he took over just after the battle of El Alamein and, with a short break of four months as a Staff Officer in Algiers, remained with 205 Group until the end of the war. He died on 29th December 1985.

Sergeant Austin was transferred with Paul Harris to help rearm No. 7 Squadron with Stirlings, and he took part in the first operational raid with Stirlings to bomb oil tanks at Rotterdam. He was later promoted to Squadron Leader and after the war was chosen for a permanent commission, being only the second navigator to be so selected.

AC2 Watson was later promoted to Sergeant and it is believed that 'Jock' was shot down over East Anglia by an intruder when returning from a raid on Germany in a Stirling.

AC1 Doxsey was later promoted to Sergeant and is thought to have been 'reported missing' over Germany.

AC1 Mullineaux was later commissioned and subsequently shot down over Germany in 1943 and captured. He escaped three times and was once adrift for three months, passing himself off as a Walloon. He was eventually captured by the Gestapo who beat him so severely that finally he shouted in German, 'Stop it. I'm a British Officer.' Instantly the Gestapo interrogators snapped to attention and saluted him. He was repatriated after the war in very poor health and subsequently suffered a series of nervous breakdowns resulting from the treatment he had received as a PoW.

Pilot Officer Innes was perhaps the saddest case of all. While on an astro-navigation cross-country practice on 4th April 1940, Wellington bomber

P9267 approached too low looking as if it was going to overshoot the runway. At 200 feet it turned to port, crashed into the ground and burst into flames, one mile south-east of Mildenhall. Of the seven crew aboard, five were killed and two were badly injured. Flying Officer Sandy Innes, DFC, was one of those who perished. He had been home on leave over the festive season and the entry in his diary for Christmas Day reads:

> 25.12.39 . . . Betts told me how much the family have been worrying over me. What on earth can I do to stop them except ring up every time there is a raid. . . . Why can't they realise that I love the life in the air and even if I do pass out I will do it while I am doing something I love like life itself and in the middle of the most amazing thrills it is possible to imagine. I mentioned it to them and I could see the tears forming. God knows, I am lucky to have a family like that. I think I am heartless not to feel the same except I probably do, but am too dense to realise it unless it actually happened, which God forbid.

Three months later he made the last entry in his little notebook:

> 2.4.40 More night flying – this time Searchlight co-operation. The first time I had done it and it was very interesting. We were caught properly several times sometimes with 8 or 10 lights, violent manoeuvering and also desynchronising motors and also climbing and diving threw them off. Most of the time they never got us at all which promises ill if the Blitzkrieg comes. Again had trouble in landing. This time my landing light was US. Made a dud approach and had to go round again. Hair raising for Strachan took the flap off too quick and we must have dropped to within 50–100 feet of the ground. Gardiner brushed a tree-top coming in and Griffith-Jones hit a post after landing. Quite definitely we need a lot more practice. Every time we night fly something exciting happens, which is not bloody good enough.

Thereafter, the pages of the little hardback notebook are blank. Sandy was not the pilot of P9267 when it crashed. But if it had not been a training exercise at Mildenhall, the odds were overwhelming that it would have been Cologne, Hanover, Berlin, Frankfurt or perhaps even Wilhelmshaven some night in the next five years. Likewise, most of the *Luftwaffe* fighter pilots who took part in the Battle of Heligoland Bight lost their lives eight months later in the Battle of Britain or on the Russian Front or defending 'The Fatherland' against the armada of Allied bombers that followed in the wake of our old warrior N2980, from Weybridge.

# 6

## *'Blood, toil, tears and sweat'*

Two weeks after the disaster of the Battle of Heligoland Bight, as a new year dawned, Air Vice-Marshal Arthur Harris, then serving as AOC 5 Group, (later to become famous as 'Bomber' Harris C-in-C Bomber Command), told his Commander-in-Chief at High Wycombe that so long as three bombers were in company in daylight the pilots 'considered themselves capable of taking on anything'.

That very same morning of 2nd January 1940, Squadron Leader Paul Harris was instructed to send three aircraft out on a daylight sweep into the Heligoland Bight. He selected Flying Officer Bulloch to lead the formation and gave Pilot Officer Innes his first captaincy as No. 2 aircraft. Sergeant Morrice was detailed to fly No. 3 position. Eighty nautical miles north-west of Heligoland the three Wellingtons were jumped by a 'Schwarm' of Me 110s led by Leutnant Herget from Schumacher's I/ZG 76. Two of the Wellingtons were shot down and only P/O Innes succeeded in escaping. It was this sweep that really marked the end of daylight operations for Bomber Command. It brought home very forcibly to every pilot that, in daylight, they were most decidedly *not* 'capable of taking on anything'. All the Wellingtons had been fitted with armour plating in both wings and self-sealing fuel tanks. Now, there were no excuses, and even the top brass could no longer delude themselves and were forced to accept that the lessons of 18th December and 2nd January were conclusive. Bomber Command's heavy bombers were thereafter confined to the hours of darkness. Sandy Innes escaped by the skin of his teeth, and that night he recorded his experience in his little notebook:

> 2.1.40 And what a sweep. A/B at noon. Bulloch leading. Me No. 2 and Morrice No. 3, first time I had captained an aircraft on operational trip. Our own crew but Swift as 2nd pilot. We were on an offensive patrol looking for German fleet and when about 80 miles from Germany damned if we didn't run into fighters. First thing I knew was a stream of tracer apparently just missing my left ear. Intercom had more or less packed up. I was in fairly tight formation on Bull. And then everything happened. I saw Me 110s on every side. All I did was to press myself into my seat so that no bits were outside and formate and hope like hell.

I heard our gunners firing and more tracers came along then an Me suddenly appeared underneath going forward and Doxsey gave it the gun – behind it to start with but then the tracer went in, and apparently it went down. Next thing I saw was a small fire in Bull's plane on port wing – this spread and I just stared at this wondering what he was going to do and then wondering what I was going to do. Soon it spread to about half the wing and I thought this is no good, formating on a thing which might blow up at any moment and as he was going down I went up to formate on Morrice. He however was behaving oddly and proceeded to dive v. steeply in an erratic manner from side to side. I tried to formate on him but though I was at full boost and touching 300 mph at 10,000 ft, i.e. 350 mph, he was still gaining. But then he went underneath me so I pulled level and saw him no more.

Bull meantime had been seen to hit the sea, so I was left alone with all 12–15 Mes. So yours truly put his nose down and seawards also with all 12–15 Mes. This was at suggestion of Swift who came forward at intervals from fire control to tell me in dumb show what was toward. Intercom U.S. so I was left wondering what the hell was happening. He turned up once waving a Colt six shooter. I had visions of him (a) shooting the petrol tanks (b) shooting himself. Actually all he wanted to do was to take pot shots at enemy. So I said OK not knowing what he wanted. Don't think he did. Eventually got down to sea level at 20 ft and carried on there for some 80 miles and then climbed and handed over to Swift. A/C seemed to be in bad way but all lads OK, bullet holes all round but see more tomorrow.

Got back at 4 p.m. everyone v. sympathetic for it was a damned pointless sort of show not having dropped any bombs. Went along to see Mrs. Bulloch. She was with Stewart and taking it marvellously – even laughing over the baby – I couldn't understand it but women are amazing things. It was forced good humour so the sooner she broke down the better. She apparently knew when I came back alone that Bull was dead. Difficult business though. I came along to comfort her if possible and all I could do was sit around and talk of everything else. After that went back to Bird in Hand for farewell party to Lt Commander Chapman. Bed at 2 a.m.

3.1.40 Not feeling so hot this morning after last night's party, though slept v. well. Funny business this going out and some of us not coming back.

Casualties have been high in this Group and the North Sea must be piled high with bits of Wellingtons. Yet it doesn't seem to affect anyone. We talk about them and how they were shot down and it is so impersonal. A good thing really for it would be really bad if you were to get a close up. And in any case you don't consider it a human loss so much as the loss of an aeroplane. Perhaps it's callous but it makes it easier to put up with. Anyhow be that as it may. I was busy this a.m.

writing out reports, signing them, questioning gunners and crew. Went along and saw a/c U. Sure was shot about a bit, though surprisingly little damage is done. We were very lucky for the big burst went bang thro' fuselage in the only part where there is nothing. After lunch we (all the crew) were interviewed by AOC in his office with short-haired WAAF in attendance. We each told our story and many more details came out. W/C Kellett came back from leave so I had to tell him. He had his DFC up and it looks v. good.

4.1.40 This morning was interviewed with crew by three Wing Commanders and 2 Squadron Leaders from Command or Air Ministry. Wanted to know all about Me 110s and their tactics. Lasted 1½ hours. Our crew have had more experience of these Me 110s and fighters generally than any other in Command I expect. We also have quite a respect for them and their pilots. It appears it was Lt Schumacher and his Squadron again. Probably best in German Air Force and a budding Richtofen – that is unless we put a stop to him. I gather 149 are going to be given a rest for a bit for we have been in every action bar one since war began (in N Sea) and our crew most. In fact Sgt Austin said we must be bloody lucky – but maybe also with all the practice our gunners are better than most. . . .

30.1.40 Large interval due to getting a v. bad go of flu and tonsilitis at home, bed for ten days and only just back.

31.1.40 No flying with fog around. Started to thaw and everything mucky. Paul Harris is away having had gastric or Bronchial pneumonia; saw him yesterday but he won't be back for weeks. My a/c from last raid is still being repaired, nearly four weeks on it. This evening saw W/Cdr and was informed that as we were the most experienced crew in operations we were to be used to train new people coming in and also to experiment in different methods of bombing and attacks. All very interesting and should put the family in a more easy frame of mind.

*Wing Commander Bunny Austin's account of 2nd January 1940*

I would like to say something about this raid because it had a far greater impact on many people in the squadron than indeed 18th December which was much more publicised. It's often thought that 18th December raid was the last major daylight operation; indeed it was in numbers but on 2nd January 1940 three aircraft from our squadron, 149 Squadron, were detailed to do a sweep of the North Sea down the islands and back, down the Dutch coast in a general circular pattern. The object of the exercise was to see if there was any enemy shipping. I recall that at briefing we were specifically told: 'don't worry there is not likely to be any attacks from enemy aircraft.' Originally Paul was due to lead this flight of three but at the last moment he came along to the crew room and said that he wouldn't in fact be flying and Flying Officer Bulloch would lead and that Sandy Innes with Pilot Officer Swift as second pilot would take the aeroplane and we would fly No. 2 to Flying Officer Bulloch, Sergeant Morrice would be the third captain. We in fact duly set off and that's all we knew when we went; we learned a lot more about what it was all about when we came back. We were attacked by a Lieutenant Schumacher and his squadron of Me 110s and the first thing we heard about the attack was Mullineaux shouting out: 'Fighters, fighters, fighters,' and I went back to man the dustbin turret and as I let it down things were disintegrating all around. I remember almost the beauty of the situation, of seeing things in mid-air from bits of geodetic and bits of the catwalk and things. Anyway, getting into the turret, I saw that the other two aeroplanes were already going down – in fact they both went down, one in flames the other one I lost sight of. Quite clearly there would have been no survivors and no parachutes. Anyway we fought as best we could all over the sky and I remember that I personally fired some 1,500 rounds from each of my guns and during the activity I called for some more ammunition and Pilot Officer Swift came running back. In the excitement he had his revolver out and I thought he was going to shoot me for mutiny or something. Afterwards I said: 'What the hell have you got your revolver going for?' – and he said: 'Well I was standing in the astrodome and I felt I had to do something, I felt so helpless.'

Anyway the object of mentioning this raid is not to specifically highlight that event but it's perhaps stemming from that raid that I realised the great guts of the wives of the people living in the area. That evening Bill Kelly, Flight Sergeant Kelly, came along and said that Mrs Wakeham, whose husband had been in one of the aeroplanes, would like to see me and it wasn't something I relished doing but I knew her and were all friends anyhow and I went down and the first thing she said was: 'Oh do come in Bunny you must be very very tired.' She had another woman, one of the sergeant pilot's wives, with her, but insisted that she made coffee and I always recall how calm she was and she wanted to know really if there was any hope at all. I had to say that there must be very little indeed. I was deeply touched by the concern she felt for me, having just lost her husband, and this typified the spirit apertaining at that time. Later, I'm afraid, we were to lose Jock Watson, and Doxsey, I'm pretty certain, was killed later in the war as well. Jimmy Mullineaux was shot down and made a prisoner of war.

New Year's Eve 1940 saw the end of 'R for Robert'. It also marked the end of the most momentous year in British history. It was the year in which a third of a million men were spirited off the beaches at Dunkirk by a fleet of little ships. It was the year in which a handful of Spitfires and Hurricanes drove back the full might of the *Luftwaffe*. It was the year of 'Blood, toil, tears and sweat.' The war went on for another five long years, but the British did not have to endure another year struggling on alone. Deprived of

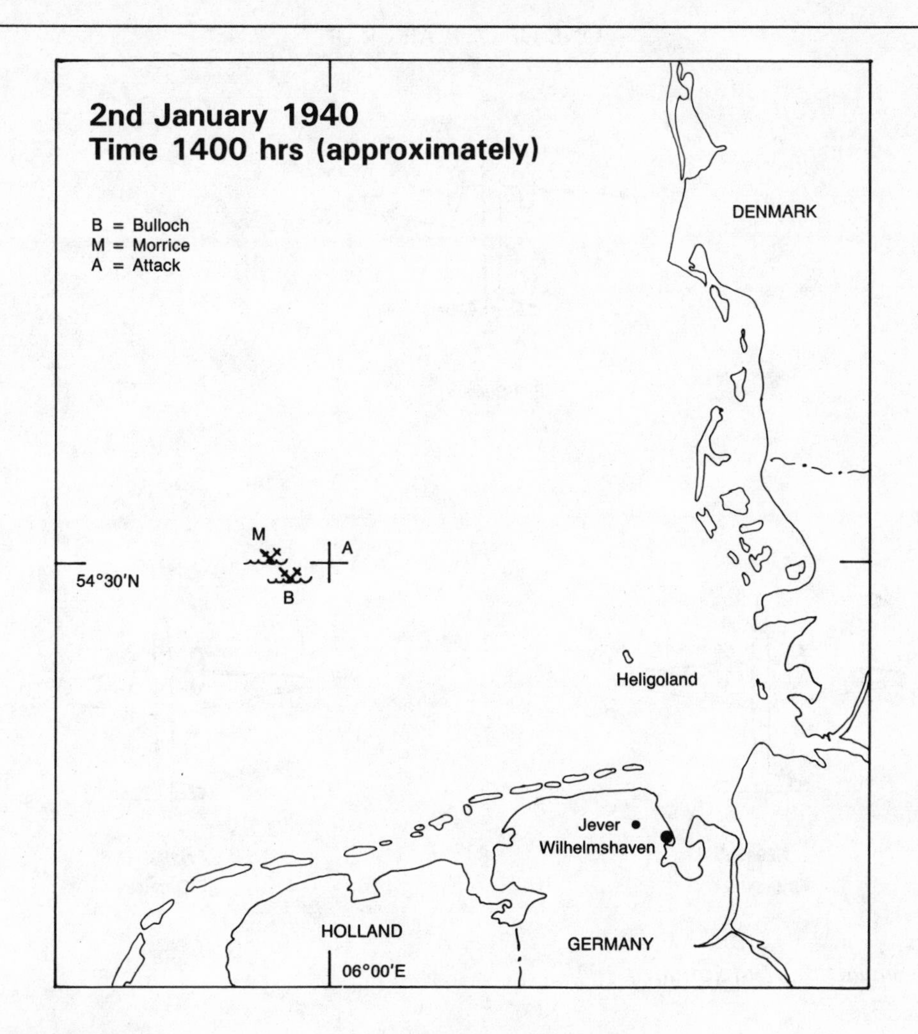


*149 Squadron*

| | |
|---|---|
| N2943 F/O Bulloch | Shot down in flames 54° 27′N, 5° 47′E. |
| N2868 P/O Innes | Claimed to have shot down two Me 110s. |
| N2946 Sgt Morrice | Last seen 54° 34′N, 5° 40′E pursued by several Me 110s. |

The three aircraft from 149 Squadron formed one of several flights of Wellingtons carrying out armed reconnaissance sweeps in the German Bight that day. (3 from 9 Sqn; 6 from 38 Sqn; 2 from 115 Sqn; 3 from 99 Sqn and 3 from 149 Sqn.) The Wellingtons were fitted with new armour plating and self-sealing fuel tanks.

*Luftwaffe*[1]

Four Me 110s of I/ZG76 led by Lt Herget attacked 149 Squadron's three Wellingtons.
Ofw. Fleischmann attacked N2943 and shot it down in flames.
Lt Habben attacked N2946 which released its bombs before crashing into the sea with its right wing on fire.
Uffz. Grams pursued a Wellington which dived towards the sea trailing black smoke (possibly N2943 or N2946).
Two Me 110s were damaged but both got back to base on one engine (one gunner was wounded).

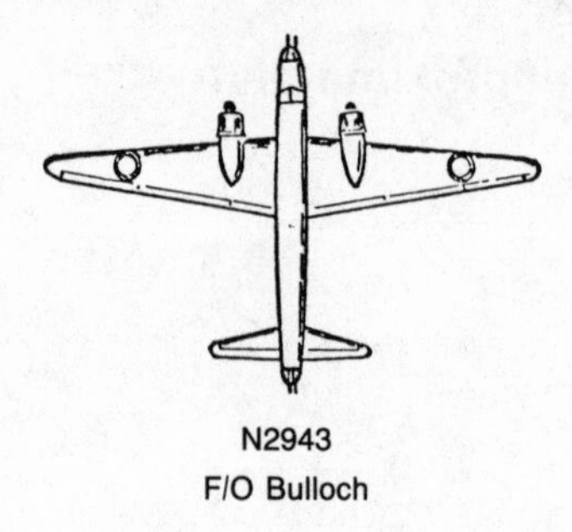


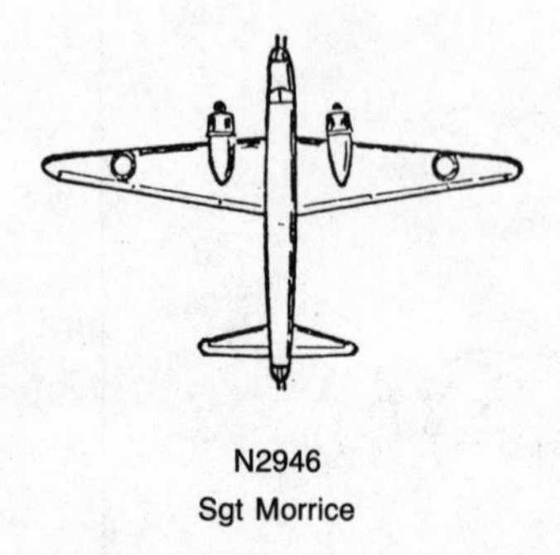


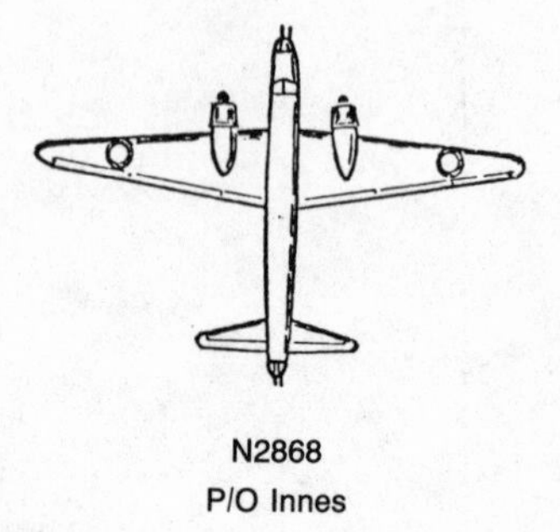


*149 Squadron, 2nd January 1940.*

his prey, Hitler turned eastward towards Russia just as Napoleon had done many years before. Japan too made an equally monumental blunder when it 'awakened a sleeping giant' at Pearl Harbor. Russia, with the unconquerable 'General Midwinter', and America, the 'great arsenal of democracy', joined forces with the little island that had firmly stood its ground. Together, they eventually crushed the tyrants Hitler, Mussolini and Tojo. But the struggle was long, hard and bloody.

By 1944 however, technology had stepped in to give a helping hand with the Mosquito as the 'speed bomber' and the Mustang as the 'long-range fighter escort' that were so sadly lacking in 1939. Now it became possible to sweep the sky over Germany clear of its defending fighters. Göring later said, 'When I saw the Mustangs over Berlin, I knew the war was lost.' The Führer came to power with a promise to the German people: 'Give me four years and, I promise you, you won't recognise your cities.' With the help of Wellingtons, Stirlings, Lancasters, Halifaxes, Mosquitoes, Fortresses, Liberators

**'R for Robert' flew fourteen operational missions to Germany.**
**In those days, the average life expectancy of a Wimpy was about six missions.**

| | | |
|---|---|---|
| 20 November 1939 | N2980 Taken on charge of Number 149 Squadron at MILDENHALL | |
| Date | Target | Pilot |
| 3 December 1939 | Heligoland | F/Lt J. B. Stewart |
| 18 December 1939 | Wilhelmshaven | S/Ldr P. I. Harris |
| 20 February 1940 | Heligoland | F/O G. P. Miers |
| 15/16 March 1940 | Hanover (Nickel raid) | F/O G. P. Miers |
| 31 March 1940 | Special Sweep (Training) | P/O H. A. Innes |
| 16 April 1940 | Special Sweep (Training) | F/O J. S. Douglas-Cooper |
| 17 April 1940 | Special Sweep (Training) | F/O J. S. Douglas-Cooper |
| 25 April 1940 | Special Sweep (Training) | F/O J. S. Douglas-Cooper |
| 5/6 May 1940 | Sylt and Borkum (Security Patrol) | F/O J. S. Douglas-Cooper |
| 14/15 May 1940 | Aachen (start of Strategic Bombing 15th May 1940) | F/O J. S. Douglas-Cooper |
| 17/18 May 1940 | Namur | F/O. J. S. Douglas-Cooper |
| 30 May 1940 | N2980 Taken on Charge of Number 37 Squadron at FELTWELL | |
| Date | Target | Pilot |
| 5/6 June 1940 | Cambrai and Munchen-Gladbach | F/O Perioli |
| 9/10 June 1940 | Rocroi, Charlesville, Meziers | Sgt Watt |
| 11/12 June 1940 | Furnay-Guspunsant, Nousonville | F/O Griffiths |
| 14/15 July 1940 | Marshalling Yards at Hamm | W/Cdr Merton |
| 6/7 August 1940 | Synthetic Oil Plant at Mors | P/O Watt |
| 15/16 August 1940 | Marshalling Yards at Hamm | P/O Dingle |
| 26/27 August 1940 | Frankfurt, Stokum, Hamm, and Brussels Aerodrome | F/O Griffiths |
| 6 October 1940 | N2980 Taken on Charge of Number 20 O.T.U. at LOSSIEMOUTH | |
| Date | Target | Pilot |
| 31 December 1940 | N2980 Ditched on Loch Ness | S/Ldr N. Marwood-Elton |

and many other kinds of bomber, this was one of the few promises he was able to keep.

Eventually the Germans were brought to a halt at Stalingrad, the Italians threw in the towel and the Japanese suffered the trauma of the atomic bomb. The war ended in 1945 with everyone worn out. Sickened by the carnage and appalled by the revelations of the concentration camps, we turned away from all the instruments of war. Historical preservation was the last thing on our minds as we picked ourselves up, dusted ourselves down and looked round at the ruins all about us. Away with all the impedimenta of war. Away with all the aeroplanes that had served us so faithfully. Away with them *all* to the scrapyards. Not one single battle-scarred Wimpy was set aside for posterity to gaze upon and help commemorate the courage and bravery of all those who flew in them. Group Captain Marwood-Elton unwittingly did us a great favour when he ditched N2980 on Loch Ness. Later in the war, on the night of 22/23 March 1944, his Halifax was shot down over Giesen by a nightfighter. He bailed out at 16,000 ft and landed in a snow-covered forest. He was repatriated on VE Day.

It is also worth relating the subsequent fate of other 149 and 37 Squadron aircrew associated with N2980. It helps to gauge the terrible losses suffered by Bomber Command. 'R for Robert' was only one of over 100,000 military aircraft produced by British industry during the war. Of the twenty-one officers who flew in her, only five are known to have survived the war.

| | |
|---|---|
| Wing Commander J. B. Stewart (Canadian) | Retired |
| Group Captain P. I. Harris DFC | Retired |
| Flying Officer H. A. Innes DFC | Deceased |
| Wing Commander G. P. Miers DFC | Deceased |
| Flying Officer C. G. Birch DFC | Deceased |
| Squadron Leader A. J. Strachan | Deceased |
| Squadron Leader M. Bryan-Smith DFC | Deceased |
| Flying Officer J. S. Douglas-Cooper | Deceased |
| Pilot Officer M. B. Dawson | Deceased |
| Pilot Officer J. R. Swift | Deceased |
| Flying Officer Griffiths | No Trace |
| Wing Commander W. N. Perioli OBE, DFC | Retired |
| Pilot Officer G. H. Muirhead | Deceased |
| Squadron Leader D. F. Benbow DFC | Retired |
| Flying Officer A. A. Scott | Deceased |
| Air Chief Marshal Sir W. H. Merton KCB, CBE, OBE, CB | Retired |
| Pilot Officer Watt | No Trace |
| Flying Officer A. C. Dingle | Deceased |
| Pilot Officer Hayes | No Trace |
| Pilot Officer Turner | No Trace |
| Pilot Officer Littlejohn | Deceased |

As for all the other thousands of Wellington bombers, they soldiered on with Bomber Command right into 1944. Their final mission was laying mines off Lorient on the night of 3/4th March with No. 300 (Polish) Squadron. By then they had also become the mainstays of Coastal Command and the Operational Training Units (OTUs). The last Wellington ever built was RP590, a MkX which was handed over from its Blackpool factory to the RAF on 25th October 1945, two months after the Japanese surrendered. The Wellington was the only Allied bomber to fly first line operations from the day the war started to the day it finished. It completed its last mission for the RAF (a training flight) in March 1953. During its service career it served everywhere, with everyone and was universally loved by all who flew in it or spent their time servicing it. It bombed, laid mines, swept mines, hunted submarines, dropped torpedoes, towed gliders, transported troops, acted as an air ambulance, dropped the first 4,000 lb Blockbuster, helped Barnes Wallis test his bouncing bomb, developed the first high-altitude pressure chamber, assisted with early electronic counter-measures and acted as a test-bed for the first jet engines. Perhaps it was because of this incredible versatility that it never acquired a specific pinnacle of achievement on which to hang its own claim to fame. The Lancaster has the Dam Busters, the Mosquito has the breaching of the walls of Amiens prison, maybe 'R for Robert' and the Battle of Heligoland Bight can accord the old Wimpy a similar place in our affections. The Wellington was built in greater numbers than any other multi-engined aircraft in Britain, a staggering 11,461.

It is outside the scope of this book to elaborate on the history of the Vickers Wellington bomber because it has been done so much more ably elsewhere.[2, 3, 4, 5, 6, 7] It is sufficient to say that it did the job for which it was designed (and a lot more besides) most efficiently but, like all the other early thirties aircraft, it was overtaken by the ever-growing pace of wartime technology. It was an unique aircraft that evolved from the previous age of giant airships. It could never exist today. Metal fatigue showed up after prolonged use as cracks and fractures in the structure, a malady well understood today but unheard of in the 1930s. As a 'cloth bomber', its further development was limited by its fabric covering, which peeled off at the increased air speeds demanded of later bombers. But – it was there when we needed it. It could be repaired like a Meccano set with new pieces of geodetic or spare bits scrounged from wrecked aircraft, with the joins hidden under fabric patches. On more than one occasion a Wimpy returned from Germany to confront a team of astonished erks* with great chunks shot out of its wings or fuselage. On more than one occasion those same erks worked round the clock and had it flying again in a few days, ready for its next trip back to Germany.

The official historians of the British air offensive against Germany, Webster and Frankland, view the three actions which were fought on 3rd, 14th and 18th December 1939 as 'among the most important of the war'. This is

* Erk, a slang term used in the RAF for an aircraftman.

certainly true as regards the effect they had upon Air Ministry thinking. It was from these three raids that their policy of daylight operations by self-defending bomber formations was found to be, quite simply, 'not on'. Surprisingly enough the *Luftwaffe* did not grasp the fact that this lesson also applied to them. It is true that they were able to provide their bombers with strong fighter escorts from conveniently based airfields in France. But the lesson was exactly the same; it just took longer and was much more painful to learn. The Americans, on the other hand, were confident that once they had fitted their bombers with power-operated gun turrets* and protected them with armour plating, they would succeed where the British and Germans had failed. With their thirteen 0.5 in. Browning machine guns bristling all over the place and flying at 30,000 feet, the U.S. 8th Airforce's B17s embarked on deep-penetration raids into Germany in daylight. In an incredible feat of arms, the *Luftwaffe* fought them to a standstill. On 17th August 1943, 376 Flying Fortresses set out on precision attacks on ball-bearing factories at Schweinfurt, Regensburg and Wiener Neustadt. Sixty of these huge machines were shot down. The Americans tried Schweinfurt again a few months later only to suffer a further paralysing loss of 60 more B17s out of a force of 291. After 'Black Thursday', 14th October 1943, the U.S. 8th Airforce was forced to abandon, temporarily, its deep-penetration raids into Germany.

The theory of the invincible bomber subjugating an entire enemy nation was first mooted in 1921 by the Italian General Guilo Douhet in his book *The Command of the Air*. Guilo Douhet had not reckoned with the then unheard-of invention called radar. Eventually the British and American air forces triumphed by sheer weight of numbers, the arrival of the long-range escort fighter, the *Luftwaffe*'s chronic shortage of fuel and its rapidly diminishing stock of trained pilots. Three dates are engraved on the tombstone of the 'bomber will always get through' philosophy – 18th December 1939, the Battle of Heligoland Bight; 15th September 1940, Battle of Britain Sunday; and 14th October 1943, Black Thursday. Each represents a decisive defeat of intruding enemy bombers by defending fighters. The British and the Germans switched to night bombing. The combat wings of the U.S. 8th Airforce in Britain received their first North American P51 Mustangs on 1st December 1943.

Battle of Britain Sunday and Black Thursday are well documented and analysed in numerous official and popular publications. While the importance of the Battle of Heligoland Bight is acknowledged by Webster and Frankland in the official history[8], it is conspicuous by its absence in most popular accounts of the Second World War. This may be due to the not unnatural tendency to play down a defeat, but is more likely caused by the obscurity of the events that occurred during the Phoney War. To most people in Britain, the war really only started on 10th May 1940 when Hitler invaded Holland, Belgium and Luxembourg. But to those servicemen who fought between

* As originally conceived, the B17 had no power-operated gun-turrets.

3rd September 1939 and 10th May 1940 there was nothing phoney about the war. Another reason for the obscurity of the December 1939 raids on the German navy may be the fact that, even to the people who took part in them, their real purpose was unclear. The official reason given at the time was to mount 'a major operation with the object of destroying an enemy battle-cruiser or pocket-battleship'. Though goaded into action by a hard-pressed Winston Churchill, Bomber Command had no traditional interest in battleships, nor for that matter had they the foggiest idea how to sink them.

Battleships were the province of the Royal Navy, and, as relations between the two organisations were particularly strained at this time, so co-operation between the two services was strictly limited. In 1939 there were really only two ways to sink a battleship using aircraft. The first called for the use of torpedoes dropped from a very low level and the other required *precisely* placed bombs released from dive bombers. Only by these two specialist methods could the overriding constraint of the Phoney War be met: NO GERMAN CIVILIAN MUST BE HURT. In the opening months of the war Bomber Command knew next to nothing about torpedoes and for many years had set its face firmly against the use of dive-bombers. By far the riskiest method of trying to hit a battleship was to drop bombs on it from a great height, a notoriously random process at the best of times. If the ship happened to be in dock at the time, the chances of avoiding civilian casualties were indeed slim. In the contemporary Bomber Command reports on the three December 1939 raids, it is significant that there is a total lack of concern at the highest level in Bomber Command regarding the failure of these raids to even dent let alone sink a German battleship with a bomb. After being shot down and captured on 18th December, Flying Officer Wimberley and Sergeant Ruse attempted to mislead their captors by saying that no attack had been intended and that they were only on a 'navigation flight' over Heligoland Bight[9]. No bombs were found on board Ruse's crashed aircraft and this reinforced the German belief that it had only been a training flight to initiate new pilots and observers. While Wimberley and Ruse thought they were giving false information to the enemy, they were, in point of fact, not far from the truth.

In a letter from 'Jackie' Baldwin, the AOC No. 3 Group, to his C-in-C, Sir Edgar Ludlow-Hewitt[10], the following extracts are significant.

> 18. *Tactics*. Now to return to tactics, and the question of how to improve formation flying under A.A. fire. I am afraid I can only hark back to the experience of the last war when carrying out long raids into Germany.
>
> 22. The other lesson we learnt was that in order to 'blood' the formations, it was necessary to give them a short raid to some appropriately placed enemy aerodrome or other suitably placed target, in order to subject them to A.A. fire and a limited attack by E.A., but giving them a chance to return across our lines before straggling became too pronounced.

23. At the present moment, we are pushing out these formations unaccustomed to the war issues, almost to the limit of the aircraft's endurance, and into heavily defended areas, and exposing them to a somewhat lengthy attack during which there is no possibility of assistance or respite, should straggling become apparent.

In his reply to this letter[11], Sir Edgar Ludlow-Hewitt made the following point:

3. . . . I had welcomed an opportunity to carry out high-altitude bombing operations on the north-west coast of Germany for the very reason which you gave in paras 22 and 23 of your letter, namely in order to give our formations experience under conditions in which enemy opposition was unlikely to be severe. In this, of course, we were disappointed and admittedly surprised, the opposition being far stronger than anything we had expected. Actually, as you suggest, there is no other means by which we can get our formations this experience except by operations against the fringe of the enemy's defences on the north-west coast.

It emerges from this correspondence between Air Vice-Marshal Baldwin and Sir Edgar Ludlow-Hewitt that the two sweeps on 3rd December and 18th December 1939 were most probably conceived as a 'test of bomber-force fighting efficiency and morale'. Put more simply, they were to 'blood the formations'. The sweep by No. 99 Squadron on 14th December was slightly different in that it was called for by Coastal Command for the express purpose of finishing off the *Nürnberg* and the *Leipzig*. Jackie Baldwin likened No. 99 Squadron's experience to the 'Charge of the Light Brigade', but nevertheless he telephoned Air Commodore Bottomley at Bomber Command HQ at High Wycombe at 3 p.m. on 17th December to urge a further operation against Wilhelmshaven.

Wing Commander Kellett and his captains were of course unaware that their missions were primarily intended to probe the enemy's defences and find out how bomber formations would fare in modern war when 'subjected to A.A. fire and a limited attack by E.A.*'. This they discovered, but at the same time they unwittingly revealed an infinitely more profound truth about the new form of aerial warfare. Stanley Baldwin had been dead wrong in his assertion that 'the bomber will always get through'. For the first time in warfare, radiolocation, later known as radar, picked up Kellett's Wellingtons as they approached Heligoland on 3rd December 1939, thereby making 'R for Robert' one of the first hostile aircraft to be so detected. The defending anti-aircraft guns and fighters were given eight minutes' warning of the attack. On that occasion Kellett's formation just escaped by the skin of its teeth because the bulk of the defending fighters took off that little bit too late to intercept the

* Enemy Aircraft.

intruders. Gone forever were the days when you could nip over the trenches to drop a few surprise bombs on an enemy airfield or ammunition dump and then race back to the safety of your own lines. Formations could no longer be 'blooded' by this simple World War I tactic. For quite a different reason to that intended, the three December raids by the Wellingtons into the Deutsche Bucht were an unqualified success. They jolted most senior officers in the RAF out of the past and into the present, into the sudden realisation that they were not engaged in a simple continuation of World War I as so many of the top brass had expected. Ludlow-Hewitt quickly recognised 'that penetration into enemy territory was practically nil, and it is the amount of penetration which is the real criterion of the severity and difficulty of the operation'. On the 14th and 18th December raids, Bomber Command lost half their aircraft just skirting the fringes of the German defences.

It was just conceivable that the fifty per cent loss suffered by 99 Squadron could have been a fluke, but for 149, 9 and 37 Squadrons to suffer a fifty-five per cent loss was conclusive evidence that there had been a dramatic change in aerial warfare since 1918. It is not known if Ludlow-Hewitt was aware that the Germans had been using radar, because he attributed the heavy losses to 'strong reinforcements by crack squadrons from elsewhere'. Throughout Bomber Command there was now a general realisation that pushing ahead with the Ruhr Plan, deep into Germany in daylight with no defence other than gun-turrets, would be suicidal. Bomber Command could not risk having its meagre resources completely wiped out. On the other hand, the Whitleys of No. 4 Group had been penetrating deep into Germany on Nickel* raids and returning unscathed *night* after *night*. For the price of 22 Wellington bombers, the Royal Air Force discovered they were in a different war from the one they had been expecting and acted accordingly. At a cost of 1,733 aircraft shot down in the Battle of Britain, Göring was forced to the same conclusion.

But the final word on the outcome of the early raids into the Heligoland Bight must be left to the professional historian. In his book[12] *The Fight at Odds 1939–1941* Denis Richards has this to say:

> The offensive (if such it may be called) against enemy warships during the long months of inactivity on land was singularly unimpressive in its immediate results. In the course of 861 sorties Bomber Command dropped only 61 tons of bombs; and the material achievement – some slight damage to the *Emden* and the *Scheer*, the sinking of a U-boat and a minesweeper, and the destruction of ten fighters – was not worth the loss of forty-one bombers. But the lessons learned in the process – learned, that is to say, not in some disastrous major campaign, but in the course of a few minor operations – were of the highest value to our cause. The improvement of operational technique; the fitting of

* Nickels; propaganda leaflets.

> self-sealing petrol tanks; the policy of using the 'heavies' of the time only by night – these were the real consequences of our failure. And, as lessons, they were learnt not only at little cost but in full time for the days of stress that were to come. Had this not been so, had the Air Staff been less sensitive to the early promptings of experience, the bomber force might well have been exposed, in the catastrophic days of May 1940, to losses that would have blunted its power at the moment of our greatest need.

Five-and-a-half years after Richard Kellett with his twenty-four Wimpys first spotted Heligoland through a gap in the clouds one mile away to the east, Bomber Command returned. The date was 18th April 1945 and the war in Europe was virtually over. This time more than 900 bombers pulverised* the island fortress where the naval radar had first detected Kellett's tiny force.

> The island fortress of Heligoland and the Dune airfield were attacked by more than 900 bombers on April 18. There were three A/Ps, the main island, the naval base and the airfield. Whole areas were laid waste – only photographs could convey the utter devastation. Marking, from the initial *Oboe* TIs to the last Backer-up, was of a high standard and the Master Bombers kept a tight rein on an enthusiastic Main Force. The next day, 33 Lancasters of 5 Group, 6 carrying Grand Slams† and the remainder Tallboys‡, sent to flatten anything left standing, reported that the centre of the island was still ablaze.[13]

Nine hundred bombers was a force big enough to have levelled Brunsbüttel, Heligoland and Wilhelmshaven in one go. The five-and-a-half years had changed Bomber Command from a puny token force to the instrument of Armageddon. The aircraft, the bombs, the radio navigation equipment, the tactics and the sheer professionalism of the organisation had transformed those young, eager and naïve faces we first saw in *The Lion has Wings* into 'the most highly trained front-line soldiers in the history of warfare'. The day before Heligoland took its final pasting, the Chiefs-of-Staff of the Allied war effort issued a communiqué to the effect that 'area' bombing was to end. Two weeks later Hitler shot himself and a week after that the British Prime Minister, Winston Churchill, stood up in the House of Commons to say that Germany had surrendered unconditionally. Japan held out for another three months before the world entered the Atomic Age.

Richard Kellett flew a little slower and Peter Grant stuck close to Paul Harris so they lived to tell the tale. Thereafter, Bomber Command switched to night-time operations and survived to grow into a mighty force of retribution. Knowing this, it now seems inappropriate to compare the early raids of December 1939 with that futile escapade of the Light Brigade. So, to what

* 5,000 tons of bombs were dropped.
† 22,000 lb penetrating bomb.
‡ 12,000 lb penetrating bomb.

can we compare Bomber Command's first hesitant steps? In an age when our sensibilities have been blunted by lavish films and spectacular television sagas, it is not easy to find a modern epic that adequately conveys the simpler sentiments and emotions of 1939. To compare like with like we must turn the clock back to those less sophisticated days when it was easy to tell the 'good guy' by his white hat and the 'bad guy' by his black one.

In 1939, as No. 149 Squadron was being marched down to the Comet cinema in Mildenhall to see a preview of *The Lion has Wings*, another film was packing them in round the country. *Gunga Din* provided a splendid piece of escapism with the swashbuckling adventures of Douglas Fairbanks Jnr., Cary Grant and Victor McLaglen. In it, the peace and stability of the British Raj were being threatened by a bunch of murderous Thuggees led by an evil Guru. Our three heroes, accompanied by Sam Jaffe as the faithful water bearer Gunga Din, had tracked the Thugs to their lair in the mountains, only to be captured and held prisoner in their stronghold called the Golden Temple. As the Regiment marched to the rescue, pipes playing and banners waving, little did they know that they were heading straight into an ambush set-up by the scheming Guru. The film reached its climax with the four prisoners escaping to the roof of the Temple, only to watch helplessly as the Regiment marched unsuspectingly towards the valley where the Guru had concealed his massive forces poised in readiness to spring the trap. Courageously, the frail Gunga Din climbed painfully up to the dome of the Golden Temple, stood up in full view of the enemy, put his beloved old bugle to his lips and blew a warning call. Alerted, the Regiment formed up into battle order and, after a mighty punch-up, defeated the Thugs – their evil Guru committing suicide. After saving the Regiment, Gunga Din fell from the dome mortally wounded. For his bravery he was made a posthumous Corporal in the Regiment and buried with full military honours to the time honoured words, 'You're a better man than I am, Gunga Din.' This was hilariously corny stuff by today's standards but, to the uncritical eye of a wee schoolboy in 1939, pure magic. So it is with those hazy recollections of a film from the days of the Phoney War that I see our old warrior 'R for Robert' helping to blow the bugle call that alerted an unsuspecting Bomber Command and saved it from charging headlong into the Ruhr Valley – to almost certain annihilation.

# 7

## *One of our Aircraft comes home*

Prior to 1981, no serious consideration had been given to salvaging the old Wimpy. The stumbling block was the depth of water in which the aircraft lay. N2980 was submerged almost five times deeper than the *Mary Rose*. On that project they had been able to call upon the help of a multitude of volunteer SCUBA* divers to study and eventually recover the wreck. But seventy metres is too deep for SCUBA divers. At that depth nitrogen narcosis, or 'raptures of the deep', causes SCUBA divers to hallucinate and lose their powers of concentration. Also, at that depth, it takes a long time for divers to decompress on their way back up to the surface. The decompression stops must be rigidly observed if divers are to avoid getting the 'bends'. Because of these dangers, professional diving companies are not allowed, by law, to exceed a depth of fifty metres without using special breathing gases consisting of a carefully controlled mixture of oxygen and helium. As a further safety precaution, professional deep divers must also be provided with a diving bell so that they can be brought to the surface under pressure in an emergency. These facilities are extremely expensive.

The only exception to the rule is the Royal Navy Fleet Diving Group. Because of the nature of the tasks they are called upon to perform, naval divers are granted a special dispensation to allow them to work down to seventy-five metres without the requirement of an attendant diving bell. They are specially trained for this task by carrying out a series of 'working-up' dives every year to keep them in condition. Even at that, their time on the bottom is measured in minutes and their decompression time on the way back to the surface is measured in hours. From 1978 to 1980, the Fleet Clearance Diving Team had been using the Loch Ness Wellington as one of their working-up sites. The Navy, however, cannot normally be called upon to undertake civilian salvage operations, and the cost of employing a North Sea diving company was prohibitive. One way round the problem was to attempt a salvage operation using an unmanned, remotely operated vehicle called an ROV.

* SCUBA – Self Contained Underwater Breathing Apparatus.

1978

1981

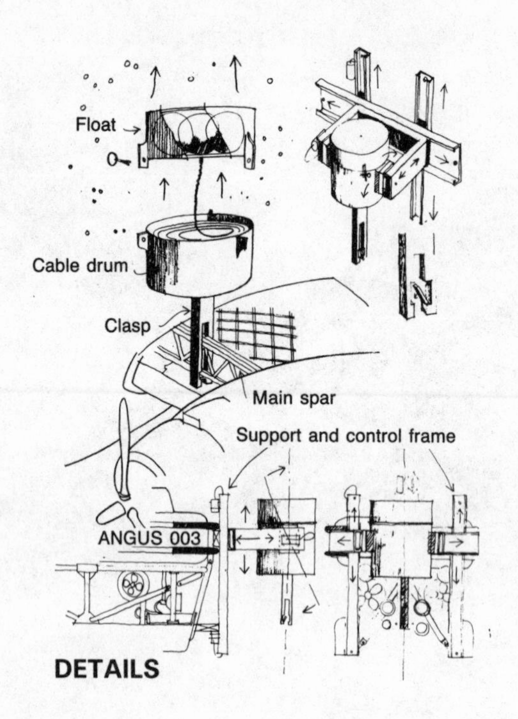
Float
Cable drum
Clasp
Main spar
Support and control frame
ANGUS 003
DETAILS

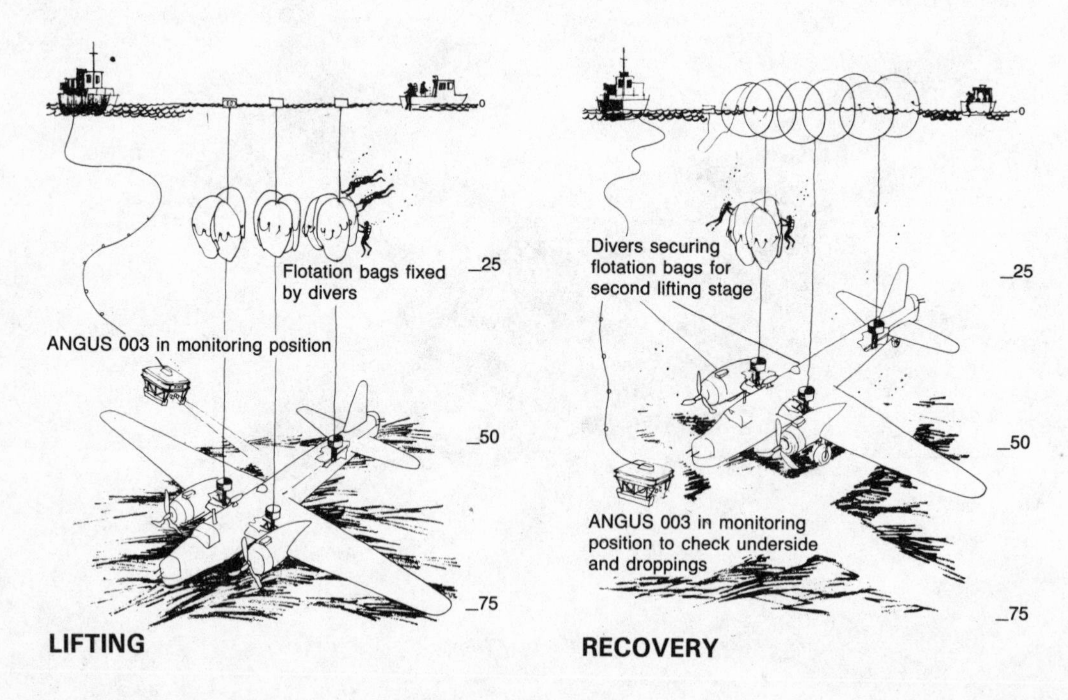
Flotation bags fixed
by divers
ANGUS 003 in monitoring position
_25
_50
_75
LIFTING
Divers securing
flotation bags for
second lifting stage
ANGUS 003 in monitoring
position to check underside
and droppings
_25
_50
_75
RECOVERY
BELL'87

As part of a SERC*-funded programme extending over a period of ten years, the author, in collaboration with colleagues in the Underwater Technology Group in the department of Electrical and Electronic Engineering at Heriot-Watt University, had designed and developed three such vehicles. The original vehicle, called ANGUS 001, was the first ROV built in Britain to achieve its design depth of 335 metres (1,100 feet) in December 1973. The second vehicle, called ANGUS 002, was built to study the problems associated with computer control of tethered submersibles. This was successfully demonstrated during the summer of 1981. The third and final vehicle, called ANGUS 003, was built to investigate the last frontier in underwater vehicle technology, the unmanned, tetherless submersible. The concept called for ANGUS 003 to carry a small, battery operated tetherless submersible called ROVER. This was to be launched and recovered from 003 on the sea bed and then transmit slow scan television pictures back to 003 by means of an advanced, computer controlled, acoustic communication link. Because of its role as a 'mother' submersible, ANGUS 003 had to be large and powerful. For this reason, it was an ideal vehicle to carry heavy payloads and was well suited for salvaging the Wellington bomber. The idea was conceived of fixing to the front of ANGUS 003 clasps for hooking over the main wing spar at the specially strengthened jacking points located between the engines and the fuselage, as shown in the diagrams. Once these clasps had been placed in position and locked in place, flotation modules could be released to carry lifting ropes to the surface. Three lifting points were essential to keep the aircraft horizontal during recovery. The third lifting point was to be the tail main frame. The lift was to be carried out in stages by SCUBA divers attaching large open-bottomed buoyancy bags to the three lift lines at selected points down the cables. Once the aircraft had reached a depth of twenty-five metres, the SCUBA divers could then place a large cargo net under the fuselage and attach it to closed air bags on the surface. When this had been done, the plan was to tow the aircraft into shallow water up at Lochend where it could be dismantled and recovered in sections by a crane on the shore. This plan had one big advantage in that the aircraft could be recovered at absolutely minimum cost by using existing University equipment and volunteer SCUBA divers. Before detailed plans could be drawn up, however, it was essential to find out if the main wing-spar jacking points were clear of obstructions so that the clasps could slip straight down over the spar and lock-on. Drawings provided by British Aerospace at Weybridge indicated that this would be so, but, before any effort was expended, this had to be proved by a visual survey. Details of the proposed salvage attempt were published in the first May/June 1981 edition of a new magazine called *FlyPast*[1]. As a result of this article, public donations were received which, together with a grant from the RAF Museum at Hendon and a donation from *FlyPast*, helped to finance the underwater survey of N2980 in July 1981. This survey, described in detail in Chapter 1,

* SERC – Science and Engineering Research Council.

revealed that the old Wimpy had sustained serious damage since it was last examined in 1978*. The top of the fuselage from the DF loop position right down to the rudder, had been torn open. The port and starboard upper longerons had been wrenched out and with them all the geodetics that made up the upper fuselage aft of the astrodome. With the longerons and fuselage geodetics missing, the strength of the fuselage had gone, taking with it any hope of getting the aircraft up in one piece by remote-control. The low-cost scheme, using ANGUS 003 to recover N2980 intact, was now clearly a non-starter. Some form of very large framework, to act as a strongback, was now called for if there was to be any hope of getting the aircraft up in one piece. As such an endeavour was outside my financial and technical resources, all thoughts of mounting a salvage attempt on the Wimpy were abandoned.

Later that year, whilst in London on business, I telephoned Paul Harris at his home to suggest that we meet and have a chat about his old bomber. 'Splendid idea – come down and have a meal – I'll pick you up at Redhill station – I'll be driving a mini,' came the reply. Bunny Austin had told me that Paul was 'larger than the average' and later that day an ancient mini duly turned into the forecourt of Redhill railway station with a larger than average driver behind the wheel. 'So you're the chap that found my old Wellington are you?' came the greeting as the car window was wound down. 'Better come and have something to eat. I'm a jolly good cook you know,' he said as we both sat squeezed into the front of the mini heading for Crab Hill Farm. He lived alone in a delightful old farmhouse at South Nutfield close by his son and daughter-in-law. The meal, cooked by himself, was indeed excellent and, as we sat down afterwards in front of a roaring log fire, he drew my attention to all his mementoes. There, on the mantlepiece, were fading photographs of young men in RAF uniform. The room itself had a sense of nostalgic familiarity about it, with dark oak beams, leaded glass windows, ingle-nooks in the fireplace, plaques with squadron badges and a painting of a Wellington bomber on the wall. During the war, such rooms had been filled with the noisy banter of fighter pilots, pint in hand, recounting their day's bag of downed Dorniers and Heinkels, or perhaps they had been aircrew lustily singing 'OPs in a Wimpy' as they unwound after a long and dangerous mission over Germany. Images like that are now long gone, but the room still spoke of a man surrounded by such cherished memories. Old and stooped, burdened with a weak heart, Paul Harris retained that intangible air of authority gained from years of command. In his day, I suspect he was a strict disciplinarian but a fair one. Now, he was just another senior citizen, but one with some truly fascinating recollections. As we sat by the fire that evening he recounted tales of the very early days of the war.

The day after war was declared, he had just finished lunch when the Station Commander strolled into the mess and across to where he stood chatting to a group of fellow officers. While he couldn't remember the exact words

* Bad weather prevented the 1980 survey from seeing anything other than the port engine.

used, the gist of the conversation went something like this: 'Afternoon, Paul. Just heard that there's a couple of Jerry battleships; *Scharnhorst* and *Gneisenau* they say, at a place called Brunsbüttel, somewhere near the Kiel Canal. Off you go and take a crack at them.' So Paul called his pilots together and told them that there was a 'flap' on. As he went through his pre-flight check-out he found that his particular Wellington was unserviceable. They all climbed down and looked for another machine and found L4302 had been bombed up so they took it. Later he learned that another of his pilots had been taxiing towards the runway when he felt the plane a bit on the light side. A check on the bomb bay revealed that the aircraft hadn't been bombed up. When all the various delays had been sorted out, 149 Squadron took off on the first bombing raid of the war. After a short while there came a request over the intercom from Sergeant Austin, the navigator, who wanted to know where they were going. 'As navigator of the lead machine I would find it useful to know,' commented Bunny later. A search of an old Admiralty chart eventually located Brunsbüttel, and Paul decided to take a dog's leg to the north of Heligoland to 'fox the enemy'. Half way across, he ordered the guns to be tested, only to hear the gunners report that not one of their machine-guns was operating. I don't know what Biggles would have done, but Paul Harris decided he was jolly sure he wasn't going to miss the first raid of the war just because his guns weren't working. He pressed on, looking for two of the most heavily defended battleships in the German navy. Five of his squadron turned back early because of bad weather and dropped their bombs in the sea. He lost contact with the remaining two Wellingtons of his flight and one went on to bomb neutral Denmark while the other was observed hovering over Kiel, eighty km off target. His own aircraft took a direct hit on the rear turret from flak and he bombed a bridge over the river Eider before turning for home. No. 149 Squadron's first sortie of the war was a somewhat disorganised affair. Paul had been with the Squadron for just a week and he told me that the only thing his new Commanding Officer ever flew was a desk.

As the evening wore on, I listened to how the 3rd December raid on Heligoland led Bomber Command up the garden path, and how the shock of the 14th December raid on the Schillig Roads caused many pilots to question the sanity of pressing on with further daylight raids against heavily defended targets. Most fascinating of all, however, was the story of the 'Battle of Heligoland Bight'. I sat engrossed as he recounted the events on the day he flew N2980 to Wilhelmshaven. That particular exploit was not one with which I was familiar, having been brought up on a diet of post-war films portraying the real life heroism of the Lancaster crews of 617 Squadron and the fictitious derring-do of the Mosquito crews of the imaginary 633 Squadron.

I was so intrigued by all these stories of the Phoney War that I asked Paul Harris that night if he would record his personal recollections of Bomber Command's first faltering footsteps. This he agreed to do and they are included in Chapters 5 and 8.

Before boarding the last train back to London that night, I thanked Paul for a truly fascinating evening and made him a promise that I would do my utmost to reunite him with N2980, the Wellington bomber in which he won his DFC. For a man who had been prepared to take on the *Luftwaffe* single-handed in a completely defenceless Wimpy, in order to bomb two of the most heavily defended battleships in the German fleet, it was the least I could do.

Now resolved to recover N2980, I was faced with the task of trying to raise £50,000. At a rough estimate, such a salvage operation would take divers about five days to complete at a cost of £10,000 per day, the then commercial North Sea rate. Unfortunately, there seemed little enthusiasm for such a project among those who handled purse strings. This was borne out by a year of fruitless writing to companies, banks, breweries, charitable trusts, etc. The big problem lay in the fact that the old Wimpy had no intrinsic value and World War II was a long time ago. Because it contained no bars of gold, like HMS *Edinburgh*, there was nothing to tempt the professional diver, nor were there any Tudor artifacts, as on the *Mary Rose*, to seduce the archaeologist. Its only value lay in its uniqueness as the sole survivor of its breed that fought back against Nazi tyranny. In November 1982, the Carnegie Trust agreed to sponsor a survey of the Wellington by ANGUS 003, but bad weather prevented worthwhile results being obtained. Publicity from this operation, together with an earlier article in the *New Scientist*[2], brought in many small donations from individuals, and Heriot-Watt University kindly agreed to act as accountant for my unofficial Loch Ness Wellington Association. Another year of soliciting donations from industry and commerce again proved to be fruitless. However, a belated bonus from all the earlier publicity was a phone call, in September 1983, from Aberdeen that resulted in a meeting with a North Sea diving company called K.D. Marine (UK) Ltd. They expressed interest in the project and suggested carrying out a survey of the aircraft the following November using one of their ROVs called UFO. The encouraging results of this survey prompted K.D. Marine to suggest that the Wellington could be salvaged at much reduced cost by using their Atmospheric Diving Suit called SPIDER. This was, in effect, an armoured diving suit that enabled divers to exceed the fifty metre limit by keeping them at atmospheric pressure while permitting them to work at great depths by means of arms controlled from inside the suit by the diver. In the underwater salvage business such a suit is called an ADS system. The cost of the recovery was quoted as £69,680. If this was a 'much reduced cost' from using divers, then clearly my original estimate of £50,000 was seriously wide of the mark. In February 1984, K.D. Marine contacted me to say that they were considering the possibility of recovering N2980 as a publicity exercise to help promote their ADS capability. A visit to British Aerospace at Weybridge with K.D. Marine engineers followed in March when detailed planning to recover the Wimpy was started.

A couple of months later, in May, K.D. Marine phoned to say they would have to withdraw their proposed sponsorship of the project. If, however, external funding could be found, they were still prepared to undertake the job. That same month I received a visit from the Secretary of the National Heritage Memorial Fund, with whom I had been corresponding for over a year and a half. The outcome of his visit was an offer of a grant of £20,000 to help recover the Wellington, provided my unofficial Loch Ness Wellington Association could get charitable status. This needed legal advice so Messrs Balfour and Manson, solicitors in Edinburgh, were consulted and the necessary wheels were set in motion. On 23rd July 1984 my unofficial Association was disbanded and the Loch Ness Wellington Association Limited was incorporated as a registered charity. Air Commodore Richard Kellett and Group Captain Paul Harris were invited to join the Executive Committee along with representatives from UNILINK (Heriot-Watt University's industrial liaison division), the Institute of Offshore Engineering (another University body) and the Royal Scottish Museum in Edinburgh. Fifty people who had a long association with the project or were related to members of N2980's crew were invited to form the Membership. Balfour and Manson agreed to act as legal advisers, and the Secretary of the University confirmed that the new Association could still rely on the University's Finance Department to handle the accounts. Ownership of the Wellington bomber was formally transferred from my unofficial Association to the new Loch Ness Wellington Association Limited. After three years of struggling to raise money, with only the National Heritage Memorial Fund offering to help, I was very pessimistic about our chances of finding the extra cash for K.D. Marine. Another tack was called for.

During the planning phase with K.D. Marine (UK) Ltd, a meeting had been held at Weybridge with British Aerospace, K.D. Marine and an organisation called the Vintage Aircraft and Flying Association (VAFA). This latter group consisted mainly of British Aerospace employees who were interested in building and flying replica vintage aircraft like the Vickers Vimy, now in the RAF Museum at Hendon. They had expressed a desire to help recover and restore the Loch Ness Wellington. At that meeting the Chief Metallurgist at British Aerospace, Weybridge, who was also a member of VAFA, had asked the LNWA to obtain a sample of the aircraft's structure so that it could be analysed to determine its strength characteristics after forty-four years under water. The Underwater Technology Group in the Department of Electrical and Electronic Engineering at Heriot-Watt University was at that time engaged in a joint research programme with the Royal Navy Experimental Diving Unit at Portsmouth. The object of this work was to study the interaction between Royal Navy divers and Remotely Operated Vehicles (ROVs). As part of this study, it was agreed that the RN Fleet Clearance Diving Team would carry out one of their annual working-up dives on the Wellington in collaboration with two commercial ROVs called Scorpi and RCV 225. This was duly carried out at the end of September 1984, and the divers brought up a section of the fuselage geodetics together with the Direction Finding Loop which had been lying on the port mid-wing. Both items were carefully sprayed with preservative and rushed to British Aerospace for analysis. A further meeting at Weybridge at the end of November 1984 revealed that the metal from the fuselage was in remarkably good condition and, in the opinion of Mr Hugh Tyrer, the Chief Metallurgist, a recovery should be perfectly feasible.

Present at this meeting was Mr Norman Boorer who had at one time been Chief Designer with British Aerospace at Weybridge and had worked under Barnes Wallis on the original design of the Wellington bomber. Now retired, 'Spud' was also the Chairman of VAFA. At the meeting, Spud was invited to design a suitable lifting frame by which the aircraft could be lifted in a horizontal attitude and brought to the surface in one piece. This he kindly agreed to do. The problem still remained of finding a suitable home for N2980 once recovered. It had originally been hoped to donate the aircraft to the Museum of Flight at East Fortune near Haddington, an outstation of the Royal Scottish Museum in Edinburgh, but as our visits to British Aerospace became more frequent, it transpired that a new museum was in the process of being formed in Weybridge at the Brooklands Clubhouse. This building had been the social and administrative centre of the Brooklands Automobile Racing Club that used the world's first banked motor racing track there until the Second World War when motor racing ceased. Post-war, it housed Vickers Research and Development Department, headed by the redoubtable Barnes Wallis. Just across the road from the Brooklands Clubhouse stands the 'Wellington' hangar, also owned by the Brooklands Museum. In 1939, N2980 would have spent some time there prior to its dispatch to No. 149 Squadron at Mildenhall. With the wealth of knowledge, talent and goodwill still existing in that area and a direct historical link with Weybridge and Brooklands, it seemed altogether more appropriate that the old girl should come home to her birthplace. The Co-ordinator of the new Brooklands Museum, Mrs Morag Barton, who was also present at that November 1984 meeting, was asked if she would accept 'R for Robert' back home. This she agreed to do in the knowledge that it could be more readily preserved and restored by loving hands familiar with its every nut and bolt. While the representatives of the Museum of Flight on the LNWA Executive Committee were disappointed, they agreed that there was really only one home for 'R for Robert' – the 'Wellington' hangar at Brooklands Museum.

During the planning phase for the 1984 diver/ROV interaction study, meetings had been held in Portsmouth and at the Royal Air Force Museum in Hendon to study their Wellington. At these meetings, and during the actual diving operations on N2980 in September 1984, the possibility had been discussed of the Royal Navy team returning to Loch Ness during the summer of 1985. Because the availability of the Fleet Clearance Diving Team depended upon their having no other more pressing service commitments, they could not be called upon to do the actual recovery of the aircraft. However, it was proposed that the Royal Navy divers might return to Loch Ness sometime in 1985 to attach special pop-up buoys to the lifting points on the aircraft.

These pop-up buoys would be on similar lines to those suggested for the 1981 recovery by ANGUS 003. The installation of the pop-up buoys could be done anytime between April and August 1985 by the RN divers while on one of their statutory working-up exercises.

The plan was then to come along at a suitable fixed date in September with the large lifting frame to act as a strongback. By means of underwater acoustic command signals, the buoyancy modules from the buoys would be released and pop-up to the surface bringing with them guide ropes. Once on the surface, these guide ropes could be fed through special eyes on the lifting frame. The strongback would then be lowered down the guide ropes to within a metre or so of the aircraft. Specially strong lifting ropes would, by then, have been fed by the guide ropes through the eyes into one-way clamps on the frame. Once everything was in position and the aircraft and its lifting frame had been inspected by an ROV, messenger weights would be dropped down the guide ropes to trip the locking mechanism on the frame's rope clamps. A single lifting wire from the strongback to the surface could then have large, open bottomed, buoyancy bags attached at selected points down the cable by SCUBA divers operating within their permitted depth limit. Once inflated with air from a surface compressor, these air bags would be used to carry out a staged lift of the aircraft to the surface.

That was the plan proposed after the successful September 1984 dive on the aircraft and a subsequent meeting at HMS *Vernon*, the Royal Navy's diving establishment in Portsmouth, in early January 1985. Everything proceeded on that tacit understanding. To minimise the cost, VAFA offered to build the lifting frame to Spud Boorer's design. The LNWA Ltd contacted British Alcan Tubes Ltd and their Managing Director, Mr Pontin, agreed to provide all the material necessary for the construction of the lifting frame, free of charge. J.W. Automarine Ltd, a company specialising in the manufacture of underwater lifting equipment, was also contacted and asked to quote for the provision of all the air bags. Their Managing-Director, Mr John Wise, replied that because of the historic nature of the aircraft his company would provide all the equipment and personnel, free of charge. British Aerospace likewise agreed to lay on the transportation of the aircraft back to Weybridge. The Underwater Technology Group at Heriot-Watt took on the task of supplying the pop-up buoys. The Institute of Offshore Engineering (IOE) at Heriot-Watt agreed to co-ordinate all this activity under the direction of Dr Bob Allwood, whilst UNILINK, would provide back-up under its Director, Ken Crichton. The sixteenth of September 1985 was set as the target date for the lift to be carried out.

At Weybridge, further meetings were held to discuss all the technical aspects of the recovery, and the first few months of 1985 were taken up with the preparation of drawings, ordering material and obtaining all the various permissions necessary to operate up at Lochend. In April, we heard from the Experimental Diving Unit in Portsmouth that the Fleet Clearance Diving Team would not, after all, be able to install the pop-up buoys, because changed circumstances meant they could not do any of their working-up dives in Loch Ness that year.

What to do now was the big question. Commercial divers were clearly out of the question on the money we had available from the National Heritage Memorial Fund. The only alternative was another ADS system. Organisations operating that kind of equipment could be counted on the fingers of one hand. However, nothing ventured – nothing gained, so I picked up the phone and called the best in the business, Oceaneering International Services Ltd in Aberdeen. I explained our predicament to Chris Jenkins, their Sales Manager for the Northern North Sea Area, and asked if Oceaneering would help. The answer was as short as it was gratifying – Yes. The big boys don't hang about. Six days later a meeting was held at British Aerospace Weybridge with Tony Pritchard, Oceaneering's ADS Manager and Alfie Lyden, their expert on underwater salvage operations. A week later a further meeting was held at the Royal Air Force Museum at Hendon. After carefully studying their Wellington, MF628, Alfie Lyden pronounced that the recovery of our Loch Ness Wellington, N2980, by Oceaneering's ADS system, should be perfectly feasible. On 20th June a further meeting between all the interested parties was held at Oceaneering's headquarters in Aberdeen where suitable terms were agreed and a contract drawn up. The budget for the operation exceeded our grant from the National Heritage Memorial Fund so they kindly agreed to provide a further £5,000. Modifications were immediately put in hand to alter the attachments on the lifting frame to take special locking straps suitable for handling by a diver in an Atmospheric Diving Suit. Two ADS systems would be provided by Oceaneering, WASP to do the actual recovery and JIM as an emergency back-up. The surface support vessel was to be the M.V. *Eilean Dubh* (the old Kessock car ferry) attended by Oceaneering's diver support ship the M.V. *Work Horse*. A large dumb-barge with a flat 120 ft × 30 ft wooden deck was to be provided to transport the aircraft once recovered. The salvage operation on the old Wimpy, 'R for Robert', was scheduled to take seven days, starting on Monday 9th September 1985.

At British Aerospace, work progressed feverishly on the construction of the lifting frame. The work was carried out by a dedicated team of VAFA enthusiasts in their own time, using the material supplied free of charge by British Alcan Tubes Ltd. The lifting frame was finally tested on 10th August 1985 and successfully lifted the weight for which it had been designed. Everything was now ready for transportation up to Lochend and the hoped-for recovery of N2980.

Thanks to the generous support of the National Heritage Memorial Fund, sufficient money was now available to contract Oceaneering International Services Ltd for a period of seven days. That was the time estimated by Oceaneering to complete the recovery. The LNWA Ltd recognised that once the aircraft had been recovered, a tremendous amount of work still lay ahead of the Brooklands Museum to preserve and restore the old Wellington bomber for display to the public. For this preservation and restoration phase, a great deal of money would be needed. It seemed logical to try and capitalise on the publicity associated with the recovery in Loch Ness to help raise funds for the Brooklands Museum. So British Aerospace offered to contribute by printing a brochure on the history of N2980 entitled, *The Story of 'Another' Loch Ness Monster,* for sale up at Loch Ness.

Just prior to the start of the operation I was contacted by the BBC who told me that they were currently making a series of programmes on underwater archaeology, and the techniques involved in the recovery of the Wellington were relevant to this programme. They asked if they could send a team up to Loch Ness to film the operation as they would like to include some excerpts in their underwater archaeology series. The answer was clearly yes.

*Monday 9th September 1985*

Muirtown basin, at the Inverness end of the Caledonian Canal, had never seen anything like it before. The old Kessock ferry, *Eilean Dubh,* was being loaded up with high-technology equipment normally seen only on the decks of North Sea diving support ships. Bright flashes from welding torches combined with the roar of a huge mobile crane to create the illusion of a science fiction film set. Generators, compressors, winches, a Hiab crane and a control cabin were swung onboard and welded to the deck of the old ferry. Space age technology had invaded this normally quiet little backwater. In pride of place on the deck of *Eilean Dubh* stood two man-like monsters cradled in their support frames. The largest was painted bright yellow and had a huge clear plastic dome in place of a head. Two great ball-jointed arms hung down in front and a label on its back proclaimed OCEANEERING. This was WASP, the ADS system that would be used for the actual recovery of the aircraft. Beside him stood his friend, JIM. He was there for emergencies should WASP get stuck on the bottom and need rescuing. Directing all this feverish activity was Alfie Lyden, dressed in his dark blue overalls and peak cap. In the midst of all this endeavour, a huge blue articulated lorry with British Aerospace on its cab turned onto the wharf. The lifting frame had arrived. By now the mobile crane had departed, having deposited the Institute of Offshore Engineering's (IOE) container and small Portakabin on the wooden deck of the cargo barge. The sections of the lifting frame were manhandled from the lorry onto the flat deck of the dumb-barge. The BBC were also there, recording the events for their archaeology series. Late into the night the Oceaneering team laboured to connect up and test all the multitude of wires, cables, pipes and hoses that would bring WASP and JIM to life.

*Tuesday 10th September 1985*

First thing in the morning, Alfie Lyden and his Oceaneering team set off to work *Eilean Dubh* through the locks. He wanted to get out onto Loch Ness as soon as possible to start laying the anchors and attaching the shore lines that would hold *Eilean Dubh* directly over the aircraft on a four-point mooring. At Muirtown basin, the *Work Horse* was lashed securely alongside

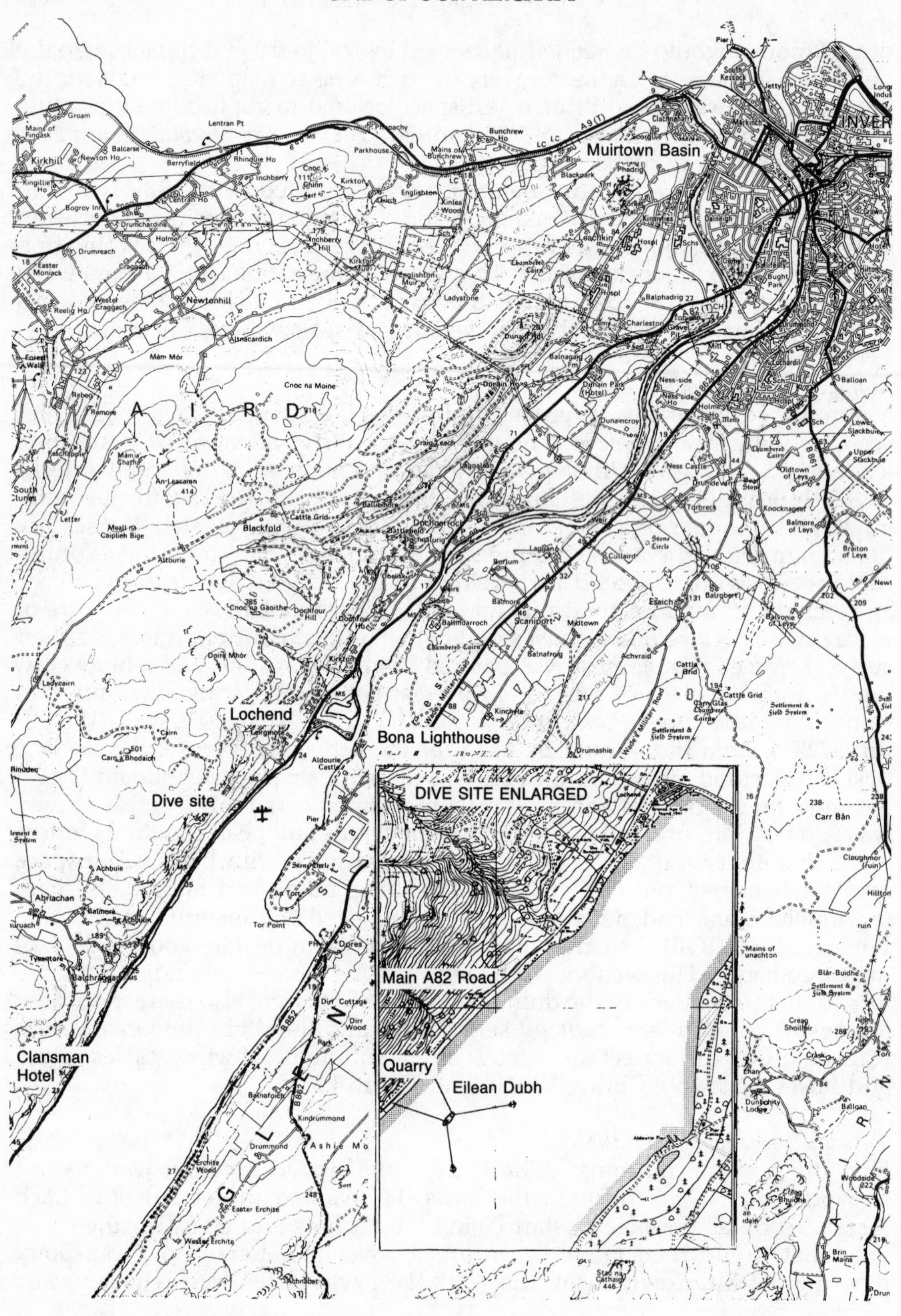
Muirtown Basin
Lochend
Bona Lighthouse
DIVE SITE ENLARGED
Dive site
Main A82 Road
Quarry
Eilean Dubh
Clansman
Hotel

the dumb-barge, and later the unwieldy pair squeezed their way into the first lock with about twenty centimetres to spare. It was a glorious sunny September day with hardly a breath of wind to ruffle the surface. The team from J.W. Automarine Ltd had by now arrived and offered to lend a hand coaxing the *Work Horse* and its seemingly self-willed charge through the succession of locks. By 4.30 p.m., the task had been accomplished with the rusty old barge secured alongside the little landing at Bona Lighthouse. It was the intention to keep the barge there to act as HQ, with the big IOE container as the workshop and the little Portakabin as the 'Office' from which the recovery of the Wellington bomber would be co-ordinated. *Work Horse* detached itself from the barge and headed out to give support to Alfie and his lads struggling with the lengthy shore lines and massive anchors.

The main VAFA team were not due till the following day but Hugh Tyrer decided there were enough bodies around to start assembling the lifting frame. Amid grunts and groans of unaccustomed heavy labour, the huge aluminium sections were manhandled into the upright position and pushed and shoved until they all fitted together. Much middle-aged sweat was expended before Spud and Hugh pronounced themselves satisfied that the huge aluminium cruciform framework was ready and the last nut and bolt were tightened up. While the now completed lifting frame was being lashed down for the night, *Work Horse* drew alongside the barge with an exhausted Alfie and his team, back from the dive site. *Eilean Dubh* was now positioned directly over the old Wimpy and held securely in place by two long cables to the shore and two hawsers, leading from the bow and stern, to anchors out in the loch. It had been a struggle, with one of Alfie's lads getting dragged away from the shore on the end of an unco-operative cable to which he had had to cling as it was hauled all the way out to *Eilean Dubh*. Fortunately he got away with nothing more serious than a good ducking. But Alfie was now satisfied with the day's work. So far, everything was going according to plan.

*Wednesday 11th September 1985*

The weather forecast for the next couple of days was good. Lying at an angle of forty-five degrees across the north of Scotland, Loch Ness acts as a natural funnel which channels the prevailing south-west winds straight along its thirty-five km length. The dive site was located two km down from the north end of the loch, so a south-west wind had over thirty-three km in which to build up very big waves should it decide to blow. *Eilean Dubh* was moored two hundred metres off the West bank just above the point where the loch narrows at Tor Point. In fact, that area was famous for its waves because, just round the corner in Dores Bay, Manchester University had at one time carried out a series of experiments on their 'Nodding Ducks' to test the possibility of extracting energy from waves. Weather was all important for the Wimpy recovery because the old ferry had nothing to shelter behind should the weather turn nasty.

Following a technical conference to plan the day's activities, *Work Horse* departed Bona Lighthouse for the dive site carrying the divers, the BBC film team and a number of newspaper men. By now, the spectacle of *Eilean Dubh* moored in full view of passing motorists on the main A82 road had started to attract the attention of the media. Items on BBC television news alerted the public to what was going on and a convenient lay-by allowed motorists to pull off the road and get a grandstand view of the proceedings. Through their binoculars, the spectators in the lay-by watched as WASP was swung out over the side of the ferry and lowered gently into the water. In his control cabin, Alfie Lyden was in direct voice contact with the diver in WASP and the winchman controlling its descent. 'Down easy on the diver,' instructed Alfie as the winchman paid out the lowering wire that sent WASP heading for the bottom of Loch Ness. The winchman's depth recorder was just coming up for the seventy metre mark as the diver's voice came over the intercom: 'Bottom in view.' 'All stop on the diver,' instructed Alfie. WASP had reached the bottom, but where was the Wimpy? For half an hour WASP searched for that great long twenty-six metre wing and couldn't find it. Visibility was bad down there with the stirred up silt helping to obscure the diver's view. Shortly there came a relieved voice over the intercom: 'I've found it.' By varying the power to his thrusters, the diver manoeuvred WASP over to the aircraft and grasped the geodetics with the remotely controlled gripper at the end of his ball-jointed arm. The first task was to attach a surface line to the aircraft so that, in future, WASP could follow it down, thereby avoiding time-wasting searches. But it wasn't to be as easy as that. Several times he released his grip on the aircraft to attach the surface line, only to drift away and lose the aircraft in the murk. Precious time was lost in finding it again. At 4.45 p.m. WASP was recovered, ostensibly for the diver to report progress to Alfie but actually to have the surface line removed from round a thruster in which it had become entangled. The offending rope was cut away from the propeller and after a comfort break and a mug of hot tea, the diver climbed back into WASP and headed for the bottom once again. The problem was that *Eilean Dubh* was not positioned directly over the Wellington, and the diver had to thrust the WASP in towards the aircraft and grab hold of it. As soon as he let go he swung away. Alfie had to move *Eilean Dubh* by slacking off the anchor lines and tightening in the shore lines. All of this, of course, took time. Eventually WASP dangled directly above the aircraft without having to use its thrusters, indicating that *Eilean Dubh* was now spot-on position. Attaching the surface line was then a simple task. It was pitch dark by the time *Work Horse* brought Alfie and his team back to Bona Lighthouse. We were now a day behind schedule.

*Thursday 12th September 1985*

Seven days had been allocated for the recovery operation. By Thursday the lifting frame should have been down on top of the aircraft with the lift taking place the following day. Now, this clearly was not going to happen. The first task that morning was to heave a ten-metre-long stiffening beam onboard the *Work Horse*. Because of the missing centre section in the fuselage, Spud and Hugh wanted to insert a strengthening beam down inside the fuselage to take the strain of lifting the tail section and its heavy gun turret. It was vital to try and lift the aircraft in a horizontal position because that way the main wing spar would contribute its maximum possible strength. The weight of the tail section was needed to balance the aircraft and keep it level on its way up to the surface. Thursday was spent with WASP trying to manoeuvre the stiffening beam into the fuselage and being frustrated by pieces of debris. A large loose section of fuselage kept getting in the way, impeding progress. WASP had to take time off to hook a lift line round this obstinate structure and haul it clear to be lifted to the surface. When the offending item was deposited on the deck of *Eilean Dubh*, Hugh Tyrer and Spud Boorer examined it minutely and were ecstatic about its condition. Beneath a layer of protective paint, the duralumin appeared as good as new. A nut and bolt attached to the framework could be loosened by fingers alone, and inspection stamps on the metalwork looked as if they had just been punched the day before. This prize was transported ashore to be cleaned up and treated with preservative.

With the lift originally scheduled to take place on the Friday, invitations had been extended to Group Captain Marwood-Elton and his wife to come up for the big event. The only other crew member from the ditching to survive the war was the wireless operator, Flight Lieutenant Bill Wright, who had landed safely after bailing out. He and his wife and family had also agreed to come up to Loch Ness for this nostalgic occasion. This was made possible by a generous offer from Mr Yeaman of Dan Air Services Ltd, who flew them up to Inverness.

A great deal of public interest was now being taken in the project. Charlie Stuart of Moray Firth Radio organised a press conference at Inverness Airport for David Marwood-Elton and Bill Wright, who had not seen one another since they last flew together in 'R for Robert' on New Year's Eve 1940.

After depositing the Marwood-Eltons and Wrights at their respective hotels, I later returned to the Clansman hotel where the recovery teams were staying. I was met by Spud and Hugh, enthusing over another piece of the Wimpy that had been brought up that afternoon. There, in the lounge, being fussed over by the VAFA contingent, was the rudder from N2980. Their excitement was not simply because they had got their hands on another bit of the aircraft but because, when the electric cable from the rear navigation light had been connected to a 12-volt battery, incredibly, after forty-five years on the bottom of Loch Ness, the tail-light lit up and shone as brightly as ever.

*Friday 13th September 1985*

It could be argued that anyone attempting to lift a Wellington bomber from the bottom of Loch Ness on a Friday the Thirteenth was tempting providence. Well, providence wasn't having any of it. During the night the wind got up, a south-west wind blowing straight up the Loch. All the teams arrived down at Bona Lighthouse that morning to watch the waves pounding up the beach at Lochend. We gazed helplessly as the wind whipped the tops off the 'white horses'. It was pointless even thinking about launching WASP under such conditions. That afternoon, Mr Harris, from the National Heritage Memorial Fund, arrived to see how things were coming along. He and his wife had been in the area and decided to drop in. He was quite taken aback by the scale of the operation, not realising the need for the high technology and extensive logistical backup involved. We attempted to take them out to inspect *Eilean Dubh*, but the *Work Horse* pitched about so badly, with spray breaking right over the wheelhouse, that any attempt to come alongside *Eilean Dubh* would have been highly dangerous. Injuring one of our benefactors would have been imprudent. We had to be content with showing them the lifting frame and the souvenirs previously recovered, including the magic tail-light. The weather forecast was depressing, with forty-knot winds predicted for Saturday and Sunday, perhaps moderating late on Sunday night to force two or three.

The lay-by was jammed solid with cars, everyone expecting to see the aircraft recovered that afternoon. The best we could do was post large notices, borrowed from the local constabulary, explaining that the lift had to be postponed due to the high winds. Everyone was disappointed except perhaps the lady in the fish-and-chip van that had earlier taken up residence in the lay-by and was doing a roaring trade.

*Saturday 14th September 1985*

All that night and into the following day the wind whistled up the loch. The lay-by was still stiff with cars, the public having been informed on the television by the BBC News that the recovery was imminent. The verges were lined with vehicles for a couple of km either side of the lift site, reducing the A82 to single file traffic in places. Notices were again posted in the lay-by explaining the delay caused by the high winds and offering, as a small compensation, a free video film on the history of the Loch Ness Wellington, at the Clansman hotel. Mr MacKenzie, the proprietor, had granted us the freedom of his upstairs lounge to show off the bits of the aircraft already recovered. Not one to miss a business opportunity, Mrs Morag Barton and her retinue from the Brooklands Museum, ably assisted by the VAFA wives, spent the day selling souvenir T shirts, postcards, tea towels and the British Aerospace brochure – *The Story of 'Another' Loch Ness Monster*. Plying the host of visitors with afternoon teas, Mr MacKenzie quietly prayed for the wind to keep up for another couple of days.

*Sunday 15th September 1985*

Overnight the barometer needle crept up from 'Stormy' to 'Change' and the wind dropped noticeably. The Oceaneering team set off early for *Eilean Dubh*. The anchors had dragged in the storm and precious time was spent repositioning the ferry to get it once more directly over the aircraft. WASP

1. Group Captain Paul Harris at the time of El ´Alamein, October, 1942

2. Squadron Leader David Marwood-Elton

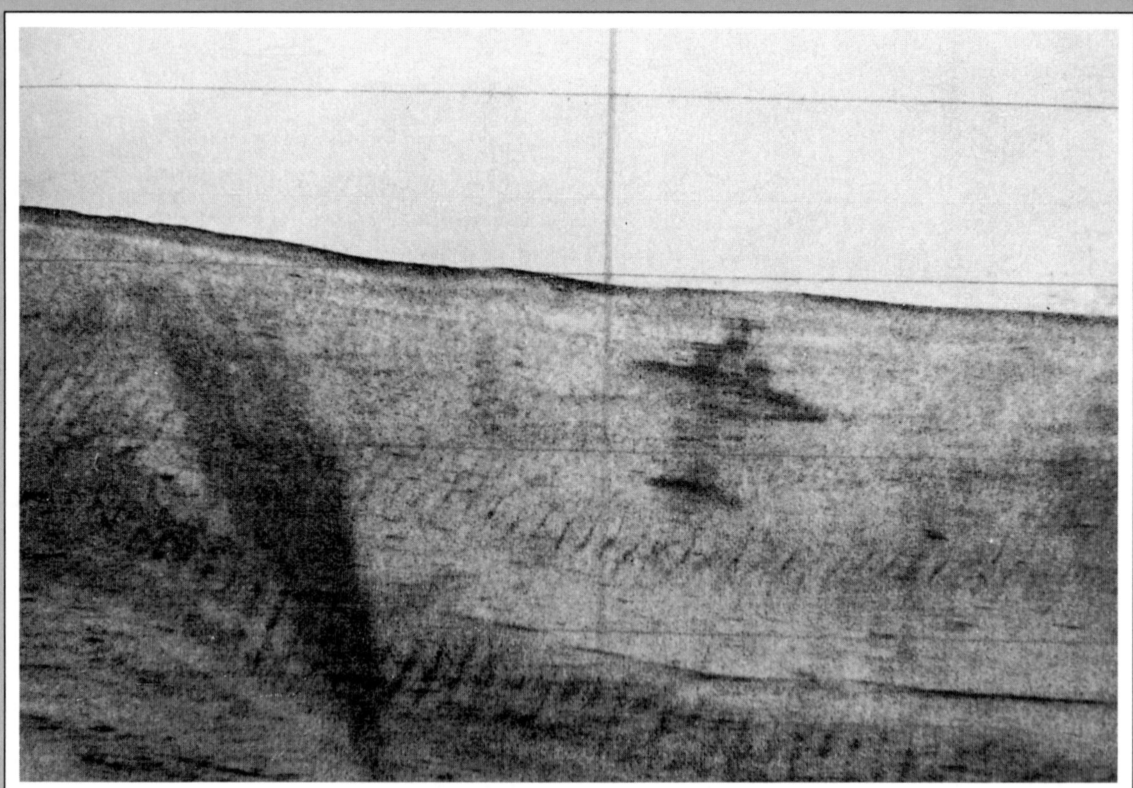

3. Klein Side Scan Sonar trace of an aircraft in Loch Ness. This trace was made by Martin Klein & Charles Finkelstein in 1976. It was thought to be a PBY Catalina but was later identified as a Wellington

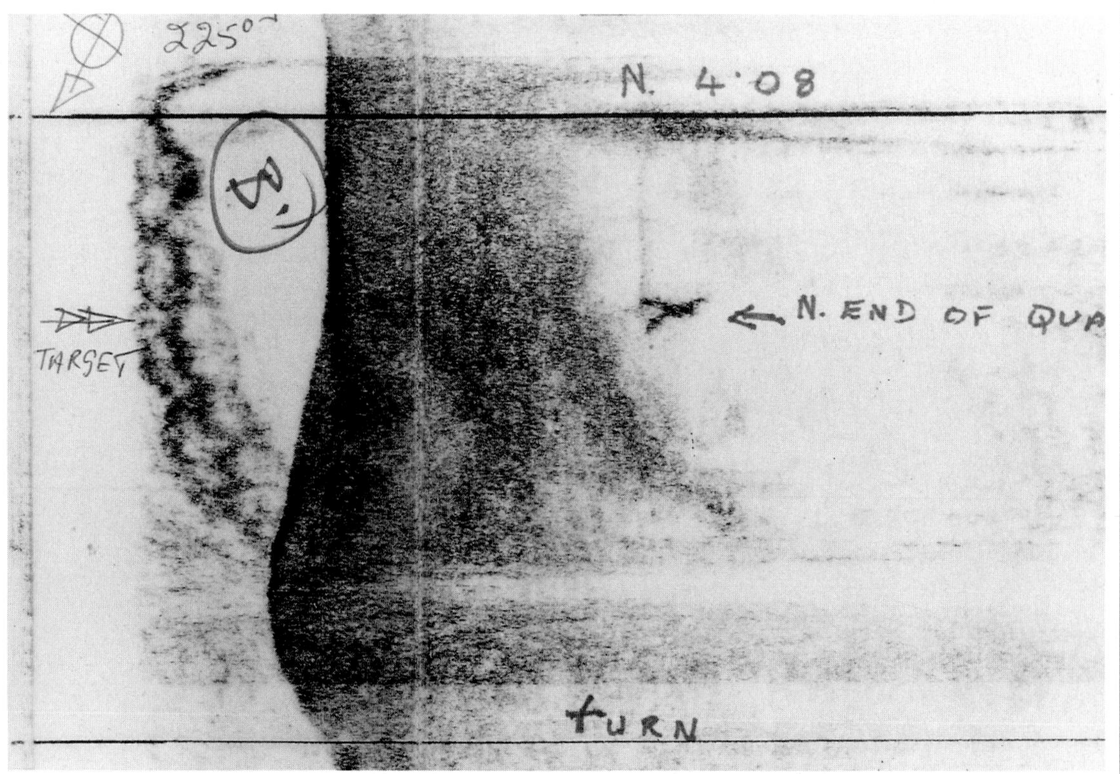


4. Side Scan Sonar trace of the Wellington taken from *Seol Mara* in September 1978

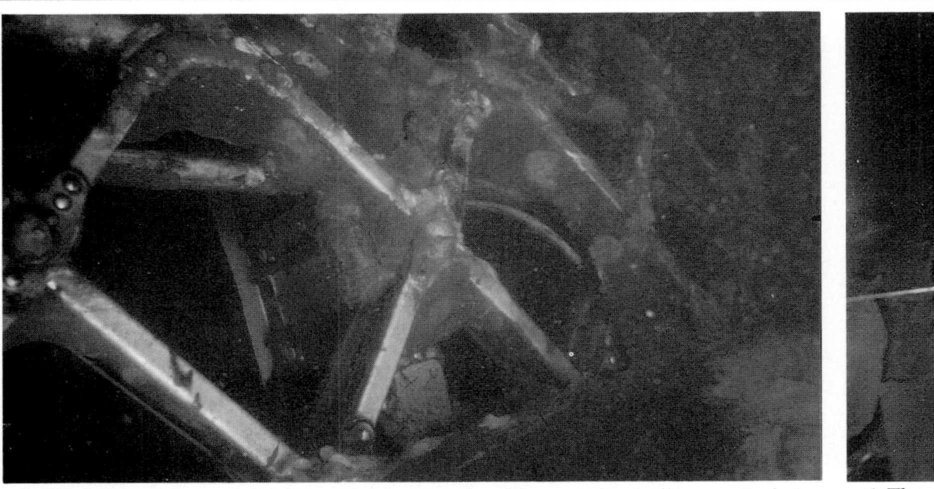

5. The bright shiny metal strips connected together like a garden trellis were in fact geodetics at the tail main frame of a Wellington bomber

6. The astrodome hatch with the high frequency aerial showing as a bright line. The plastic  dome was not in place as it was standard procedure to remove it into the aircraft prior to ditching

7. The port wing root where the leading edge joins the fuselage, showing the air intakes for the cabin heater along the leading edge

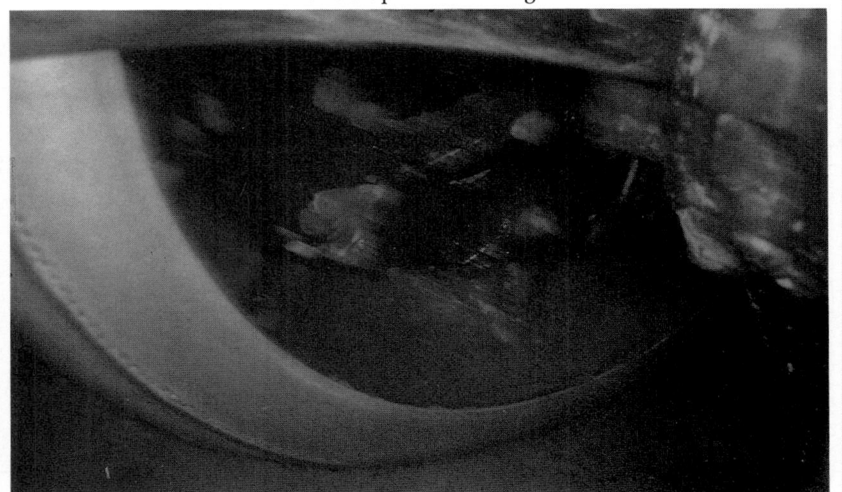

8. The bottom half of the port engine showing the exhaust collector ring and one of the propeller blades embedded in the silt

9 The Scottish Marine Biological Association's research vessel *"Seol Mara"*

10. Heriot Watt University's underwater television and 35 mm camera frame PK1 on board *Seol Mara* in September 1978

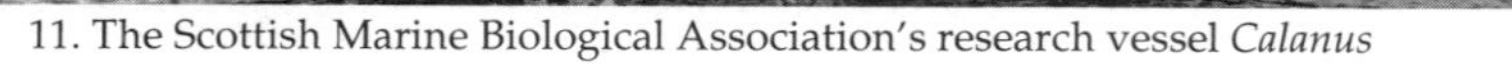

11. The Scottish Marine Biological Association's research vessel *Calanus*

12. ANGUS 002 ready for launching over the stern of *Calanus*

14. Sea Pup being launched over the side of the pontoon

13. The Loch Ness and Morar project's survey pontoon with Sea Pup ready for launching over the side

15. 'Only another thousand miles, Charlie, and we'll be home'

16. Sergeant Fensome was killed when his parachute failed to open properly after bailing out of N2980

17. Sergeant Bill Wright landed safely after bailing out of N2980 on New Year's Eve 1940

18. Fairey Battle

19. Bristol Blenheim

20. Vickers Wellington Mk1

21. Heinkel III

22. Dornier 17

23. Göring's new 'Wonder Bomber', the Junkers 88, was still in the experimental stage in 1939. His opinion that it was fast enough to elude fighters proved over optimistic

24. Handley Page Hampden

25. Junkers 87

26. Acting Flight Lieutenant K. C. Doran

27. Flying Officer A. McPherson

28. Paul Harris photographed just after the 3rd December raid on Heligoland. Snap taken by Sandy Innes. "Three direct hits on enemy ship from 10,000ft" reported Paul Harris

29. Barnes Wallis

30. Early Wellington Mk 1 bombers under construction at Vickers Armstrongs' factory at Weybridge in 1939

31. A crowd, including women and children carrying their gas masks, watch as the coffins of two German airmen who were shot down in the raid on the Firth of Forth are escorted to the cemetery by men of the RAF

32. Wing Commander Griffiths photographed with Corporals Pettitt (right) and Bickerstaff (left). Two days after the raid, His Majesty King George VI conferred the DFC on Griffiths and the DFM on Pettitt and Bickerstaff

33. Air Vice-Marshal Baldwin and Air Chief Marshal Sir Edgar Ludlow-Hewitt (left)

34. Air Commodore Bottomley (shown here later as an Air Vice-Marshal)

35. Number 149 Squadron's 'B' Flight crew room

36. Pilot Officer Herome Alexander Innes with his dog Astra. Sandy kept a diary of events during the Phoney War

37. Wellington Mk1s of No. 149 Squadron over Paris on the 14th July, 1939 (Bastille Day). Wellington G-LY (L4272) was F/Lt. Duguid's aircraft on the 4th September, 1939 raid on Brunsbüttel

38. A rare photograph showing a Wellington Mk1A, of Number 9 Squadron, with its 'dustbin' turret lowered for action *(Photo: T. Mason via Chaz Bowyer)*

39. Richard Kellett

40. A tantalising glimpse of "R for Robert" in the background

## The crew of Wellington bomber N2980 on the 18th December, 1939

41. Pilot: S/L Harris

42. 2nd Pilot: P/O Innes

43. Navigator: Sgt. Austin

44. W/Op: A.C.2 Watson

45. Front Gunner: A.C.1 Doxsey

46. Rear Gunner: A.C.1 Mullineaux

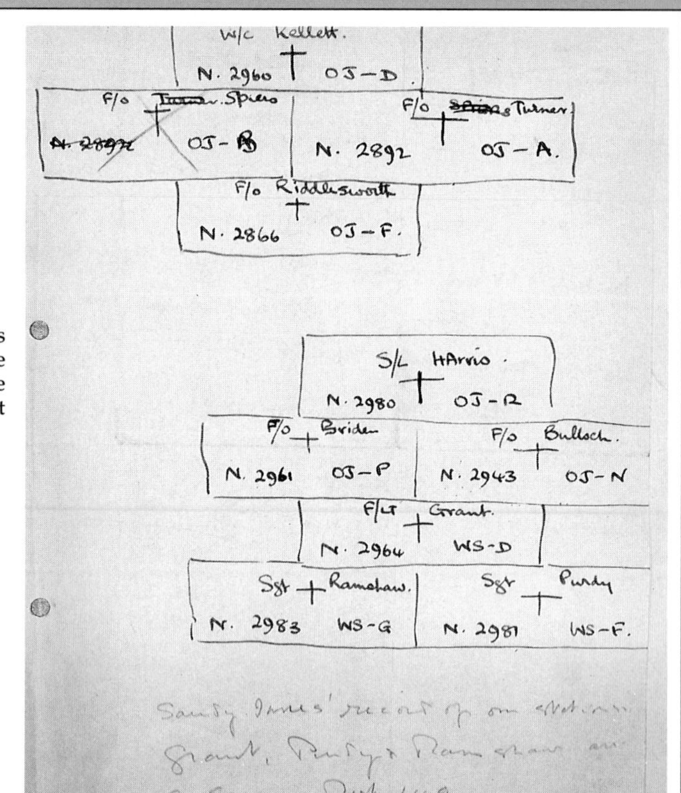


47. Sandy Innes's record of the stations kept by 149 Squadron and the three aircraft of 9 Squadron during the Battle of Heligoland Bight

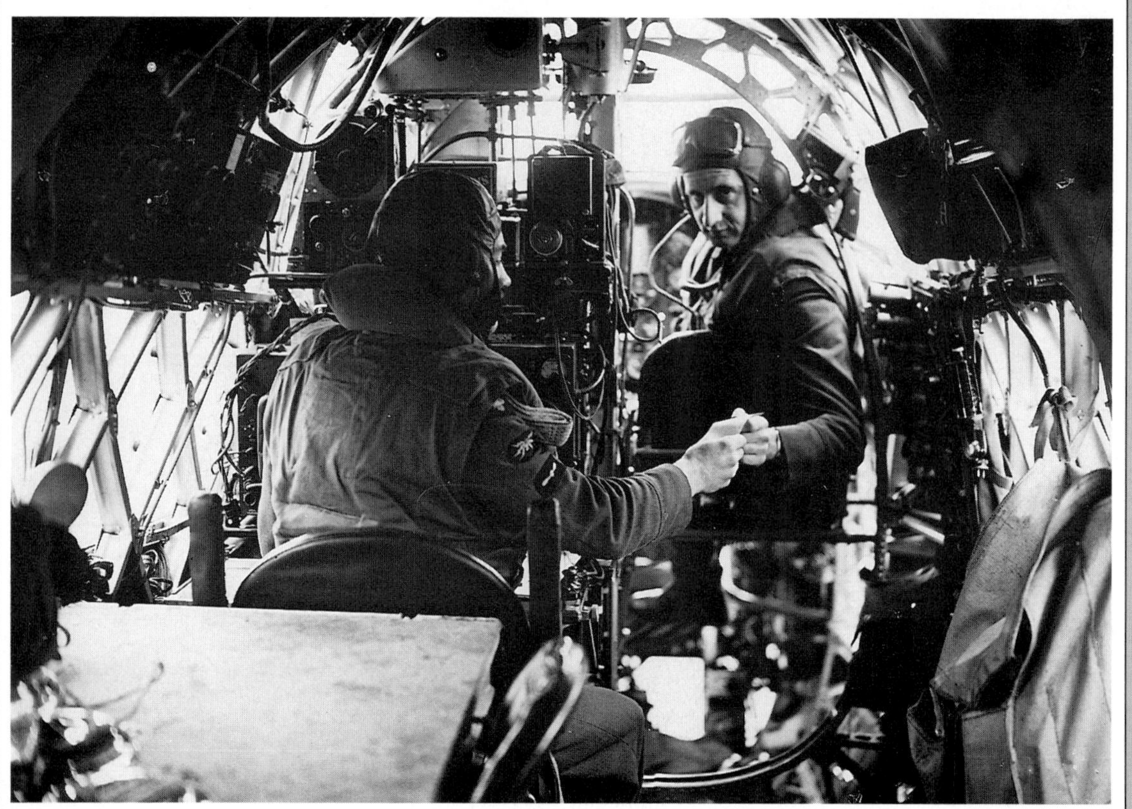

48. Here the second pilot of a Wellington bomber is taking a message from the wireless operator who is located in a tiny compartment behind the pilot

49. Photograph taken by Wellington A OJ (F/O Turner) of 149 Squadron while flying over Wilhelmshaven on 18th December 1939

50. The pilots of the Marienkäfer Squadron (2/ZG76) with a Me 110c

51. Oberstleutnant Carl Schumacher survived the war as a Generalmajor with the Ritterkreuz (Knight's Cross of the Iron Cross)

52. Major Harry von Bülow-Bothkamp was awarded the Ritterkreuz for his leadership in the West

53. Staffelkapitän Johannes "Macki" Steinhoff went on to become one of the great leader personalities of the Luftwaffe. He was awarded the Ritterkreuz and achieved the remarkable total of 176 victories. He was seriously wounded on 18th April, 1945 during take-off in a Me 262 but survived the war to become Inspector General of the German Air Force

54. Staffelkapitän Wolfgang Falck later rose to command the Luftwaffe's premier nightfighter force, Nachtjagdgeshwader 1 (NJG1). He became a key figure in the development of radar-guided interception and was awarded the Ritterkreuz

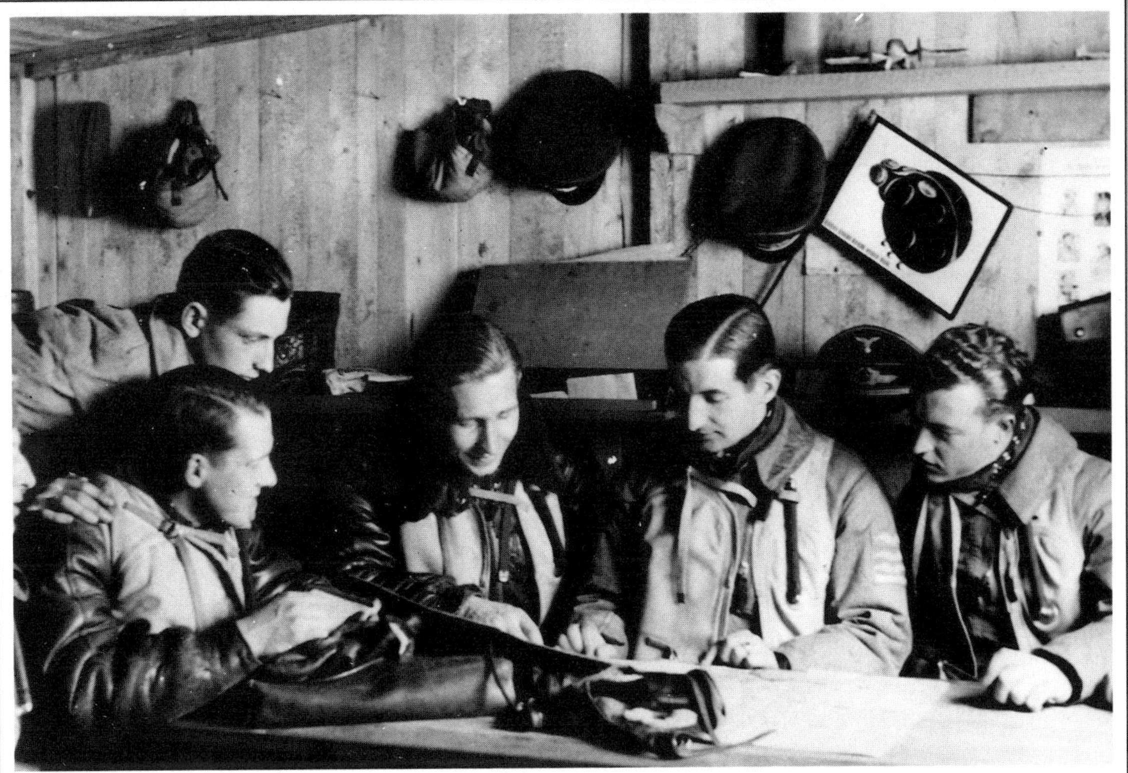

55. Pilots of 2/ZG76 in their hut waiting for the next 'scramble'. Second from the left, sitting, is Unteroffizier Fresia, the Rottenflieger or 'Kaczmarek' of Hauptmann Falck

56. The " well camouflaged aerodrome at Schillig Point" was called JEVER, shown here with a Me 109 and a Me 110 during the winter of 1939

57. Me 109E of II/JG77 being readied for combat

58. Oberleutnant Gordon Gollob went on to become one of the Luftwaffe's top fighter Aces with 150 victories to his credit. He was one of only twelve Luftwaffe pilots to add the much coveted 'Diamonds' to his Ritterkreuz

59. Oberleutnant Helmut Lent went on to become one of the outstanding personalities of the Luftwaffe. He was one of their top Aces with 110 victories to his credit. Like Gordon Gollob, he too succeeded in adding the 'Diamonds' to his Ritterkreuz. During a daylight landing on the 5th October 1944 one of his engines failed and his aircraft touched a high tension wire and crashed. Lent was critically injured and died two days later

60. Sergeant Herbert Ruse (pointing) of 37 Squadron being briefed for an operation. On the far right is the Squadron CO, W/Cdr Joe Fogarty with F/O Vaughan-Williams. On the left is F/O Lewis

61. The remains of N2936's forward section, Herbie Ruse's Wimpy

62. A copy of a painting of the battle was given by the artist, Norman Wilkinson, to S/L Harris and his wife

63. Aircraft wreckage burning on the sea after the Battle of Heligoland Bight

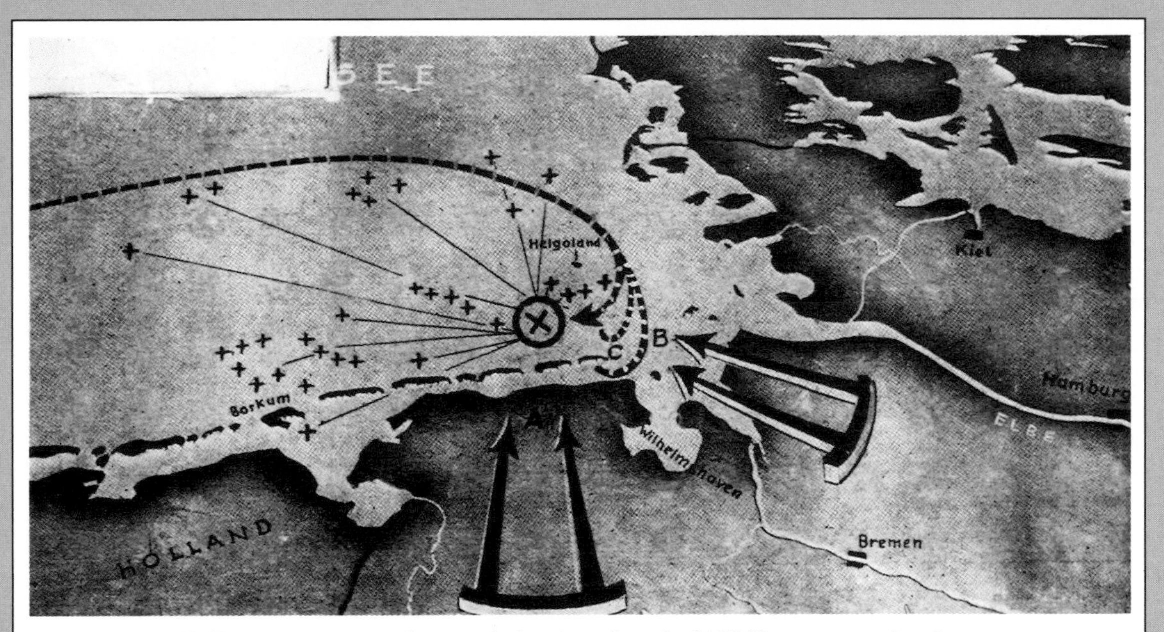


64. German newspaper photograph showing where the 34 Wellingtons were shot down

In order to avoid the fire from the Heligoland batteries the English flew in a broad arc round the island and then turned south (dotted line). The German fighter squadrons attacked the enemy from both sides (A & B), broke up their closed formations (C) and then pursued the individual Vickers-Wellingtons until they ended up in the "drink" (see crosses). Individual aircraft which managed to evade the fighters came under fire from flak batteries on the islands and on the coast. They had to turn back without managing to release their bombs

65. International press conference in Berlin to report on the 36 bombers shot down on 18th December 1939

66. "Airmen who proved their worth. Heroes of Heligoland air battle"

No. 1,290. SUNDAY, DECEMBER 24, 1939. TWOPENCE.

VICTORY

# Inside Story of War's Biggest Air Battle

## Won 'Great Glory'

MEMBERS of the Royal Air Force who took part in the dramatic fighting over the Heligoland Bight.

In a "Sunday Graphic" picture they are seen at their base "somewhere in England," discussing plans of attack before a flight.

67. Paul Harris and his men on the front page of the *Sunday Graphic*

Il sergente inglese Herbert Ruse prigioniero della battaglia aerea di Helgoland del 18 dicembre. Il Ruse, benchè con l'apparecchio colpito e incendiato potette atterrare in un'isoletta del Mar del Nord

THE ENGLISH SERGEANT HERBERT RUSE, A PRISONER FROM THE AIR BATTLE OF HELIGOLAND ON 18 DEC RUSE ALTHOUGH WITH HIS AIRCRAFT DAMAGED AND IN FLAMES WAS ABLE TO LAND ON AN ISLET IN THE NORTH SEA.

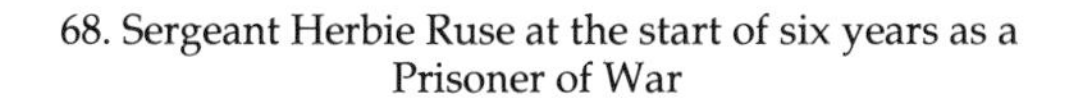

68. Sergeant Herbie Ruse at the start of six years as a Prisoner of War

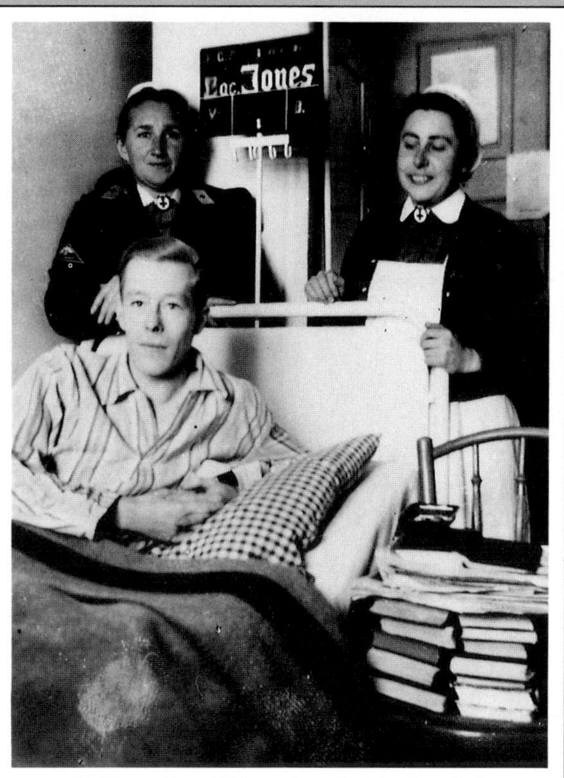


69. Harry "Jonah" Jones in a German hospital after being rescued by Herbie Ruse from his burning aircraft on the island of Borkum

70. The bodies of Sgt Holley, Sgt Tilley, Cpl Taylor and A/C Geddes were buried on Borkum with full military honours

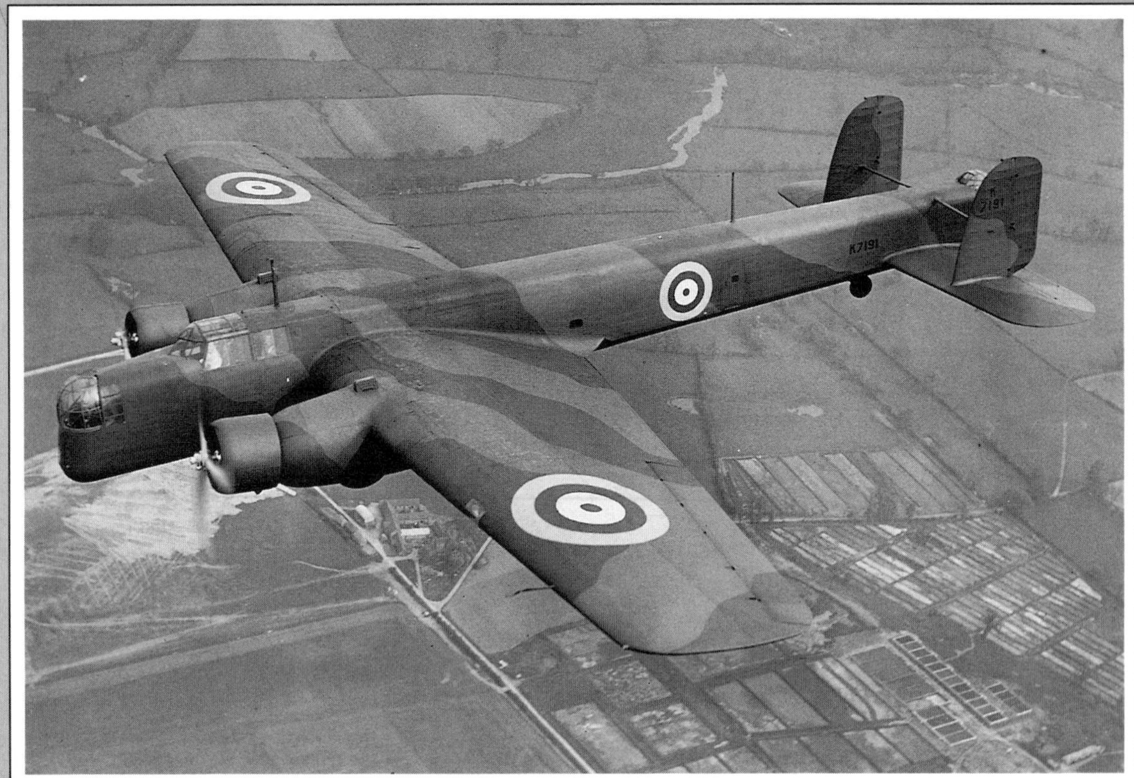


71. Armstrong Whitworth Whitley

72. Kellett's three Wellesleys on the record-breaking flight from Ismailia in Egypt to Darwin in Australia

73. Heriot-Watt University's three unmanned, remotely operated submersibles; ANGUS 001, 002 and 003

74. RCV 225 was provided by Hydro Products Ltd

75. SCORPI was provided by Sonat Subsea Services (U.K.) Ltd

76. The VAFA framework successfully lifted the weight for which it was designed, on 10th August 1985, at the British Aerospace factory in Weybridge

77. The assembled lifting frame on the barge at Bona Lighthouse

78. *Work Horse*

79. *Eilean Dubh*, now moored directly over the aircraft

80. WASP being swung out over the side of *Eilean Dubh*

81. Paul Harris and Wolfgang Falck enjoying one another's company at the 1984 Farnborough Air Show

82. Robert MacFarlane, Rhiannon Naismith, Naomi Leech and Robert Duncan (left to right) presenting the Marwood-Eltons with souvenirs of their visit to Loch Ness

83. Two air bags shot to the surface and floated high in the water, indicating that they carried hardly any weight – something had gone disastrously wrong

84. Once clear of the water, everyone could see that the lifting frame was now nothing more than a tangled heap of scrap. The attempt to recover the Wellington bomber had failed!

85. Spud Boorer looks really dejected as he and Hugh Tyrer survey the remains of the lifting frame. Morag Barton, Ann Huckins and Davida Crichton share the overwhelming feeling of despondency

86. The author recalling those immortal lines by Scotland's national bard
Robert Burns:
"The best laid schemes o' mice an' men
Gang aft a- gley,
An' lea'e us nought but grief an' pain
For promised joy"

87. This time there was no mistaking their message. The two air bags floated deep in the water. Something very heavy was hanging on the end of the lifting cable. We had done it! "R for Robert" was off the bottom of Loch Ness – for good

88. Peter Grant, over from Canada specially for the recovery of 'R for Robert', handles the old Wimpy's control column. It was with this control column that Paul Harris held his bomber in tight formation under the Luftwaffe's onslaught and with which Nigel Marwood-Elton struggled while ditching on Loch Ness

89. 'R for Robert" reaches for the sky after forty-five years on the bottom of Loch Ness
A close-up of the starboard wing clearly shows the 1940 RAF roundel

90. To the accompaniment of cracks and bangs from stress members within the geodetics that had not experienced loads for forty-five years, the old bomber finally emerges, dripping wet, from Loch Ness
Many of the spectators were taken by surprise when they saw just how big the Wellington really was

91. For a few brief moments
"R for Robert" is airborne again

92. Only when the tail section was lifted clear of the water to reveal the gun turret, did the real significance of the aircraft dawn on the majority of the spectators. 'R for Robert' was a war machine from a bygone era

93. Ammunition boxes containing thousands of rounds of machine gun bullets were removed from inside the fuselage by Warrant Officer Jack Harrison (left) and Chief Technician John Atkey, of the RAF Explosive and Ordnance Disposal Team

94. Over from Canada specially for the occasion, Peter Grant photographed N2980 as he flew over it in a light plane piloted by the crane's owner, Mr James Jack. By a remarkable coincidence, this is exactly the same view Peter Grant would have had of N2980 as he flew above and behind Paul Harris in formation during the Battle of Heligoland Bight

95. The convoy carrying the mortal remains of the only surviving Wellington bomber that saw action during the Second World War draws into the car park in front of the aircraft's final resting place – Brooklands Museum

96. The old warrior poses for a very historic photograph, right under the office window of its creator, Barnes Wallis

97. At long last Paul Harris is reunited with the old Wimpy in which he won his DFC at the Battle of Heligoland Bight. Assisted by Squadron Leader John Rootes, Paul visited Brooklands Museum in November 1985. Less than two months later he died peacefully at his home

98. Morag Barton, the Co-ordinator of the Brooklands Museum, presents Air Commodore Richard Kellett with the alarm clock, marked off in "Vickers Time", that the RAF Long Range Development Flight presented to Mr Gordon Montgomery in 1938. Standing between Morag and Richard is Jeff Montgomery, Gordon Montgomery's son

99. On 13th May, 1987, the Royal Navy Fleet Diving Group recovered the front gun turret

100. The RAF Kinloss sub-aqua club with the items they recovered at Lochend over the 1987 Christmas and New Year period

101. The Loch Ness Wellington Association Ltd. Executive Committee Members. Left to right: Don Storer; Ken Crichton; Robin Holmes (Chairman); Richard Kellett, Morag Barton and Bob Allwood

102. Oceaneering International Services Ltd. On the right is Chris Jenkins, Sales Manager for the Northern North Sea area

103. Oceaneering International Services Ltd. Left to right: The ADS team: Dave Weddle, Neil Brock, Andy Griffiths, Alfie Lyden, Dave Foot and Eric Hammons

104. Oceaneering International Services Ltd. The *Work Horse*'s crew: Norman Brown and John McKenzie (Skipper)

105. J. W. Automarine: Left to right: Richard Allen, Malcolm Felmingham and John Wise

106. Brooklands Museum, British Aerospace and VAFA. Back row, left to right, John Mitchell, Frank Hack, Alan Jeffcoate, Norman Barfield, Morag Barton, Jack Wheeler, Dorothy Hancocks, Angus Grant (local boat owner), Joan Mitchell, Josie Price, Jean Jeffcoate
Front row, left to right, Alex Delaney, Tony Large, Martin Cutler, Andy Pither, Peter Hancocks, John (Peter Hancock's grandson)

107. Vintage Aircraft and Flying Association (VAFA). Left to right, John Mitchell, Norman Boorer and Hugh Tyrer

108. The author with his two sons, Drew (left) and Keith (right) who helped to dismantle the Wimpy

109. A second celebration dinner to mark the successful recovery of "R for Robert" from Loch Ness was hosted by Mr McKenzie, the owner of the Clansman Hotel. All those who took part in the operation, in one way or another, are shown

110. Volunteers at work on the Wellington fuselage
Brooklands Museum 1st August 1991

went down to start attaching the securing straps to the lift points on the wings and fuselage. One of these lifting points was just behind the front gun turret, up at the nose of the aircraft. On its chest, WASP carried a television camera that allowed Alfie to see what the diver was doing. 'All stop on the diver,' ordered Alfie, as he peered at his television monitor to make out an object the diver had spotted through the murk. Something was draped round the nose of the Wimpy. It was a trawl net. Either someone had been trying to capture Nessie or had been intent on snatching a souvenir from the wreck, but there was now a potential hazard festooning the front turret that hadn't been there in 1983 when we examined the aircraft with K.D. Marine's UFO. From the size of the net, it could only have come from a fishing boat. More precious time was wasted as WASP very carefully cut away the strands of the net and eventually hauled it clear. We could well have done without that time-waster!

According to our contract with Oceaneering, Sunday was the day they were due to pack up and go back to Aberdeen, having delivered the Wellington safely on board the cargo barge. Obstinate debris, bad weather and now this fishing-net all conspired to push us three days behind schedule. Alfie went off to make a phone call to Chris Jenkins in Aberdeen. Again, Oceaneering came up trumps. We were granted another three days to make up for the lost time.

By now, N2980 should have been sitting at Bona Lighthouse being dismantled by VAFA. To celebrate our anticipated success, a dinner, hosted by Heriot-Watt University, had been organised at the Clansman hotel for the evening of Monday 16th September. Four years before, almost to the day, I had promised Paul Harris I would reunite him with the Wellington bomber in which he won his DFC. To keep this promise, he had been invited up to Loch Ness to be joint guest of honour with Group Captain Marwood-Elton at the celebration dinner. Paul's old adversary from the Battle of Heligoland Bight, Wolfgang Falck, was also flying over from Germany for the event and even Peter Grant was making a special trip from Canada to be there. With so many people coming such long distances, the dinner couldn't be postponed. I duly set off for Inverness Airport that afternoon to welcome Paul and his family. It had been some time since I last saw him and in the intervening period his heart condition had deteriorated. I was saddened to see him being wheeled across the tarmac in an invalid chair. Janine, his daughter, who had also flown over from Canada specially for the occasion, whispered to me that her father was very ill and it was only by sheer willpower that he had summoned up enough strength to make the journey north to see his old Wimpy. He was also greatly looking forward to meeting Peter Grant and Bunny Austin again after all those long years. Wolfgang Falck had flown up to Inverness on the same flight and greeted Paul warmly. They had got to know and respect one another at the Farnborough Air Show the previous year. In contrast, at seventy-five, only three years Paul's junior, Falck looked as fit as a fiddle. I don't think anyone would have been surprised if he had stepped out of his Me 110 instead of Dan Air's BAC 111. After settling everyone into their accommodation, I headed back to Bona Lighthouse.

The barometer needle had been steadily edging upward from 'Change' to 'Fair'. The wind had dropped and the surface of the loch was down to a gentle swell. WASP had been busy attaching the lifting straps to the fuselage and wings, having got rid of the troublesome fishing net. The ten-metre-long strengthening beam was proving difficult to manoeuvre into its correct position inside the fuselage. One of the WASP divers likened it to working inside a washing machine while trying to tie knots with pairs of pliers instead of fingers. A simple job that would take ten minutes on land could take WASP over an hour to complete on the bottom of the loch. A dinghy was sent ashore to the fish-and-chip van in the lay-by, and dinner that evening was a fish supper on the deck of *Eilean Dubh*. Alfie had been keeping a careful eye on the weather and at eleven o'clock he sent a message by radio to the HQ on the barge at Bona Lighthouse for the lifting frame to be launched. Every available hand was rounded up as VAFA, IOE and J.W. Automarine manhandled the bulky aluminium structure over the side and eased it gently down into the water. Some wag had fixed a dummy barrel of beer to the front of the frame and there had even been suggestions of attaching halved lorry tyres along the top of the frame to look like 'humps'. Fortunately, nobody could find scrap lorry tyres or we might have been plagued with reports of monster sightings. It was clear this was going to be an all-night job. At midnight, *Work Horse* arrived back at Bona Lighthouse ready to tow the lifting frame out to *Eilean Dubh*.

*Monday 16th September 1985*
By 1.00 a.m. the wind had dropped until it was nothing more than a cat's-paw. By 1.45 a.m., the waves had abated to a gentle swell. Over the barge radio came the request from Alfie for the lifting frame to be towed out. Very slowly *Work Horse* took up the strain on the tow rope and the ungainly frame, supported high in the water by its five big yellow buoyancy bags, eased away from the side of the old barge and headed out into the loch towards the dive site. Following along behind, illuminated by the bright light of Bona Lighthouse, was a flotilla of hired cabin cruisers, their searchlights playing on the shiny aluminium of the frame and its bright yellow air bags. One of the cruisers darted about as the BBC film team looked for the most dramatic shots of *Work Horse* and the frame passing between the closely spaced red and green navigation buoys at the mouth of the river Ness.

It was just coming up for 3.00 a.m. when *Work Horse* manoeuvred the lifting frame gently alongside *Eilean Dubh*. The powerful flood-lighting on the ferry clearly illuminated all the equipment on deck, where the Oceaneering team bustled about checking out WASP as it sat in its support frame beside the wheelhouse. Two surface divers from *Work Horse* jumped into the water to make final adjustments before the lifting frame was submerged. When all the securing straps had been released to dangle down under the frame, ready for quick connection to their corresponding attachment points on the aircraft, John Wise shouted to the divers to open the vent valves on the buoyancy bags. The air gushed out and the lifting frame settled lower and lower in the water until finally the buoyancy bags themselves disappeared beneath the surface in a froth of bubbles. The thick steel lifting hawser was shackled to the top of the frame and the remaining air let out of the buoyancy bags. The frame disappeared beneath the surface on its way down to the aircraft. When the full sixty-five metres of lifting cable had been paid out, WASP was hoisted back into the water ready to start connecting up the aircraft to the frame. Dawn was just breaking behind the mountains as WASP was recovered and dropped into its support, beside its companion JIM. Andy Griffiths and Eric Hammons, the two WASP pilots, had been working non-stop for eighteen hours and were absolutely exhausted. Six out of the eleven straps securing the aircraft had been done up when Alfie decided that his WASP pilots had had enough and called it a night. Everybody clambered aboard *Work Horse* and headed for shore and much needed rest. Surprisingly, the lay-by was still packed with cars as their owners kept all night vigil. Once word got round that the diving operations were packing up till Tuesday morning, most of the cars gave up their precious vantage points along the wall and headed off to give their drivers a sleep as well.

That afternoon, as the Oceaneering team enjoyed their well-earned rest, Charlie Stuart from Moray Firth Radio was busy conducting an interview with Group Captain Marwood-Elton and a group of children from the nearby Drumsmittal primary school at North Kessock. Previously, their headmaster, Mr Benzie, had contacted me to ask if he could bring along a deputation to meet the pilot who had ditched the Wellington. In a very touching little ceremony at Polmaily House hotel, Rhiannon Naismith, Naomi Leech, Robert Duncan and Robert MacFarlane (average age eleven) presented Mrs Marwood-Elton with a beautifully carved walking-stick and the Group Captain with a handsome tie embroidered with a Scottish Thistle. The presentation was entirely the children's own idea and it was clear that the elderly couple were deeply touched by this thoughtful gesture. I too received a tie and there was also one for Group Captain Paul Harris, who was unable to attend the presentation because he was resting before the dinner. Rhiannon later wrote a poem* for Group Captain Marwood-Elton to commemorate the recovery of the Wellington he thought he had 'hidden away for all time' at the bottom of Loch Ness, an aeroplane that belonged to an age before even Rhiannon's parents were born.

The celebration dinner that evening had originally been planned to mark the successful recovery of N2980 and formally hand over ownership to the Brooklands Museum. Now, circumstances outside our control dictated that the old Wimpy remain temporarily on the bottom of Loch Ness but everyone was supremely confident that that would be rectified the following day. With

* See Appendix C.

only half-a-dozen connections to make, Tuesday should see the aircraft lift gently off the bottom and rise triumphantly to the surface. It was in a mood of quiet optimism that the assembled guests sat down to dinner. Mr and Mrs MacKenzie and their staff laid on a meal worthy of the Savoy. In pride of place on the menu was, of course, Beef Wellington followed by Bombe 'Nessie'. After the meal, the guests of honour, Group Captain Marwood-Elton and Group Captain Harris regaled the assembled guests with some of their more amusing memories of flying Wellington bombers to Germany, while Oberst Wolfgang Falck later contributed some light-hearted anecdotes on how he had tried to stop them.

*Tuesday 17th September 1985*

Things got under way a little late that day. It was not until after lunch that WASP went down to make the final connections and position the strengthening beam. Difficulty was experienced in locking the beam under the trailing edge and tail main frames. By 5.00 p.m. Alfie decided that no more time could be expended on this task and the additional air bags, planned for under the strengthening beam, would have to be dispensed with. Squeezed into the tiny control cabin, Spud and Hugh gave Alfie the benefit of their experience as WASP adjusted the eleven securing straps to allow for the angle at which the aircraft was lying. It was now or never. Tuesday was the last day WASP was available on our extended charter. *Eilean Dubh* was due to be unloaded on Wednesday afternoon at Muirtown basin. Oceaneering had been more than patient. At 5.00 p.m., Alfie instructed the winchman to start bringing up WASP. Once the big yellow machine was safely secured on deck, the order was given to cut the port rear anchor cable to allow a clear passage to shore for the aircraft when it surfaced. Five minutes later John Wise ordered the valves on the air hoses from the compressor down to the 'parachute' lifting bags to be cracked open. Compressed air surged down to the two 5 tonne lifting bags secured to the steel cable five metres below the surface.

At that time, I was holding on to a thin surface line attached to the nose of the Wellington. From seventy metres below, vibrations started to be transmitted up this line to my finger-tips in much the same way as a nibbling fish announces its presence to an anxious angler on the surface. Yes, I could quite definitely feel movement down there. Suddenly great volumes of air bubbled to the surface alongside *Eilean Dubh*. The lifting bags were now full of air and exerting 10 tonnes of upward pull on the lifting frame. Still the excess air spilled out of the bottom of the bags and frothed on the surface. The trembling on the rope between my fingers increased until I could actually see the vibrations coming up the line. The tension in the rope suddenly eased a little and I could take in about five centimetres, then ten centimetres, then a metre. All at once, I was hauling in the line, hand over hand. The Wimpy had broken free from the suction of the mud and was heading for the surface. I now had about two metres of slack on deck. Quite suddenly my surface line stiffened and wouldn't come up any further. The

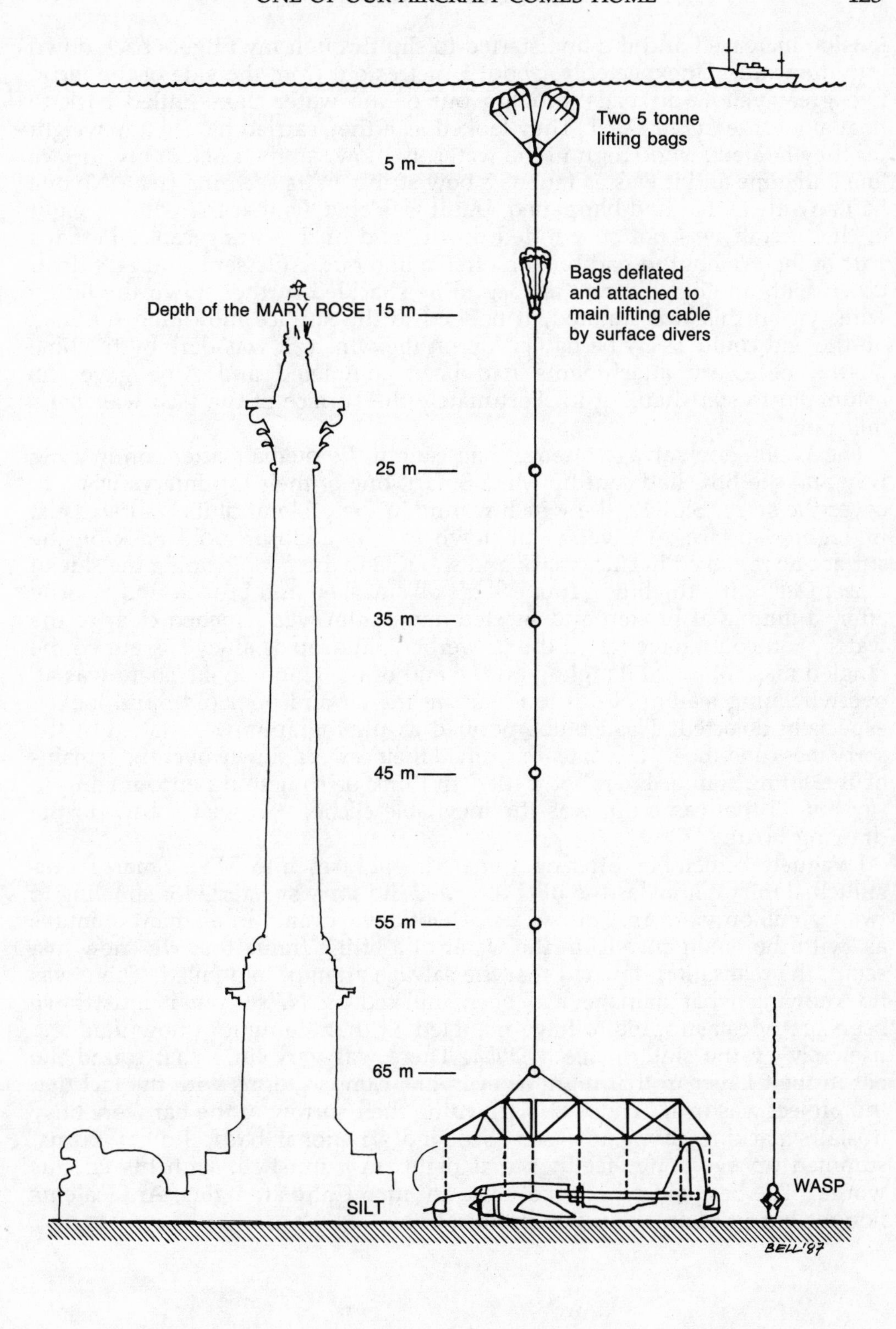
Two 5 tonne
lifting bags
5 m
Bags deflated
and attached to
main lifting cable
by surface divers
Depth of the MARY ROSE 15 m
25 m
35 m
45 m
55 m
65 m
SILT
WASP
BELL '87

tension increased and the line started to slip through my fingers back down into the water. Unexpectedly, about 5 metres out from the side of the ferry, two great yellow air bags shot up out of the water then settled back to float alongside *Eilean Dubh*. They looked as if they carried hardly any weight for they floated far too high in the water. By now, all the slack in my surface line had gone and it was as taut as a bow string on its securing cleat. No one had any idea what had happened, but it was obvious that the whole weight of the aircraft was not suspended on the end of the lifting cable. Perhaps part of the Wellington had broken off. To find out, Alfie sent a surface diver down with another 5 tonne air bag to be shackled further down the lifting wire. When this was inflated, it bobbed to the surface indicating the load on the end could safely be hauled up on the winch. It was dark by the time all the necessary attachments had been completed and Alfie gave the command to start hauling in. Fortunately the surface of the loch was like a mill pond.

The Wellington salvage attempt had caught the media's attention in a big way and the BBC had sent up Mike Smart, one of their top interviewers, to cover the story. Slowly, the winch wound in the cable until its load was just under the surface. A diver went down to take a closer look. Back on the surface he removed his face mask and shouted to the people lining the side of *Eilean Dubh*: 'It's the lifting frame – it's all smashed and broken up.' Shortly after, a jumble of broken and twisted aluminium was winched clear of the water. You could have heard the proverbial pin drop as all eyes scanned the tangled mass of metal dangling on the end of the crane hook. There was an overwhelming feeling of despondency in the air and poor old Spud looked especially dejected. Flash bulbs popped as photographs were taken of the sorry mess and the BBC film team panned their camera slowly over the remains of the lifting frame. Everybody tried to think of something encouraging to say but all that came out was the inevitable cliché, 'Ah well – back to the drawing board.'

I vaguely remember uttering some trite phrases into Mike Smart's outstretched microphone as the BBC recorded the sorry spectacle for showing to twenty million viewers. Four years of work evaporated in as many minutes as, with the emergence from the water of a lifting frame that was now just scrap, the realisation dawned that the salvage attempt had failed. There was no knowing what damage had been inflicted on N2980 but it must have been pretty catastrophic to have mangled all that aluminium now dangling uselessly by the side of *Eilean Dubh*. There was very little chat round the bar in the Clansman that night as everyone came to terms with the fact that the project was over. Those not drowning their sorrow at the bar were busy upstairs packing their suitcases. Scotland's national bard, Robert Burns, summed up everyones feelings that night, in a nutshell, with his famous words; 'The best laid schemes o' mice an' men Gang aft a-gley, An' lea'e us nought but grief an' pain For promised joy.'

*Wednesday 18th September, 1985*
Breakfast that morning was a sombre affair with little, if any, conversation in the Clansman's dining-room as everyone lethargically went through the motions of eating their sausage, bacon and eggs. The lifting frame was now a heap of scrap, the money had run out, our allotted time was up and the hotel foyer was piled high with suitcases ready for the journey back south. The VAFA team carefully wrapped up their rudder and other assorted bits and pieces of the aircraft – all there was to show for eight days of hard graft.

Having said my rueful farewells, I was busy packing luggage into the boot of the car when Bob Allwood, IOE's project co-ordinator, shot out of the hotel and across the car park. 'Alfie wants a word with you,' he said as he ushered me back into the hotel. Alfie was standing in the public phone box in earnest conversation with Oceaneering's office in Aberdeen. The BBC film team had faithfully recorded the previous night's débâcle and the whole sorry story had been watched by millions of viewers waiting expectantly to see a Wellington bomber emerge, Phoenix-like, from the depths of Loch Ness. Mike Smart had done a real professional job, interviewing all the principals against a backdrop of the mangled lifting frame. Spud's dejection that night came across as almost tangible, and the universal air of despondency among the rest of us who were interviewed moved a number of people to reach for their chequebooks. That Tuesday night, Alfie had put in a long-distance call to the President of Oceaneering International Services Ltd in Houston, Texas, and been given the go-ahead to keep *Eilean Dubh* on site for another five days, provided sufficient money could be found just to cover the costs. This was now Alfie on the phone to his Aberdeen office to confirm the arrangements. Apparently, as a result of the previous night's trauma, Chris Jenkins, Oceaneering's Sales Manager had received pledges of sufficient money to keep *Eilean Dubh* on station for five more days. 'Would the Loch Ness Wellington Association agree to another salvage attempt?' asked Alfie from the phone box. 'Yes', I replied, 'provided the money is guaranteed.' When this had been relayed back to Aberdeen, Alfie put the phone down and said, 'Confirm it with Chris Jenkins and we're back in business.'

At that point, Chris was engaged in conversation with a gentleman in the car park. I went out and enquired. Chris Jenkins replied by handing me two cheques, one from a company called Water Weights Ltd for £300 and the other from a company called AOC International Ltd for £2,000. At that, the man to whom Chris had been talking, a Mr Don Roedecker of Gas Supplies Ltd, took out his chequebook and wrote me a cheque for another £2,000. Chris confirmed that he could guarantee the remainder.

The Wellington lift was on again. The news spread round the Clansman like wildfire. Suitcases were hauled out of car boots, rooms were rebooked and suddenly everyone started talking at the same time. To describe the atmosphere as electric would be an understatement. Adrenalin started to flow once more as everyone animatedly discussed how they would go about recovering the aircraft now. Everything, of course, hinged on the state of the

Wellington. How had it survived being lifted a couple of metres then dropped back onto the bottom of the loch? Like greased lightning, Alfie and his boys were off to *Eilean Dubh* to inspect the damage to N2980. Crowded into his little control cabin we all peered anxiously at the television monitor as WASP surveyed the aircraft. I think everyone was staggered to find the old girl virtually intact. The tail section had snapped off from the front fuselage but, apart from that, there seemed to be no major damage. All the lifting straps were still in place, having been torn off the frame.

Obviously, there was now no point in trying to lift the aircraft in one piece. The wings, engines and nose section could come up as a unit, provided the wing spar would take the strain. The tail section should prove no trouble to lift on its own. The legendary strength of geodetics had stood the test of forty-five years underwater, *and* a two metre drop, to prove once again the genius of Barnes Wallis. But for that damaged centre section we would, more than likely, have been successful on the first lift. Why the lifting frame collapsed can only be a matter of conjecture. The ten-metre-long stiffening beam was observed to be buckled into an inverted V shape, sticking up out of the fuselage behind the trailing edge main frame. Clearly, the weakened centre section of fuselage had folded, throwing all the weight on to the front part of the frame. Perhaps the tail section, with its heavy gun turret, had caused the back end of the lifting frame to twist sideways and collapse in the middle. Perhaps the aircraft had been embedded deeper in the silt than had originally been thought and the extra suction imposed too great a load on the frame. We will never know exactly what happened down there, but the important thing was the Wellington had survived, albeit in two pieces. The remainder of that afternoon was spent around a table in *Eilean Dubh*'s cabin discussing how to go about recovering the aircraft in the light of the new situation. In the best tradition of the engineering profession, a new lifting frame was sketched on the back of an envelope and one of Oceaneering's team headed for Evanton to get Cromarty Firth Engineering Ltd to make it. There, they worked all through that night to construct the new *steel* lifting frame ready for delivery – *next day*.

Sadly, the further delay meant that Paul Harris could not be reunited with his Wimpy on that occasion. He had to leave with his family and friends as they headed home to attend to pressing business commitments. Likewise, the Marwood-Eltons, Bunny Austin and Wolfgang Falck had to leave Loch Ness as well.

*Thursday 19th September, 1985*

I arrived at Bona Lighthouse later that morning to find Hugh Tyrer wading in his wellies by the side of the barge. He was happily scrubbing down fourteen oxygen bottles that WASP had earlier recovered from the aircraft. The cleaning had to be done with the bottles submerged underwater because some of them were still full of oxygen at high pressure, even after forty-five years. Indeed, one of them had 'popped-off' as they were being brought ashore in the rubber dinghy, fortunately without causing any harm. The new lifting frame duly arrived at 4.00 p.m. and the separate pieces were off-loaded from their lorry by a mobile crane. The white paint was still tacky. Hugh Tyrer scratched his head and turned to me and said: 'You know, it would have taken a certain large aircraft company I know six months – just to order the material.' Welding torches were lit and the men from Cromarty Firth Engineering Ltd got down to the task of welding the sections of the frame together. When they had finished, it looked strong enough to lift a jumbo jet. Next, John Wise and his men descended on it and started strapping on three huge flotation bags. By the time everybody packed up that night, the new lifting frame was all set to be craned into the water and WASP had re-rigged the Wimpy ready to accept it. Tomorrow was the big day, a Friday, yes, but not the thirteenth this time.

*Friday 20th September, 1985*

Driving past the lay-by on the way to Bona Lighthouse that morning, we could see quite a few cars had returned to take up vantage points along the wall. With the sudden and dramatic collapse of the original lifting frame, and the project, Mike Smart and the BBC film team had left Loch Ness along with all the disappointed spectators. Now, news had spread that the lift was on again. Half-way to London, Derrick Towers and his BBC film team got a message to turn round and head back north. They were waiting for us aboard their cabin cruiser as we parked beside the barge at Bona Lighthouse. The wind was fairly gusty, so Alfie was holding-off ordering the launch of the new frame. Come lunchtime, he felt the conditions had moderated sufficiently to call for it. When craned into the water, it sank from view so that all that was visible were its three yellow buoyancy bags.

Once again, *Work Horse* eased gently ahead to take up the strain on the tow rope. Following along in the wake was another flotilla of hired cabin cruisers, with the BBC film cameras rolling and everyone keeping their fingers crossed that nothing would go wrong this time. By late afternoon, the new frame was alongside *Eilean Dubh*, with the surface divers busying themselves making the final preparations. Once again, John Wise shouted to the divers to open the vent valves on the buoyancy bags, and the new frame started its journey down to the aircraft, suspended on the end of the lifting wire. This time, WASP completed the connections to the aircraft in record time, just over an hour. The WASP pilots had become so adept at threading the lifting straps through the aircraft's structure and round the wire loops on the frame that Alfie was heard to comment: 'After this, Dave and Eric will be able to take up macramé as a hobby.' By 8.30 p.m., the task was completed. N2980 was all laced up to its frame and ready to go. Looking ashore we could see the lay-by was once more full of cars with their occupants scanning the water with binoculars. A radio telephone had been given to one of the VAFA team in the lay-by to try and keep the spectators ashore informed of progress. Everything now depended on J.W. Automarine. Over the side of *Eilean Dubh* went the bundled-up lifting bags to be taken down by the surface divers for shackling on to the lifting wire. It was 10.30 p.m. by the time John Wise was satisfied that all the connections were secure and the safety checks completed. After one last inspection of the aircraft, its frame and the lifting straps, Alfie ordered WASP out of the water. This was it. Once again, I was standing up at the bow of *Eilean Dubh* holding on to a thin surface line attached, this time, to the tip of the starboard wing. Everyone not directly involved in the lift was ordered up onto the flat cabin roof as the deck was cleared for action. Alfie nodded to John Wise who in turn nodded to his companion to crack open the valves. The air hoses on deck straightened out and went rigid as the high-pressure air surged down to the first set of lifting bags, five metres below the surface. There, as before, were the familiar vibrations coming up the line to my finger-tips. There, as before, was the great explosion of bubbles on the surface as the lifting bags overflowed. Once again, the tension in my hand line eased a little and I was able to pull in a few centimetres, then a little more, until I was hauling it up hand over hand. All at once a tremendous cheer went up from everyone standing high up on the cabin roof. Down through the water they could see the great yellow 'parachute' bags heading for the surface where they broke amid a cauldron of frothing bubbles. Up they bobbed, their tops shooting a couple of metres above the surface, to settle back low in the water. Every eye was riveted on these two great buoyancy bags. This time, there was no mistaking their message. They floated deep in the water. Something very heavy was hanging on the end of the cable. The little line lay motionless in the palm of my hand, showing no desire to slip back down into the depths. 'R for Robert' was off the bottom of Loch Ness for good. By now, everyone was jumping up and down with joy, slapping backs, shaking hands. It was just like scoring the winning goal at the Cup Final in the last minute of extra time. A couple of bottles of champagne materialised as if by magic. Mike Smart appeared with his outstretched microphone and the BBC film team recorded beaming smiles all round, in stark contrast to the previous occasion. The sense of relief was overwhelming. We had finally done it. We had wrested N2980 from the murky depths of Loch Ness after its forty-five years of peaceful slumber.

'Right then, lets get on with it,' shouted John Wise as the air valves to the second set of buoyancy bags were opened. By 11.00 p.m., the second set of bags were on the surface indicating that the aircraft was a further ten metres up off the bottom. Three-quarters of an hour later the third set of lifting bags had broken the surface confirming that 'R for Robert' was well and truly on its way up.

*Saturday 21st September, 1985*

Conditions on the loch that night can only be described as idyllic. A mirror calm surface combined with a hint of drizzle to lend the stillness an almost mystical quality. Looking shoreward from the deck of *Eilean Dubh*, I could clearly see twin rows of fairy lights strung out along the shoreline as the lights of the parked cars reflected on the still waters. There was no thought

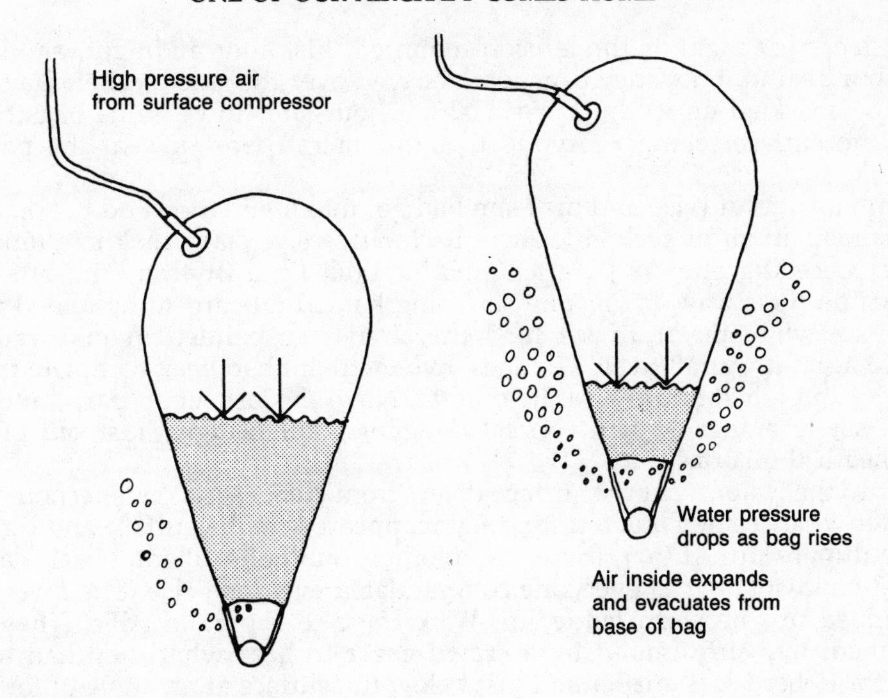


PARACHUTE BAGS

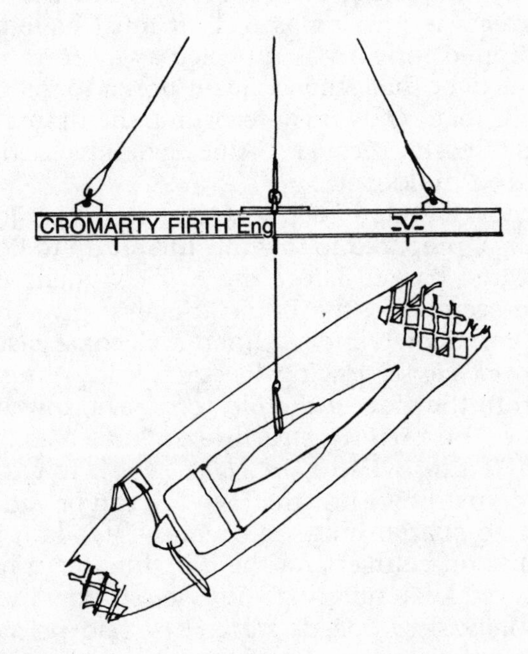


LIFTING FRAME

BELL '87

of sleep that night as the tension mounted. Just after midnight, another set of bundled up buoyancy bags were heaved over the side on their way down to be shackled on to the cable. Half an hour later those same bags bobbed to the surface telling everyone that the aircraft was now at the half-way mark.

By now, John Wise and his team had got into their stride and the operation assumed an air of slick efficiency. Each successive stage took less time than the preceding one, as J.W. Automarine built up a rhythm with one set of bags on their way down, one set being hauled inboard to be folded up for re-use, while the third set held the aircraft suspended in mid-water. At 2.03 a.m., it was all over. The sixty-five metre lift had been completed in just three-and-a-half hours – to the minute. Now, the last set of 'parachute' bags lay safely alongside with N2980 dangling, tantalisingly, just out of sight beneath the surface.

Into the water went the surface divers from *Work Horse* to inspect our catch. After what seemed an eternity, they reappeared on the surface and signalled the thumbs up. At that, there was another round of exuberant back-slapping and hand-shaking as everyone congratulated everyone else. The divers then climbed up the stern ladder on *Work Horse* to report to Alfie. They were immediately surrounded by a crowd eager to hear what they had to say. 'R for Robert' was suspended just below the surface at an angle of forty-five degrees, nose down. Without the balancing weight of the tail section, the massive engines transferred the centre of gravity well forward of the lifting frame. We had not been expecting the tail section, but the divers reported that the front gun turret was missing as well. It must have been wrenched off when the aircraft tipped forward as it peeled away from the bottom. No matter, WASP could recover that when it went down to get the tail section.

All the while, the BBC team were busy recording the drama on film. When asked to sum up the successful recovery, Alfie Lyden likened it to 'trying to pick up a cobweb with a bulldozer'.

The operation was now handed back to Oceaneering as John McKenzie, the skipper of *Work Horse*, prepared to tow the aircraft up to Bona Lighthouse for craning onto the cargo barge. Before the tow commenced, another two 'parachute' bags were secured to the lifting frame to give the set-up more stability in the water. Very slowly indeed, John McKenzie eased the throttles gently forward and *Work Horse*, towing its four yellow mushrooms, drew imperceptibly away from the side of the old ferry. The tow had to be done extremely slowly because the aircraft's structure could be damaged by the drag of the water. It was 3.00 a.m. when *Work Horse* set off to cover the two km up to Bona Lighthouse. Just how slow the tow was can be judged by the fact that it took five and three-quarter hours to cover the two km. A slight breeze kept blowing *Work Horse* off-course, and the BBC film team had to assist by using their cabin cruiser to keep nudging *Work Horse*'s bow in the right direction. At that exceptionally slow speed, *Work Horse* had no steerage way. It was broad daylight by the time the aircraft grounded close by the beach at

Lochend, to complete what must surely have been one of the slowest tows in history.

With the aircraft grounding, a team of divers went down to assess the situation. Because of the steep angle at which the Wellington was suspended, its nose was now scraping along the bottom. To get it over an underwater spit at the mouth of the river Ness and in under the crane, it had to be re-rigged. This meant removing the steel lifting frame and strapping buoyancy bags directly on to the main wing spar while, at the same time, attaching a set of flotation bags to the two propeller bosses in an attempt to get it floating level. While this work was going on, one or two items were hauled out of the fuselage and brought up for safety. The largest of these was the unit containing the pilot's seat and control column. VAFA took charge of it and carefully placed it on the grass beside the barge where they sprayed it with dewatering fluid. Surprisingly, the control column still moved back and forth quite freely and the rudder bar swivelled effortlessly on its bearings. Re-rigging the aircraft, however, was a painfully slow process. Oceaneering and J.W. Automarine divers worked non-stop, in relays, for seven hours to prepare N2980 for her début before the assembled audience on the beach at Lochend. Up on the main road, every available space in the lay-by and on the grass verges was packed with parked cars for miles in each direction. As the police struggled to keep the main A82 road from Inverness to Fort Augustus open to traffic, their good humour and patience attracted many appreciative comments from the crowd of 'local Derby' proportions.

At long last the lifting frame floated free of the aircraft and was taken in tow by *Work Horse* round the corner of the lighthouse to the waiting crane, where it was lifted out of the water, its job done. Just after 4.00 p.m., John Wise surfaced and indicated that everything was now ready for the air lines to be taken down and plugged into the re-rigged buoyancy bags on the aircraft. A fleet of cabin cruisers milled around, jockeying for position to get the best view. At a signal from John Wise, the air supply from *Work Horse*'s compressor was turned on. For a minute or two nothing seemed to happen. Then a solitary blob of oil appeared on the surface and spread out into the familiar rainbow patterns. More blobs of oil followed, then one or two small air bubbles burst on the surface. Suddenly all the onlookers were taken by surprise, for we had no idea what to expect. The flat calm was broken by a great frothing, up out of the middle of which poked a wing tip. It rose slowly and majestically skyward to reveal a perfectly formed but strangely unfamiliar kind of wing. With water cascading from every nook and cranny, it surged upward to a peak where it seemed to hang motionless for a brief instant. There, for all to see, were Barnes Wallis's geodetics with their unique criss-cross pattern revealed in places under a torn and tattered brown fabric covering. But the most emotive sight of all was the large blue circle with a red centre prominently displayed on the upper surface – a 1940 RAF roundel. The sight of that roundel brought home to those spectators with grey hair the full significance of the event. The last time that great wing had cleaved its natural

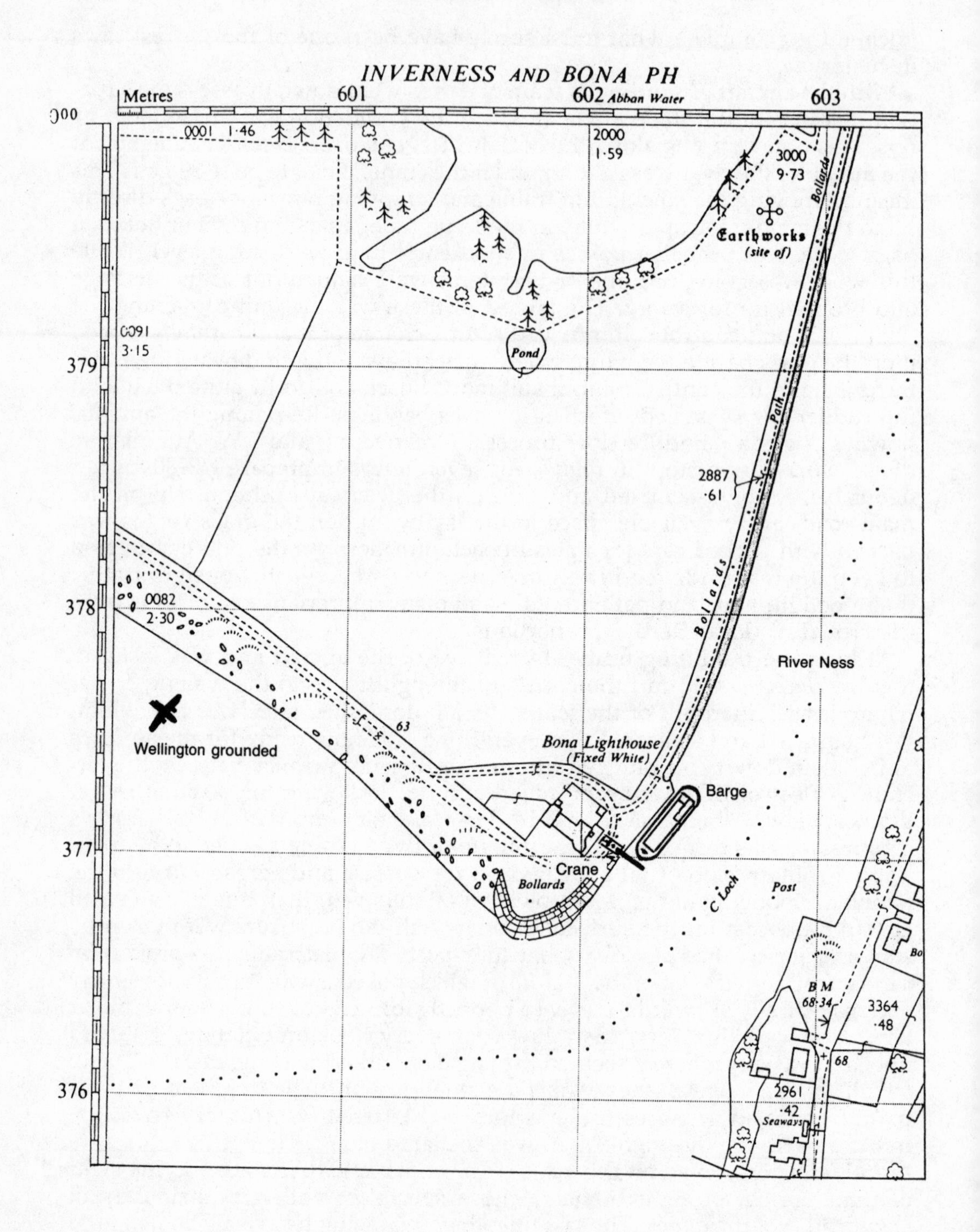

INVERNESS AND BONA PH
Metres
601
602
Abban Water
603
0001 1·46
2000 1·59
3000 9·73
Bollards
Earthworks (site of)
0091 3·15
379
Pond
Path
2887 ·61
Bollards
378
0082 2·30
River Ness
Wellington grounded
63
Bona Lighthouse (Fixed White)
Barge
377
Crane
Bollards
C Loch
Post
B M 68·34
3364 ·48
68
2961 ·42
Seaways
376

element, London was reeling under the impact of the Blitz, with the City having just suffered its worst attack of the war so far from 30,000 incendiary bombs that gutted the square mile, including the Guildhall and eight Wren churches.

The wing slid smoothly back down beneath the surface of Loch Ness. Seconds later it bobbed back up again to float almost horizontally on the surface alongside its yellow buoyancy bags. A multitude of cameras on shore and in the flotilla of cabin cruisers snapped that unique moment as 'R for Robert' reached for the sky. To those lining the shore it must have been a little disappointing to see nothing more exciting than a wing tip and some jagged bits of metal sticking up out of the water. Looking down over the bow of *Work Horse*, however, we could see the full extent of our catch. There, just below the surface, floated a huge Wellington wing with its two Pegasus engines, spanning a rather torn-up fuselage. All that had to be done now was tow it round to the waiting crane where all would be revealed once it lay safely on the deck of the barge. John McKenzie, *Work Horse*'s skipper, nudged the throttles forward to take up the slack in the tow rope. Rounding the lighthouse corner, the submerged aircraft started to pick up speed where the previously still waters of the loch funnelled in to the river Ness. The current now assisted the little flotilla of boats, with the Wellington just clearing the submerged spit at the mouth of the river. The aircraft came to rest right underneath the crane's towering jib extended out over the water. Hanging from the crane hook was the lifting frame with six wires dangling ready to pick up the load. The fleet of Caley Marine cabin cruisers stood-off in a semi-circle round *Work Horse* watching it cast-off the tow rope, back away then turn round and head out to give *Eilean Dubh* a helping hand. Divers at once jumped into the water and swam the narrow gap to climb up onto the wing in readiness to start shackling up the lifting wires to the main spar.

Suddenly, someone on shore shouted a warning. They had spotted the buoyancy bags drifting away from the side and out into the middle of the river. With unexpected rapidity, the current took charge and swept the aircraft out past the moored barge and on down the river. By this time *Work Horse* was well on its way so a bit of a panic ensued. Like the 7th Cavalry charging to the rescue, two of the Caley cruisers revved up and gave chase. A bit of deft manoeuvring followed as they tried to get a line to the aircraft. Eventually they succeeded in slinging a couple of ropes round the wing spar. Straining on these ropes, engines going flat out, they finally reined in the reluctant celebrity. It seemed for all the world as if our old Wimpy had taken stage fright at the thought of appearing before the huge crowd that had, by now, gathered at Bona Lighthouse. Engines roaring, the two cabin cruisers strained to make headway against the current. To cheers of encouragement from the assembled throng, they gradually inched their way forward, with a combined pull that just managed and no more to overcome the drag of the current. Eventually, their gallant rescue bid was rewarded with the sight of the aircraft safely back underneath the crane. No mistakes were made this time, with a stout rope securing the aircraft to a bollard. After the excitement had died down, the divers were not long in shackling up the lifting wires. Glancing at my watch, I noticed that it was coming up for 7.45 p.m. The recovery team had not closed an eye for over thirty-six hours. We listened as the engine note from the huge crane dropped an octave, telling us that the load was coming on. In slow motion, the trailing edge of the wing broke surface and the buoyancy bags flopped down as the weight came off them. With the greatest of care, the aircraft was gently lifted up out of the water. Those spectators lining the opposite bank across the river and the people in the cabin cruisers were treated to a perfect full frontal view of the twenty-six-metre-long wing as it emerged, dripping wet, from the river.

The blades of the port propeller were bent backward and those of the starboard propeller were almost straight, just as we had observed them four years before on Sea Pup's television camera. There were quite a few gasps of surprise among the spectators when it dawned on them just how big the Wellington really was. The lift was carried out to the accompaniment of loud cracks and bangs from stress members within the geodetics as they took up loads they had not experienced for forty-five years. Finally, the entire remains of the bomber hung clear of the water for all to see. The great wings were immaculate, in absolutely perfect shape, showing little damage apart from the torn and tattered fabric, but the poor old fuselage was in a sorry state. Above the wings, where the fuselage and tail should have been, there was nothing but fresh air. The nose in front of the cockpit had disappeared as well and it looked as though someone had taken a tin opener along the top of the fuselage between the wings. Nevertheless, everyone stood transfixed, gazing in wonder at this relic from a bygone age.

The towering jib slewed round till the suspended aircraft hung directly over the barge. Ever so carefully the aircraft was lowered to the sound of more cracks and bangs from the Wimpy as it made a perfect landing on deck. For a few brief moments 'R for Robert' had been airborne again, with the help of the mobile crane. The starboard wheel hung down only to be partially pushed back into its housing when the aircraft was lowered onto the barge. Once more the crane's engine note changed, rising an octave as the barge settled deeper in the water. The recovery team could not wait to climb aboard for our first close look at the Wellington. After seven years of studying the machine on remote underwater television cameras, it had become a very old friend, and I couldn't resist the temptation to stroke the dripping wet port propeller and then pat the oily, smelly engine and say, 'Welcome aboard, old girl.'

The crowd surged forward, right up to the edge of the landing, for a closer look at this strange machine with its trellis-like metal skeleton showing through the torn fabric. Many were surprised to learn that such an aircraft had ever existed. While everyone knew of Barnes Wallis's bouncing bomb, few, especially among the younger ones, had heard of his Wellington bomber. Lancasters and Mosquitoes – yes, but an aeroplane made out of thin strips of aluminium covered with cloth was a revelation. By now it was getting dark and too late to think about doing any work that night, apart from the fact that everyone on the recovery team was absolutely exhausted. The floodlighting on the barge was switched on and two of the VAFA team offered to mount an all night guard so that we could all go and get our heads down.

Before leaving for the Clansman hotel, I had a chance to chat to Mr James Jack who owned the crane and I was struck by an ironic twist of fate. The great huge crane that had just lifted 'R for Robert' up out of the water and laid it so gently on the barge had been delivered that very week from Germany. It had just been built by the famous World War II armaments firm of Krupp at its factory in, of all places – Wilhelmshaven. Was Somebody up there trying to tell us something?

*Sunday 22nd September, 1985*

The first people to climb aboard the aircraft that morning were two members of the RAF's Explosive Ordnance Disposal (EOD) Team. Their job was to recover any dangerous pieces of ordnance lying about. After prodding around gingerly in the silt at the bottom of the fuselage, they removed what looked like four little silver bombs. These turned out to be sea marker floats. Boxes of ammunition were also recovered and taken ashore. Inside were belts of 0.303 inch machine gun ammunition. Most of the bullets were still bright and shiny and their connecting links still flexed quite freely. Once the EOD team were satisfied that they had removed all the dangerous material, they allowed the VAFA team on to the aircraft. To help clear out the silt, the local fire brigade arrived with a small portable pump and started hosing down the inside of the fuselage.

Forty-five years of mud and silt drained away to reveal a little time capsule full of poignant souvenirs. The navigator's log book with a NAAFI pencil attached by a piece of string; a tin of Wills' Woodbine cigarettes; a device for coding secret messages; a large aerial camera with the film cassette still attached; a betting slip dated 31st December 1940; a Type R1082/T1083 wireless set; navigating instruments and a box of tuning coils for the radio transmitter – these were just some of the nostalgic bits and pieces that ended up on the grass bank for cleaning and spraying with preservative. While all this excavation of the fuselage was going on, *Work Horse* appeared round the point towing the tail section buoyed up by three large air bags round the rudder. Not until the tail unit was lifted out of the water by the crane did many people in the crowd appreciate the real significance of the aircraft. Prominently situated at the back end of the tail section was the gun turret with its two Browning machine guns poking out through the perspex dome. Only now did N2980's function really sink home. This was a war machine from a bygone era totally unfamiliar to the majority of spectators who had grown up in the age of supersonic jet aircraft and guided weapons. But there were one or two elderly gentlemen wistfully gazing at the turret. One senior citizen confided in me that he had been a tail gunner and spent many cold, cramped hours of lonely isolation in just such a turret until his Wellington had been hit by flak over Duisburg in 1943 and he had to bail out and spend the rest of the war as a PoW. The crane swung the tail section up over the barge and deposited the back end of the Wimpy on the banking because there was no room for it on the deck of the barge.

After one of the EOD team had pulled the machine guns' cocking handles back and removed two rounds of live ammunition from the breeches, the crowd surged round to gaze into the tiny turret. How anyone ever managed to sit for hours in that cramped and exposed position was hard to comprehend and filled me with tremendous admiration for all tail-gunners. When the crowd started to peel off bits of fabric from the tailplanes as souvenirs, they were ushered back behind the barrier. A member of the EOD team removed the head from one of the bullets taken from the rear turret to find it was full of water and therefore quite inert. Amazingly, large areas of the fabric covering the tailplane were still drum tight and you could bounce a fifty pence piece off it. Also recovered from the tail section were a flying helmet, a parachute, an escape axe and two magazines of ammunition.

All afternoon the crowd watched the removal and preservation of items of equipment from the Wellington as the VAFA team prepared the aircraft for dismantling the following day.

*Monday 23rd September 1985*

After almost two weeks of enforced inaction, the VAFA team now came into their own. Ably led by John Mitchell, they descended on the Wellington, spanners and hacksaws in hand, to start dismantling the aircraft ready for transportation back to Weybridge. In their white overalls and hard hats they looked for all the world like the famous television advert of the 'Flour Graders' about to set to work on a bag of flour. The nickname stuck. Never pausing for a meal or even the 'traditional' tea break, they squirted everything in sight with release oil, undid nuts and bolts, sawed through pipes and wires and gathered up instruments, controls, actuators and a mountain of loose bits and pieces for stowing away into tea chests. With surprising ease, Hugh Tyrer extracted the two long steel bolts that held on the starboard outer wing, and watched it being craned away to be placed on the grass banking beside the barge. He showed me the two bolts, covered in the original grease, with their ratchet handles still working perfectly after all those years underwater. Next to come off was the starboard engine and, last thing that night, the starboard mid-wing with its engine nacelle was lifted clear and over beside its engine and outer wing on the grass.

*Tuesday 24th September 1985*

By lunch time the port outer wing had been removed and lay on top of its opposite number. Off came the port engine to be followed by the port mid-wing until all that was left on the barge was the fuselage. Then came the job of rearranging all the separate sections on the barge for the short journey through the Caledonian Canal to Inverness. By 8.00 p.m. the tail unit, the last section, was being lashed down alongside the engines, wings and fuselage ready to leave first thing next morning for the lorries waiting at Muirtown Basin.

*Wednesday 25th September 1985*

The barge, now laden with the dismantled remains of the Wellington bomber, left Bona Lighthouse early for the four-hour trip back along the canal and down through the locks. We had been particularly fortunate with the weather during the second week, and that morning was especially fine, with just a hint of autumn in the still, clear air as we waved farewell to the crowds of people lining the tiny quay at Bona Lighthouse. Standing up at the bow of the old barge as *Work Horse* pushed it along the mirror-calm water of Loch Dochfour, I looked behind me at the remains of N2980. The previous day a young reporter had implied that the Wimpy was really nothing more than a heap of worthless scrap. That morning, as passing motorists tooted their horns in acknowledgement, I wouldn't have swapped our 'heap of worthless scrap' for the Crown Jewels. Neither, I'm sure, would any of the others who had shared the initial disappointment and final triumph. Arriving at the first lock at Dochgarroch, we were greeted by children from the little local school who waved us on our way.

*Eilean Dubh* had already left Loch Ness the day before, because Alfie Lyden and his ADS team urgently needed to get WASP out to another job in the North Sea. Before he left, Alfie reported that, sadly, their efforts to recover the front gun turret had been unsuccessful. For hours WASP had tried to get a lifting line round the smooth, ball like turret but had to abandon the attempt when time ran out.

After a delightful journey along the canal and a smooth passage down the final set of locks, *Work Horse* eased the heavily laden barge out into Muirtown Basin and in alongside the wharf. There was no sign of *Eilean Dubh* which had, by now, left on another charter. WASP, JIM, the control cabin, the Hiab crane, the compressor and all the other pieces of Oceaneering equipment had been lifted off the previous day by the big Krupp crane. It had journeyed round by road and now waited patiently at the side of the basin to unload the bomber. Once again 'R for Robert' became airborne. First the tail unit, then the fuselage, followed by the wings and finally the engines were delicately transferred from the deck of the barge and over on to the waiting lorries. Hugh Tyrer had managed to unearth an old 'Queen Mary' road transporter from somewhere. One of the crowd of spectators watching the proceedings commented to me just how nostalgic the whole scene was because an aircraft on its 'Queen Mary' had been a common sight up there during the war. By late evening the VAFA team had all the sections safely stowed on the lorries and secured ready for the long haul back home to Weybridge.

*Thursday 26th September 1985*
All that now remained to do was crane the IOE container and Portakabin off the barge. When they were both safely deposited in their lorry, George Heggie, the crane driver, retracted the towering jib then lowered and secured it ready for the return journey back to his base. Just delivered from Wilhelmshaven, the brand new German crane left Muirtown Basin a little after noon. Thus ended a unique operation to salvage an old British bomber that had, many long years before, also paid a visit to Wilhelmshaven.

After handshakes all round, the various recovery teams climbed aboard their cars and vans. At a signal from John Mitchell, the three lorries turned out of the wharf and set-off in convoy on the long road south to the Brooklands Museum.

*Friday 27th September 1985*
The factory had just closed for the night when the convoy of vans and lorries swung off Brooklands Road and in through the main gates of British Aerospace. Down past the old Vickers Armstrongs workshops, where it had been built forty-six years before, went N2980 and then turned the corner onto the road that had once been the finishing straight of the world famous motor racing track. In through the gates of the new Brooklands Museum went the convoy until the 'Queen Mary' was brought to a halt in front of the Clubhouse, right under the window of Barnes Wallis's old office. Morag Barton was there, along with the Mayor and other Civil Dignitaries from Elmbridge Borough Council, to welcome 'R for Robert' home. Among the assembled crowd were many people who had worked long hard hours during the war building Wellingtons; maybe some had even helped build N2980. I would like to think that perhaps even the great man himself looked down on the proceedings from his old office window, and approved.

While the recovery operation had now reached its successful conclusion, the immense task of preserving and restoring 'R for Robert' had just begun.

A few weeks later, a very frail old man in his wheelchair visited Brooklands Museum. Group Captain Paul Ivor Harris just managed to summon up enough strength to make the trip to Weybridge. There, he was finally reunited with the old Wimpy in which he won his DFC at the Battle of Heligoland Bight. Less than two months later he died peacefully in his sleep at his home, Crab Hill Farm. He just missed, by a day, a television film entitled *One of our bombers is no longer missing*. The recovery operation had proved so dramatic that BBC 2 allowed Derrick Towers and his Loch Ness film team to use the material they had shot for their underwater archaeology series and make it up into a full length, fifty minute documentary.

A year later, another elderly gentleman was collected from his home in Bexhill-on-Sea and wafted up to Weybridge in a British Aerospace limousine. Air Commodore Richard Kellett, DFC, AFC, was then conducted round the dismantled remains of the aircraft he had led to Wilhelmshaven on

18th December 1939. While there, he was entertained to lunch at British Aerospace by Mr Jeff Montgomery, whose father, Mr Gordon Montgomery, had prepared the three Vickers Wellesley aeroplanes used by Kellett's team to win the world long distance flight record for Britain in 1938. Before leaving for home that day, Air Commodore Kellett generously offered to donate a commemorative plaque to the museum. To be displayed beside the Wellington bomber, the plaque was to record the names of all those individuals and organisations who had contributed to the aircraft's successful recovery. This was a most appropriate gesture from the man who had led N2980 into battle in 1939 to those who had restored it to the nation in 1985.

In my thirty years as a professional engineer, I can recall no other such large collaborative venture that was conducted so harmoniously. At no time during those two weeks up at Loch Ness was there a single raised voice or cross word exchanged between any of the participants. Fuelled by adrenalin and lubricated by goodwill, it was a unique endeavour where victory was snatched from the jaws of defeat because everyone concerned placed the welfare of an intrinsically worthless old aeroplane above all else. It was a privilege and a pleasure to have worked with such a magnificent bunch of people.

A year and eight months after the Wellington returned to Weybridge, the Royal Navy Fleet Diving Group, assisted by Heriot-Watt University, Ametek Offshore (Scotland) Ltd, UDI Group Ltd and Caley Cruisers Ltd, went back up to Loch Ness on one of their working-up exercises and recovered the front gun turret on 13th May 1987.

Seven months after the front gun turret returned to Weybridge, the Royal Air Force closed the book on the story of the recovery of N2980. A sub-aqua team from RAF Kinloss spent the 1987 Christmas and New Year period diving on the site where the aircraft grounded at Lochend. They recovered the pilot's seat, the co-pilot's control column and rudder pedals, the throttle box, trim controls, flare chute, pitot head, aerial tuning coil and a large assortment of bits and pieces of geodetics.

Today, at Brooklands Museum in Weybridge you can see, perfectly preserved and partially restored, Wellington bomber 'R for Robert', 'One of our Aircraft' that is no longer missing.

Forty-seven years after the starboard engine on 'R for Robert' coughed, spluttered and finally died, a group of volunteer engineers from British Airways at London Airport think that they may know why the engine failed. The Wellington's two Pegasus XVIII engines had twin spark-plugs in each of their nine cylinders. The spark-plugs derived their power from two separate magnetos on each engine. When the British Airways engineers stripped them down for overhaul and testing, both magnetos from the starboard engine were found to have cracked rotors and could not produce the high voltages necessary for the spark-plugs. On the other hand, both magnetos from the port engine, once cleaned and tested, produced sparks. The engine itself, when stripped for overhaul by another group of volunteers at the Rolls Royce Heritage Trust (Bristol Branch), showed no mechanical faults or failures and the carburettor and fuel pump were still full of neat fuel (87 octane) and there was no water present in any of the fuel lines. I don't suppose anyone will ever know for certain why the engine failed, but it is possible that Squadron Leader David Marwood-Elton was forced to ditch on Loch Ness because both magnetos on his starboard engine packed-up.

# 8

## *Personal recollections of the Battle of Heligoland Bight*

## GROUP CAPTAIN P. I. HARRIS DFC.

No. 149 Squadron Mildenhall was in No. 3 Group. This group, equipped with the latest and best armed bomber in the Royal Air Force, was earmarked for day bombing which included the task of attacking the German Navy as and when found at sea.

No. 3 Group had, until immediately before the war, been a night bomber group armed with the Handley Page Harrow. Our training then had been totally different, with no formation flying, so vital to survival in daylight operations. Almost overnight we became a day bomber group, but formation flying was not our forte. This was apparent on long distance flights by the whole group, supposedly in formation, over France shortly before the war, with the idea of building up French morale. Only two squadrons, No. 214 and No. 9, formated well; otherwise it looked more like a race than a formation flight. I was then a Flight Commander in 214 Squadron. Our Commanding Officer was an old friend of mine, under whom I had served in Palestine in the middle thirties. The group did three flights to Marseilles and one to Bordeaux. No. 214 Squadron was on all of them, and in one case we led the whole group, but the other squadrons were scattered all over the sky with little semblance of any formation.

Until the invasion of France in 1940, we in the Royal Air Force suffered from what is known as the Phoney War. This is not fully understood today. Our directive was simple but silly. No civilian might be killed or injured and only naval ships attacked at sea. We were virtually not allowed to drop our bombs on land. Transgression could, and did, involve being taken off flying and put in an Operations Room. This was before Churchill came to power. A friend of mine was doing a sweep in the Heligoland Bight when he was fired at by minesweepers, he did a run up at 10,000 feet and dropped his bombs, fortunately missing his target. A few days later I happened to pass the AOC's office and I asked him what he was doing there; he said, 'I am waiting to get a rocket, actually,' and I said, 'What on earth for?' and he told me the story. He was taken off flying and put in an Operations Room as a punishment for attacking ships that had fired on him: apparently they were requisitioned trawlers and not, *ab initio* as it were, naval ships. This shows the extreme punishment that could be inflicted on people who transgressed.

I was posted to 149 Squadron about one week before the war. I brought with me my own crew and also another crew, Michael Briden as captain and Billy Brown as second pilot. I am bound to say that I was not happy with what I found. Looking back it seems that we were posted there to hot up the squadron's formation flying and prepare it for battle. Some squadrons actually had Commanding Officers of the 1914–18 War vintage, who did no flying whatever. I started the war with one, but fortunately he left shortly before we started our operations in December, when Wing Commander Kellett arrived and transformed the squadron – just in time. None of these non-flying types should have been commanding squadrons; our High Command was at fault.

You cannot lead a squadron if you cannot fly the aeroplane with which it is armed. When this is clearly understood one realises why the other squadrons did not survive, and No. 149 Squadron did, on 18th December 1939.

Initially we were armed with Wellington 1s but they had Vickers turrets which were useless. Sights did not follow the guns and the ammunition belts stuck in the ducts. But soon Frazer-Nash turrets were fitted in the 1As including a Frazer-Nash retractable under-turret, a 'dustbin', which rotated through 360 degrees and when firing aft could fire 2 degrees above the horizontal which was very useful, backing up the rear gunner against stern attacks. All turrets, front, rear and mid-under, had two .303 Brownings firing 1,000 rounds per minute; and the 1,000 round belts, one to each gun, were fed in efficiently. Our gunners were volunteer ground crew and not well trained: we had no Gunnery Leaders then and the only training they had was when they were able to come up with us when not working on the ground. We were particularly lucky in that Archie Frazer-Nash used to drive up fairly frequently in his Bentley and fly with me, testing his own turrets and guns. We also had a partner of his who came up and did much testing with us.

By 3rd December, when Kellett led 24 Wellingtons to Heligoland, we were in fairly good form. We bombed through heavy flak, but sank only one small ship. Our gunners were moderately trained, and with the turrets and guns working well, we were ready for battle. On this raid we saw but few fighters and Kellett led well but a little bit too fast, so I could not keep up with him and when we got back he asked me if he had led all right and I said, 'Go a little slower next time.' This is a particularly important point as, had we not gone on that raid together, and had he not realised the need to fly slower so that I could keep up with him, he might have led too fast on the Wilhelmshaven raid with the result that 149 Squadron and the three aircraft of 9 Squadron would have been annihilated.

On the Heligoland raid of 3rd December, N2980 was flown by Flight Lieutenant Stewart, a Canadian. Although the flak was heavy at Heligoland we all survived and we were not attacked by fighters. I see from my log book that I took over N2980 on 10th December and flew it four times with my crew before 18th December, by which time my gunners were used to the guns, could fire them well and operate the turrets efficiently, thanks to Frazer-Nash, even if we were not particularly crack shots. Now we come to the big day.

On the evening of 17th December my Commanding Officer and I were summoned to group headquarters together with the Commanding Officers of 37 and 9 Squadrons to be briefed for a group operation the next day, a sweep in the Heligoland Bight area searching for the German fleet. Kellett was to lead. As a comparative newcomer he had never had the chance to practise formation flying and bombing with the leaders of 9 or 37 Squadrons, to impose his will on them, or formulate any plan for bombing or fighting either as a group or by squadrons or by flights, or to discuss our tactics in the face of fighter attack. A brilliant pilot, no better leader could have been chosen for this impossible task and our squadron, 149, had the honour of providing nine aircraft and leading the whole group, totalling twenty-four aircraft. Kellett had Lieutenant Commander Rotherham with him, a Fleet Air Arm Officer, to identify enemy ships and aim the bombs provided the targets were not too close to land. In the event there was a battleship there, but moored in the dock. At the briefing I was told that Peter Grant was to fly with me; this was the first time that we had ever flown together and my parting words to him were: 'Stay close to me whatever happens' – and this, fortunately for us all, he did most ably.

Our twenty-four Wellingtons were divided into four flights of six aircraft each, Kellett leading with six of 149, and I in N2980 on his starboard side with three of my own flight and three of 9 Squadron's led by Grant. We were in boxes of six stepped up in order not to mask our guns, not an easy position for Grant. On Kellett's port side were six aircraft of 9 Squadron and 37 Squadron were Arse-End-Charlies, obviously the most vulnerable position, unless they kept very close and flew above Kellett. To have flown underneath and behind him would have masked the fire of his rear gunners and been obviously dangerous. I cannot remember if there was any discussion on this matter but all I know is that 37 Squadron did not stay with us for long. 37 Squadron were flying in pairs, not in 'Vic' formation of three like the rest of us, but in line astern stepped down: it was more manoeuvrable but had obvious disadvantages since the rear guns could shoot down their own people. On the run out I saw 37 Squadron, as it seemed to me, almost on the skyline. They were a long way off, not practising close formation flying on Kellett – essential for survival. Only one aircraft of 37 Squadron returned home, 'Cheese' Lemon, who lowered his flaps by mistake over the target instead of opening his bomb doors and, having leapt suddenly into the air, descended at great speed to sea level and managed to weave his way home in spite of heavy fighter attacks. Had he not made this mistake he would probably have been wiped out with the rest of his squadron. He was lucky to get home, the only survivor of 37 Squadron. I kept very close to Kellett all the way out, and ensured that Grant kept close to me. Kellett flew at exactly the right speed so I had no difficulty in formating with him. The other squadrons seemed to be far away and running their own show in an independent but dangerous sort of way. The further they were away the nearer I kept to my leader.

Kellett led us over the Heligoland Bight but saw nothing and then he steered for Wilhelmshaven. On the run in at 15,000 feet there was heavy flak, accurate for height, but fortunately trailing behind us and as it kept catching up, my rear gunner, Jimmy Mullineaux, kept saying: 'Hurry up Sir, its catching up on us.' Meanwhile, the fighters were collecting above us like flies waiting for us to clear the flak before they attacked. With my eyes glued on Kellett, I saw nothing. He told me on our return that there was a Pocket Battleship in dock but we could not attack it because of explicit instructions to this effect: no risk of bombs on land – The Phoney War!

Once clear of the flak, Kellett and I were on our own with ten aeroplanes.

There should have been twelve but two returned early about an hour out from England. The other two formations of 9 and 37 Squadrons had disappeared. One of Kellett's four aircraft went down in flames early on so the battle was finally joined for some thirty minutes between our nine aircraft and the Germans. We were entirely on our own and N2980 behaved immaculately, as did my crew. I kept as close to Kellett as possible and Grant clung to me like a limpet, flying really well. So our nine aircraft presented a concentrated but unattractive target with nine rear turrets and nine 'dustbins' to contend with. The front turrets had, of course, very little shooting and, I think, fired only once.

The events inside N2980 were exciting. I, of course, saw almost nothing, my eyes being fixed on Kellett, survival depending on maintaining formation. My second pilot, Pilot Officer Sandy Innes, a splendid Scotsman, was at the astrodome to control our gunners. This he did magnificently, like a commentator at a football match, so I knew what was going on. My rear gunner, Aircraftman Jimmy Mullineaux, eventually fired all his ammunition, 1,000 rounds per gun, so Sandy nipped down to him with short, spare belts of 300 rounds each so that Jimmy was able to keep firing one gun while loading the other in between attacks. Sergeant Austin, my navigator, manned the 'dustbin'. A/C Doxsey in the front turret had a dull time, except once.

While I could see nothing, I knew exactly what was happening from Innes's narrative. As far as I remember all our guns worked well, unlike those of some other squadrons which I believe froze at 15,000 feet. Those of N2980 worked perfectly in the Frazer-Nash turrets; we had tested them on the way out and I had done a lot of air firing with Frazer-Nash, to whose turrets we undoubtedly owed our lives.

I did, however, see one fighter, a Messerschmitt 110 which suddenly shot across my bows in a vertical turn doing a complicated and well executed attack on Kellett. It seemed to black out the sky and, considering how close I was to Kellett, his attack was brilliantly timed not to crash into me or any of my other aircraft. I do not know how he did it. Naturally, our front gunners, who had as yet fired no shots in anger, all let fly and he went down pouring out smoke. A/C Doxsey in my front turret had his foot grazed by a bullet. Naturally, all our front gunners claimed a victory and we were convinced of this. We now know from German records that no Me 110 was destroyed, although some were damaged, as ours certainly was. But that pilot certainly deserved to survive.

The crew of N2980 fought superbly. My navigator, Sergeant Austin, manned the mid-under 'dustbin' retractable turret. My rear gunner, Jimmy Mullineaux, got an immediate and well merited DFM for his efforts. I enjoyed writing his citation. Sandy Innes was decorated later but sadly did not survive long. I was fortunate with my crew. Flying with them was a pleasure.

After the battle, Kellett was accused of flying too fast by the survivors of the other squadrons. This is nonsense. He flew perfectly; I stayed with him without difficulty. He did not go too fast for me. The fact is that the others were untrained in formation flying and were not led by their own Commanding Officers, who in turn had not discussed, or practised formation flying with Kellett. It was like trying to form a football team of people who had never met each other before and had never played together as a team, and had different ideas about the rules.

The leader of a flight must know the difficulties facing each individual in his flight. Leading my box of six stepped up I had to understand the feelings and difficulties of the other five pilots. Kellett leading his lot had the task of flying in such a way that I could keep in touch with him. Neither too fast nor too slow. In a turn, it is obvious that the aircraft on the inside of the turn are going slower than those on the outside. If the leader flies too slowly the aircraft on the inside may stall and fall out of the sky. If he turns too fast the aircraft on the outside cannot keep up, while the only aircraft that can follow him without much difficulty are the Arse-End-Charlies, who, of course, are going at the same speed as the leader. A large formation can obviously be turned only very slowly, and the bigger it is the slower must be the turn. Once formation was lost it was not easy to regain it. A single aircraft can do this by opening the throttle and belting ahead to catch up but the leader of a flight cannot easily do this; he has to keep his flight together and fly a bit faster, but not so fast that the formation disintegrates. Knowing this I kept close to Kellett from the moment we took off until we finally broke up after the engagement. Formation flying requires the highest discipline, skill and practice.

We survived simply because Kellett's leading was immaculate, we kept in close formation, our guns worked and two of our formation's three losses were almost certainly due to having no self-sealing tanks.

Our squadrons had their own ideas and whimsies about formation flying. There were basically two schools of thought: close formation relying on concentrated firepower and mutual support, and loose formation relying on manoeuvrability but at the sacrifice of firepower and mutual support. The latter school unfortunately ignored the immensely superior manoeuvrability and speed of the fighter. No. 149 Squadron adhered to the former school, and had a Commanding Officer who was a brilliant leader and knew his job; the other squadrons did not. The result was that our formation was weakened and No. 149 Squadron, with three aircraft of No. 9 Squadron, ably led by Flight Lt Peter Grant, were left alone to fight the ultimate battle. There is no doubt that the other two squadrons left us because they were untrained. One cannot blame them for this because we had been given no previous opportunity to fly together, and Kellett had no chance to discuss the matter with them and impose his will upon them as a leader. Group headquarters laid on no group formation training. However, it laid on active operations in which squadrons which had never before flown together were sent into action. The lessons of the pre-war French flights were ignored – a fatal error.

## FLYING OFFICER H. A. INNES, DFC.

18.12.39 Well, bombing raid no. 2 is completed, though not so successfully as last time. Started off with 24 a/c. led by W/C Kellett. 2 dropped out on way out and remainder came on. We went out toward Denmark and south to E of Heligoland. Ht 15000 – no cloud at all and Germany was stretched out below us for miles and miles. Very fine sight and the estuaries seemed to be half frozen over. We had one fighter attack us on run south, but it was probably there to get our ht* and A/S.† We feinted toward Bremerhaven and Wessermünde and then W to Wilhelmshaven where we got the attack signal. By this time archies had opened up in great strength. At first they were up to 1000′ below us but improved to amazing accuracy later on. Some of them getting our height to within 10–12′ though fortunately to one side. A fine sight watching them explode and enlarge. At first there is a jet black splodge which immediately widens out, then you get the bump if it is close. After that you look back and it is as though you have left a large wood with all the bursts hanging about in the sky like tree tops. Anyhow I dropped my bombs. Don't expect any good for we had no time at all and aimed at a boat in outer harbour. Anyhow when bombs went we cracked off and with a goodly attention of ac ac we made the English coast – but not too easily. All the way from the target we were attacked by fighters. Fleets of them s.s.‡ and twin engine Me 110 attacks continued for 25 minutes during which they came in say 15 times from the rear.
19.12 I am always falling asleep writing this up. Hence rather involved account last night before I packed it up. Anyhow we have got an hour longer lie in bed this morning so I can complete narrative.

Their fighters were damn good. The idea we had that they were windy of us turned out to be all bunk. We had Me 109 and 110 majority of latter. These seem to be bloody good. They were thrown all over the sky and seemed to be doing all of 400 mph. God knows how many of them there were. Anything up to 50–60 and they came in without ceasing – sometimes 2 and 3 at once all from diff directions. I had moved straight to astrodome after bomb release and was controlling the turrets. It worked very well for I could see everything except underneath when I had to leave it to the centre gunner. Several times I directed the rear gun onto a target he had not seen – so I think it has justified itself. Anyhow it was not my idea of a picnic, for it was a horrible sight seeing these damned Me's coming straight for you and all you could do was to talk. Actually I had a camera and took numerous photos which relieved me of some of the jitters by having something active to do. I don't know how many times they came in – probably about 30–40. Our formation of 3 kept up magnificently and also the 3 behind and above were pretty good and by that and that alone we made good. Our fire power was grand and I think we

* height † air speed ‡ single seater
Note: 1000′ indicates one thousand feet.

got quite 5 Me's between us. Several times I could see the tracer meeting the a/c and then it would give a nasty jerk and it would crack off downwards. Never saw them right down for I always had to turn to more attacks, but rear gunner saw several into the drink. They were using canon and also machine guns and the tracer was whipping around us. Halfway through front gunner called out he was hurt so wireless operator went forward to take his place. We expected to have to pull out a corpse but a rather white faced Doxsey came out under his own steam. It appeared the bullet had pierced his boot and given him a hell of a bruise in the instep before going out. Anyhow that left me to have to carry reserve ammunition. Which I did several times. Awful job for it kept on falling out of the boxes and trailing behind and getting caught up in the Geodetics and then quick back to fire control again. We were at 14,000′ and the temp was −15 but by God I was running fit to beat records. Sweat pouring off – lack of oxygen and cold completely forgotten.

Meanwhile as it went on I saw fewer and fewer of our a/c following us. Two of ours went down with port wings blazing and like bloody fools no-one seemed to jump and then it was too late for they blew up. Suppose they thought they could get down to land. So again it is the idiocy of some bloody fool in not armouring both wings that has cost us several a/c and many lives. Another a/c of ours I saw hit almost at the end of engagement. The starboard wing just blew off, the petrol appeared to pour out and ignite in one solid mass of flame about 100′ thick and the fuselage and remaining wing went down in a sickening spin. I don't think anyone could have got out for they must have been thrown against the side by the spin and held there. It was a terrible sight and yet awe inspiring but I don't want to see it again.

Anyhow eventually the fighters broke off some 70–80 miles from the coast and we relaxed, every one pouring with sweat and throats so dry we could only croak. Paul Harris handed round the brandy* and we had one damn good swig and it put new life into us. My God it was necessary. Our formation of 6 were all there also the CO and his three and there were one or two more further back. As it turned out we must have had 7 shot down and probably two more came down in the drink on the way home. Feltwell lost 5 out of 6. Poor 37. I wonder who they were. So their pet formation didn't work so well after all. We lost Jimmy Spears and Norman Lines in one a/c over Germany and then on way home we heard Michael Briden calling CO to say he was losing petrol and could he take the shortest way home. Sure enough I could see the plume of gas coming out of his port wing. All went well till we were ½ hour off England when I saw his engines coughing and he fell away in a glide toward the sea. I was flying then and I told the S/L and he told me to follow him down. I did this though it was a bit tricky for we were 10,000′ and Mike went down behind us. Anyhow as luck would have it I just caught sight of him before he went thro′ the clouds which were broken. I circled round again and then from about 1,000′ saw him touch down. Must

* It was actually rum.

have been a good landing or alighting, for although it was down wind and the splash went right over the a/c it came to rest on an even keel having slewed round thro' 90°. Floating nicely. I came down to 300–400' and came past several times. Next time round, the dinghy was open and floating aft of the engine. Next time round it was by the nose of a/c which was settling down. I could see them by the dinghy. Next time round the a/c had almost gone and the boys – 3 of them it seemed – were in the water with the dinghy on end and it was then I had a horrible fear that it might be holed and was sinking also. Maybe though it was only because they are devils to get into. Anyhow it was then we thought of releasing our own dinghy for them. All this time we had been sending out SOS and trying to get radio fix. Anyhow I came back once more and only by a silvery patch on water was I able to see them. I gave the signal and Sgt Austin pulled the dinghy release, about 50× before them. But it was a tough break on us for it came back and burst on our tail plane and remained there, setting up the most awful juddering in the controls. There was nothing more we could do for we hadn't much petrol ourselves and in addition the elevator was holed and liable to break at any moment.

So we turned straight for home on one engine to lower the drag on the starboard side. We were only making 120 and got back in ½ hour, landing at Coltishall, a new aerodrome under construction. Here I commandeered a push bike and beat it for a phone to inform operations. Had awful trouble getting on for some fool of a girl in the exchange was behaving with bureaucratic efficiency in spite of it being a priority call. Ticked me off for my language and said she would report me just because I said 'for Christ's sake get a bloody move on'. I also said I would run her out of her job. Well after that we all got a lift from a Mr Bowles in a v. nice Rover all the way home some 50 miles, which was a damned good show. After seeing the operations and intelligence we were actually able to relax this was about 6.15 p.m. and I can't remember anything being so good as my first pint of beer that night and did I need it.

Went along to the Bird in Hand afterwards to talk it over with Paul and the boys and the G/Capt stood me supper there which was also much needed. Finally bed at 11 p.m. and I am glad to say deep sleep, possibly due to the beer. Never in my life have I ever had such a thrilling time – I wouldn't have missed it for anything but by God I don't want to go through it again. I have often heard people argue about their biggest thrill – fast run downhill on skis, 10 mile point hunting, pig sticking, but I know now quite well that I have had the biggest of the lot. And I am glad I had such a marvellous view of it all.

19.12.39 *Night* Well today has been the anti-climax. Spent the morning wandering around, everyone feeling rather flat, doubtless because I suppose everyone was celebrating their safe return. I went along to Intelligence Office to see my films and what did I find? Of my own camera which I had used

Notes: 50× indicates fifty yards. 90° indicates ninety degrees.

taking I thought some 10–12 snaps of Me's attacking us and flying near us, all were duds. Several into the sun, several of clear sky and others where I had simply not cocked the camera and no exposure was made. There was however one poor shot of the dinghy on the tail. After that I was busy writing out reports reports reports pages of them – on Fighter tactics, best formation, and finally on Michael and his landing. He was not picked up, though messages had come in saying he had been, but no-one could trace these, and he had not turned up. Boats and planes had been searching all day. Our aircraft R was brought over and we had a look at it there were about 6 bullets through it, and one burst of AA. One bullet went through the port wing but just missed the tank – lucky. Doxsey's bullet was found, still in the front turret.

20.12.39 Still writing reports – the hangover from a raid is almost as bad as the real thing. Also today the C. in C. turned up to hear all about it. I was hauled up to the C.O.'s office to say what I had seen, trying affair with 1 Air Chief Marshal, one Air Vice M, 1 G/Capt, 1 W/Cdr and 1 S/Ldr – finally yours truly (1 P/O). I had a bad cold and had to keep on blowing my nose to stop sniffing. C. in C. was very pleasant. I was jawing for about 20 mins then Mullineaux was called in and poor lad it was a bit scaring for an A/C2. He talked very well for about 5 mins and then suddenly said 'Please Sir, may I faint' – and fell slick over as cold as mutton. I caught him as he fell. Came round quick and continued sitting while he finished his story. After that the C. in C. had a few words to say to the crews. It appears that it is the biggest aerial battle that has ever taken place, over 100 aircraft being engaged and lasting for 40 mins. Our total casualties was 12 a/c and 11 crews. One crew of 9 Sq were picked up in their dinghy out of the drink. Their losses were probably about 20. Quite likely many more for we don't know how many were shot by our boys who never came back.

In the evening I went over to Methwold and Paul and Capt. Frazer-Nash came too. It was the Christmas party for B flight and all the old faces were there and they gave us a cheer when we came into the pub which felt grand but we just blamed each other for having brought us out of the fight and then went into the more serious duty of drinking. I was then taken back to Methwold and we stayed there till 1.30 a.m. and so to bed. I left my car there and came back in Frazer-Nash's Rolls Royce – more comfortable.

## ACCOUNT BY FLIGHT LIEUTENANT J. J. MULLINEAUX OF RAID ON 18TH DECEMBER 1939.

I had a false sense of security when Squadron Leader P. I. Harris told me we were going to attack shipping in Wilhelmshaven, as on our previous raid we were met by three Me 109s who soon broke off their attack when we returned fire. This instilled untold courage and made me look forward to our next engagement.

Anyhow on the morning of 18th December 1939 we were briefed and our target was to be a daylight attack right into the heart of the German naval defences. The strength of the attack was the amazing number of twenty-four Wellington bombers Mark 1A. This formation was to be made up from the whole of No. 3 Group in which Command I was serving. Our crew consisted of Squadron Leader P. I. Harris, pilot, Pilot Officer Innes, second pilot, Sergeant F. Austin, navigator, A.C.2 Watson, wireless operator, A.C.2 Doxsey, front gunner and myself rear gunner.

Bombs were loaded on the aircraft and guns and ammunition were checked, wireless and navigation tested, but during this time I am sure we were all wondering whether we should come back or not. I remember I did and was very nervous indeed.

We took off from Mildenhall and after about half an hour we joined up with other crews from the Group. The leader of the attack was Wing Commander Kellett and my captain was the leader of a formation of six aircraft.

The weather was ideal, visibility about ten miles, no clouds. We pressed on until we passed over Heligoland when we were attacked by three Me 109s but with the concentration of fire they too immediately broke off the attack and we pressed on knowing full well that the alarm had been given and that a warm reception would be given to us when we approached our target.

About five minutes' flying time from the harbour we encountered heavy, accurate flak which soon forced the formation to open up. In we went straight and level for about ten minutes, the flak getting heavier and more accurate. I could feel the bursts and very soon the whole of the sky seemed full of black puffs. I was sure one would find its mark and blow us clean out of the air.

Luck was with us, we did not get hit and very soon we altered course and headed out to sea on a reciprocal course. This was our bombing run. It was during the run that I first saw little black specks on the horizon and within seconds, as it were, I recognized them as Me 109s and Me 110s. Our bombing run completed, the fighters came in to attack and very soon the whole sky seemed full of them. I estimated their strength to be about 100. I called frantically 'Fighters'. Immediately Austin took up position in the mid under turret and Pilot Officer Innes went to the astrodome. We had not long to wait before the first fighter came in to attack our aircraft. It was an Me 110. Innes was the first to see it. In he came and I could see his machine guns blazing away. I opened fire at 300× and continued to fire until he broke away at 20×. No sooner had he broken than another attack took place and this continued throughout the engagement. During the short spells I looked around the sky and could see our bombers going down in flames. This had a great effect on me as I had been pumping bullets into the attacking aircraft and did not seem to get any results. Another fighter came up and no sooner had it attacked and I opened up than it seemed to blow up. My bullets had found their mark. The captain shouted, 'Good show, Mullineaux.' That was all I needed. I got stuck in with added zest and it was not long before the second went down. He came dead astern. I opened up at 400×. The mid under gunner was also firing at him and between us we blew the aircraft out of the air. Other attacks came again and again. I could hear the front gunner firing over the inter-com and he too shot one down. But after a while my ammunition ran out. I called frantically to the captain for more. He sent the second pilot down but in his excitement he opened the door of my turret and simply threw it at me. The result was that I had no assistance to load both guns. I did however manage to get one gun going after a while and throughout the rest of the engagement I kept it going and with the aid of the mid under gunner kept most of the fighters from firing accurately at us, from astern.

During the later part of the engagement I heard a blood-curdling scream from the front gunner. 'He has been shot,' I immediately thought. Then from the captain came, 'Wireless operator, drag the body out of the front turret and take over.' But after the engagement was over I looked back from my turret and saw the front gunner calmly sitting on the bed. A bullet had torn the sole of his boot from the upper.

Another amusing incident took place. It was when Innes had dumped the ammunition in my turret. I called to the captain for help but he thought I had stopped a bullet and immediately sent Innes back again with a bottle of his closely guarded rum. Innes opened the turret doors and asked if I was OK. I said I just wanted help with the ammunition but he did not seem to understand; all he did was to pass the bottle of rum into my hand and close the doors again. Needless to say my captain never saw his rum again.

After what seemed hours the fighters broke off their attack but I regret to say we had many bombers missing and our only consolation was knowing we had destroyed an equal number of enemy fighters.

## FLIGHT LIEUTENANT F. C. PETTS, DFC AND BAR
## OPERATION ON 18TH DECEMBER 1939.

On a number of previous occasions reconnaissance Blenheims had found German warships off the German coast in the Heligoland area and had been followed by a bomber striking force. In the short days of mid-December it was decided to dispense with the preliminary reconnaissance and to despatch a bomber force in the morning to search for and attack German warships. It was established subsequently that security about the proposed operation on 18th December was extremely poor; certainly on the evening of the 17th it was widely known in Bury St. Edmunds that 9 Squadron crews had been recalled because of an operation planned for early next day.

On reporting to the Flights at 0730 on 18th December we learned that 9 Squadron was to supply nine aircraft for a force of 24, with nine from 149 Squadron at Mildenhall and six from 37 Squadron at Feltwell. There were to be four groups of six aircraft: three of 149 and three of 9 in front, six of 149 to starboard, six of 9 to port and six of 37 in the rear. Targets were to be any German warships found in the area of Heligoland or the Schillig Roads.

To the best of my recollection bomb loads were four 500 lb GP's* per aircraft. We were airborne from Honington about 0900; by 1000 we were formed up with the other squadrons and were leaving the Norfolk coast. I was outside left of the whole formation, flying No. 3 in a Vic of three. Although the operation was planned for 24 aircraft, I believe that only 22 crossed the North Sea; I cannot now remember what happened to the other two but understand that they turned back.

We climbed on course to 15,000′. Halfway across the North Sea we left all cloud cover behind; soon all aircraft manned and lowered the dustbin turrets. We continued without substantial change of course until we were within sight of low-lying land which must have been Sylt.

I was not sure how large a navigational error was involved but I was surprised that we were so far north. The formation turned south, still at 15,000′ in a clear sky. The coast was still in sight but there was no sign of enemy opposition until my rear gunner called, 'There's a fighter attacking behind – they've got him!' Then to starboard I saw an Me 109, with smoke pouring from it, change from level flight to a near vertical dive so abruptly that the pilot could hardly have been alive and conscious after the change of direction. I remember that at this stage I thought, rather prematurely, that encounters with German fighters were 'easy'.

We left Heligoland to port and shortly afterwards turned left towards the Schillig Roads where we had been told at briefing there was likely to be warship targets. We saw none but continued on a south-easterly course and I remember wondering how far up the river we were going in search of battleships and cruisers. I have vague recollections of ineffectual ack-ack fire at this stage and earlier as we passed Heligoland.

Next came a wide turn to starboard to take the formation over Wilhelmshaven and back seawards. In my position at outside left of the whole formation I found it increasingly difficult to maintain my position. Repeated calls to my Section Leader to ask him to slow down brought no reply and in spite of opening up to a full boost and increasing propeller revs to maximum I still could not keep up.

Over Wilhelmshaven we flew into intense ack-ack fire and trying to work out whether evasive manoeuvres were any use against the black puffs bursting all round I was for a while less pre-occupied with the problem of staying in formation. The black puffs stopped quite suddenly and there in front were the fighters (thinking things over next day I decided that there must have been about 40 of them), and still in spite of full throttle and full revs I was lagging behind. I dumped my bombs, and hoped to gain a little speed. About this time Balch on the front guns got his first fighter. An Me 109 away to port was turning in a wide sweep, possibly to attack the sections

* General Purpose bombs.

in front. I saw the tracer in Balch's first burst hit in the cockpit area and the canopy or part of it fly off; the second burst also hit and the 109 immediately went into a catastrophic dive with white smoke pouring from it.

About this time I decided that, in spite of my full throttle and full revs, I should never keep up. Ginger Heathcote pointed out the 37 Squadron six, forming the rear of the box of 24, and suggested that I dropped back to them. It was as well that I did not. 37 Squadron were flying in their own formation of three pairs stepped down in line astern. As the attacks developed, one of the six – I am not sure which but P/O Kydd was the rear gunner – went to dump his bombs. To open the bomb doors he first selected master hydraulic cock 'on', not realising that he had flaps selected down. The result was sudden lowering of full flap leading to a sudden gain of considerable extra height. Enemy fighters left this aircraft alone but shot down the other five of 37 Squadron. My account of this incident is, of course, second-hand but I heard it first a day or two after the event and later from Kydd when we were both instructing at 11 OTU.

Having decided that I could not catch up with my Section Leader I turned about 40° to starboard, put my nose hard down and with the dustbin turret still in the lowered position screamed down to sea level. All the way down from 15,000' and then for some time just above the water I kept full throttle and full revs except when I reduced power for short periods in an evasive manoeuvre as fighters lined up to attack.

During the dive I was too pre-occupied with what was going on outside to pay much attention to my instruments; I did however notice my ASI* reaching the 1 o'clock position, second time round. It was not until we returned to the aircraft next morning that I looked to see what that meant in terms of indicated air-speed – it was 300 mph! This was about twice normal cruising IAS† and I could not help wondering how much faster I could have gone before something broke.

I cannot remember just how many fighter attacks there were: the first came before I left cruising altitude, there were more on the way down with Me 110s passing us as they broke away, and finally we were chased along the water by three 110s. Robertson on the rear guns kept me informed as each attack developed and there were commentaries from the other two gunners.

We met each stern attack with a drill that we had agreed as a result of experience gained in fighter co-operation exercises. The usual sequence ran: 'There's one coming in, he's coming in. Get ready, get ready. Back, back.' Throttles slammed shut and pitch levers to full coarse. Bursts from our guns and enemy tracer past the windows. 'O.K., he's gone.' Open up again to full throttle and full revs.

Mostly the tracer was on the starboard side and it was not until some weeks later when we started taking aircraft back to Brooklands to have armour plate

* Air Speed Indicator.
† Indicated Air Speed.

fitted behind the port wing tanks that I realised that previously we had enjoyed this protection only on the starboard side.

Altogether that day my gunners claimed three 110s and two 109s, but I do not know that they were officially credited with any. I saw Balch's first 109 before we left formation and a 110 which also was his, and I have a clear recollection of Robertson's jubilant shout as he got the last 110. For the other two I could not offer much in confirmation even later the same day and there may have been some duplication of claims from other crews over hits before we started the descent. If I see Bob Kemp again I must ask him about this; I met him about two years ago after an interval of 20 years but there were other things to talk about.

Balch's 110 deserves mention. The attack developed in the same way as others but immediately the tracer ceased there was a shout from Robertson, the 110 came past close to our starboard wing; next there was a burst from my front guns and the 110 was gone. This was a fine example of the effectiveness of sudden throttling back at the right moment in causing a fighter to close more quickly than he intended to. Afterwards Robertson said that he had fired without apparent effect on this 110 as it closed, and then as it overshot and passed beyond his reach the enemy rear gunner put his fingers to his nose at Robertson before opening fire. At that moment Robertson saw Balch's tracer, and that was that.

My recollection of what happened to the first of the three 110s which followed us down is now a little vague but I believe that it was hit by both Robertson and Kemp. I do remember quite clearly the end of the attacks: the drill had proceeded as before but Robertson's, 'Get ready, get ready; Back, Back,' was followed by a jubilant, 'I've got him, I've got him, he's gone in!' The 110 had of course been obliged to get down to our level just above the water for his stern attack and there was no height in which to recover any loss of control. Robertson's next comment was, 'The other one's gone home, he's had enough!'

There had already been calls from Kemp and Balch that they had been hit and Heathcote had gone back to Kemp. Whilst I started checking at my end he helped Kemp (who was losing a lot of blood from a bad thigh wound) out of the dustbin and onto the rest bunk. Kemp in full kit was a tight fit in the dustbin and this move must have called for quite an effort from both. Heathcote next let Balch out of the front turret and went aft again. Balch had been hit in the sole of one foot but he was in urgent need of attention.

Robertson reported that he had emptied his guns into the last 110 and Kemp had called that the centre guns were out of action. Heathcote reported that there appeared to be no major damage to the aircraft, although it was a bit draughty as there were plenty of holes.

For my part I eased back to normal cruising throttle and propeller settings and checking round was shaken to find the starboard oil pressure gauge reading zero. The propellers on Wellington IAs did not feather so I had to be content with pulling the starboard engine right back as with that setting it would give less drag than if switched off, and if it did not seize it might be of some use if I wanted it. I opened up the port engine to 'climb power' and found that I was able to climb gently to 1,000′ or so. During this time I had turned onto a course of 270. When Heathcote came forward again he agreed that 270 was as good as any because we did not know where we were and steering due west we ought to hit England somewhere.

Towards the western side of the North Sea we encountered some broken cloud which on first sighting raised false hopes that we were reaching land. We were finally sure that we were seeing land when we made out the shape of a Butlin's holiday camp ahead and knew that we were approaching Clacton or Skegness. I had seen Skegness some months previously and when we reached the coast I was able to confirm that this was it.

I turned south-west to skirt the Wash as there was no point in crossing additional water on one engine. I first intended to carry on to Honington but in view of Kemp's condition and deteriorating weather ahead I decided instead to land at Sutton Bridge. Preliminary gentle checks of undercarriage and flaps, a slow approach and smooth landing and we stopped after a very short landing run – our damage included a burst starboard tyre. It was just 4 o'clock; we had been airborne for seven hours.

First concern was for an ambulance for our two wounded, next a call to Honington – but no transport was available until morning – a preliminary debriefing and then something to eat. Next morning we went back to the aircraft to survey the damage and to collect various loose articles that we had left inside. The damage was mostly down the starboard side of the fuselage and on the starboard wing – the lost oil pressure had resulted from a holed oil tank. As a souvenir I took only a piece of wing fabric complete with cannon shell hole. Inside the aircraft we found that spare Irvin suits left on the rest bunk and the rear gunner's mascot had been stolen. This, I reflected, was how we were received on a Fighter Command station.

When next morning in the Sergeant's Mess at Honington I found that during the time we were thought to be missing I had lost the clean laundry which I had put to one side the morning of the 18th, I decided that no especial stigma attached to Fighter Command.

The operation on 18th December carrying, in search of warships, bombs quite unsuitable for such targets, cost 12 Wellingtons, 11 complete crews and several wounded. Among the 9 Squadron casualties was my Flight Commander and Section Leader, S/Ldr Guthrie. Among the surviving crews were Sergeant Purdy and his Section Leader F/O Grant, and Sergeant Ramshaw, who had ditched beside a fishing vessel off Hull.

## OBERFELDWEBEL O. K. DOMBROWSKI, IRON CROSS 1ST & 2ND CLASS

## THE 18TH DECEMBER 1939 – THE GREAT AERIAL BATTLE OVER THE GERMAN BIGHT.

It was a 'ripping' day – to use airforce slang. A superb day – blue sky, not a cloud to be seen. I can remember it just as if it was a few months ago, rather than 23 years.

There was something in the air that day. We were expecting the British to turn up – they had already penetrated airspace over Heligoland on 14th December and had lost 6 aircraft in the process.

Our briefing was to fly a pair of Me 110s on patrol along the East Friesian islands. We were at about 1,000m above sea level, engines throttled back, and if we hadn't been at war, one could have called it a superb flight.

Then – a radio message – enemy aircraft approaching the German Bight at 4,000m.

So much for the superb flight. . . . My leader, Lieutenant Uellenbeck, banks towards the German Bight. Let's hope we don't get there too late to engage them in combat – we're raring to go. . . .

Soon we see small dots on the horizon in front of us – flak. We're going to make it!

Suddenly – what was that? Shadows – aircraft silhouettes below us – we bank steeply and immediately recognise a flight of Vickers Wellingtons with their typical shark-fin tail. They are flying extremely low. The right-hand Wellington has lost formation and fallen behind. We'll go for this straggler. All systems go? Yes. The lights for the machine-gun and cannons are red. The magazines are in place. Lieutenant Uellenbeck nods briefly.

From the right we build up a text-book attack. 400m . . . 300m . . . 200m . . . a hail of machine-gun bullets hits the target . . . our cannons bark. As our aircraft goes into a steep climb we see a ball of fire and the bomber hits the sea. Hurrah! (at that point) – a hit! Everything has gone perfectly.

The other two Wellingtons take a course for home, flying low in close formation. Uellenbeck tries the same attack again – it worked so well first time round.

400m . . . 300m . . . the Wellington turns towards us. Our bullets miss. Another try. The two enemy aircraft have separated and their defensive fire is not so concentrated. Nevertheless, three further attacks are unsuccessful – taking quite a toll on our nerves! The pilot must be an old hand at this game. Every time we open fire he turns towards us and our shots pass over him.

Fourth attack. A brief exchange over the intercom: 'Dombrowski, shall we attack from behind?' I have no time to think or speak – our Me 110 is already on the attack!

600m . . . 500m . . . 400m . . . 300m . . . then a hammering noise followed by a hiss – we've been hit! I feel a blow to my left arm. Uellenbeck banks steeply up to a safe height. But at the same moment we can see that our attack has been successful. The Wellington catches fire and crashes into the sea. We can see the splash and a burning oil slick.

The cabin is full of smoke. A smell of cordite fills the air. I can see splashes of blood. 'Uellenbeck (no time for titles) – you're hit – up on your left shoulder – clean through'.

Uellenbeck: 'So I am!'

Then: 'Dombrowski, I've lost our bearings. Get a QDM'.*

'How are you, Lieutenant?'

'Never mind that – get a QDM!'

Ouch! My arm has gone heavy; my left hand suddenly begins to burn – blood – I'm hit too!

QDM! I slide from the receiver to the transmitter.

Pan from M8 EK QDM.

The beacon replies QDM 75.

It works smoothly – all credit to the beacon operators.

'How are you, Lieutenant?'

'OK. Have we the QDM. And why are you groaning?'

'QDM in operation. I have a wound in my left forearm.'

'Serious?'

'I'm losing a lot of blood.'

Then, on the horizon we see Me 109s and 110s. We've reached Jever. We breathe a sigh of relief. The aircraft rolls to a stop. Back to earth. Our squadron symbol, a ladybird with 7 spots, has brought us luck yet again. 'Returned from engagement with enemy. 2 shot down, crew wounded.' In the military hospital in Jever they discovered that the pilot and radio operator had been hit by one and the same shell – a phosphorus exploding shell. It had become bent and had therefore not exploded. We carefully split it in two and it served for a long time as a talisman for us. But we never again attacked another aircraft from behind.

*Notes on documentation:*

The results of this, the first major air battle, are still a matter of controversy. British claims are that only 24 Wellingtons were involved, of which 12 failed to return and three were severely damaged. It was thought that 12 German fighters were shot down.

The OKM report speaks of 52 bombers of which 36 were shot down. Two German aircraft were shot down. It would seem clear that this is a considerable overestimation, probably because of duplicated claims. What is clear is that the I/ZG 76 reported 15 aircraft shot down, of which 13 were confirmed while one aircraft shot down by each of Capt. Falk and Lieutenant Gollob were returned.

Aircraft shot down were credited as follows:

Falk 1, Fresia 2, Lent 2, Gröning 1, Jäger 1, Fleischmann 1, Gresens 1, Uellenbeck 3, Graeff 1, Kalinowski 1.

* A radio signal back to base requesting the compass heading to steer for home.

Other units serving in Squadron 1 filed reports of aircraft shot down by Schumacher, Heilmayr, Steinhoff, Holck, Jung, Schmidt and Peters. We would be interested to hear other details of this sortie from our readers. It is of interest that this was the first time that the Germans were making successful use of radar equipment.

The losses were particularly serious for the RAF inasmuch as this had not been a bombing operation but merely a navigation exercise and the aircraft were flying with double crews. Significant for the further development of the war in the air was the fact that from this point onwards daylight raids were given up as being too risky.

# *Appendix A*

## MEMORIES OF PEACE

by C. G. Grey

A German Communique was recently quoted in a London newspaper as stating that Squadron Leader Falk, a member of the Schumacher formation, had, with his command, particularly distinguished himself in recent fighting over Heligoland. The title of Squadron Leader is merely one of our usual newspaper inaccuracies. He is probably a Captain in rank and commands a Jagdstaffel of a Gruppe commanded by Oberst-Leutnant Schumacher in a Geschwader unnamed.

The German *Kette* corresponds to our Flight: a *Staffel* is a Squadron: a *Gruppe* would be a Wing if we had such a thing as a definite formation: and a *Geschwader* would correspond to our Group, but it is a single permanent entity like a Regiment in our Army, and its name is borne by all its *Gruppen* and *Staffeln*. The *Richthofen Geschwader*, purely a fighter organisation, was the first thing of the kind in the German Luftwaffe. Today, I believe, a *Geschwader* may include bomber and fighter gruppen.

Those who were at the opening of the York Aerodrome and the festivities associated therewith will no doubt have recognised Captain Falk as the right-hand figure in the photograph on page 246, of a cheerful group of German pilots with Lieut. Col. Schumacher and Dr Dietrich.

I met him first when he was Ober-Leutnant in a Staffel of the Richthofen Geschwader at Damm, near Jüterbog, where there is a monument to record that the great Immelmann learned to fly there. Incidentally, an Ober-Leutnant is a full Lieutenant. An Oberst-Leutnant is a Lieut. Col. English people are liable to mix them just as they mix our Adjutant, which is an appointment and not a rank, with the French Adjutant, who is a Non-Commissioned Officer, corresponding to our Warrant Officer, such as a Sgt Major.

Afterwards various of our English sport flyers and officers of the RAF met Falk at Frankfort meetings and at York, to which meeting he flew with about half a dozen young German pilots in sporting aeroplanes. He was particularly well liked.

His name fits him well for he looks like a falcon. He is not big enough to be an eagle. But he has the aquiline features which artists and novelists love to ascribe to heroic bird-men.

He speaks excellent English and is a charming companion. He reminds me much of our great air fighter of the last war, Jimmy McCudden, VC, DSO, MC, etc. He has the same boyish manner, the same straightforward look, and, I am sure, the same dispassionate attitude towards killing his official enemies, who might be his personal friends.

McCudden always described himself as an hired assassin, and never had any animosity against anybody. That sort is always the most dangerous fighter, for the coolness of his head is never disturbed by the heat of his emotions.

The day on which the great von Richthofen was killed McCudden came into my office really moved and said mournfully – 'And I did so want to talk it all over with him after the war.' I can only hope that Falk's English friends will be more fortunate.

McCudden was killed three days after he had finished writing that magnificent book, *Five Years in the R.F.C.*, which was republished not long ago under the misleading title, *Flying Fury*. Shortly after his death one of his best friends remarked – 'What a great argument McCudden and von Richthofen must be having.' – C.G.G.

---

The comparison in the last few paragraphs between Wolfgang Falck and Jimmy McCudden is strangely prophetic. The author had the great privilege of arranging a meeting between Oberst Falck a.D. and Group Captain Harris DFC, at the Royal Air Force Club in Piccadilly on the evening of Thursday 29th March 1984.

As Jimmy McCudden said: 'I did so want to talk it all over with him after the war', to which C. G. Grey added in his article: 'I can only hope that Falk's English friends will be more fortunate.' Well, this time they were more fortunate because both combatants survived to 'talk it all over'.

On being introduced that evening to Oberst Falck, Paul Harris smiled as they shook hands and said, with a twinkle in his eye, 'Well old chap, all I can say is you must have been one bloody awful shot, for which I am truly grateful.' Over dinner, the talk was all of Wellingtons and Messerschmitts. Forty-four years rolled away to reveal two real old professionals. There was no rancour, no animosity, but rather an instant rapport between two minds united in their common love of flying. As the evening wore on I would not have been at all surprised to have seen two shadowy figures in World War I uniforms, McCudden and von Richthofen, standing behind Paul Harris's and Wolfgang Falck's chairs listening intently as the Battle of Heligoland Bight was fought all over again.

The two veteran airmen parted that evening with the promise to meet again at the forthcoming Farnborough Air Show, and Falck handed me an envelope containing a description of his 'Lady Bug' Squadron which he commanded on 18th December 1939.

---

*The 'Marienkäfer' (Lady-Bug) Squadron by Wolfgang Falck:*
In the summer of 1939, Wing I of Destroyer Wing 76 was equipped with the Me-110. Before that date, we had been flying the Me-109. I was squadron leader of the 2nd Squadron at that time.

With the acquisition of the Me-110 a new era dawned for us, at least as far as flying was concerned: a transition from the single-engined to the twin-engined aircraft, from the single-seater to a plane that could carry a second man on board – a radio operator and gunner at the same time! In addition a reorganisation of our wing, even if in practice this was actually little more than a change of name, and the new Me 110 *Destroyer*, formerly called *Heavy Hunter*, were further elements contributing to the initiation of a new chapter in the history of military aviation. Subsequently, and in order to make our wing appear as a homogeneous unit, a new squadron insignia had to be created.

Now, to design a squadron insignia has always been somewhat problematic. In the first place, the design has to be timeless and last for a long while. In the second place, it must be a true reflection of the spirit and the tasks of the unit and, in accordance with the circumstances prevailing at that particular moment, it had to reflect and symbolise the spirit of the times.

There were several things that had to be taken into account when designing our insignia, concerning the colours. As my convictions tended to be conservative, I preferred the colours of the old German 'Reich', which were black-white-red. Furthermore, as seven had always been my lucky number, I also wanted to have it included in some way. Then we needed a symbol of good fortune, so I selected the 'Marienkäfer' or lady-bug, well known for this, and very much favoured by me. The outcome of this combination finally resulted in a red lady-bug with seven black spots on a white field in the shape of an escutcheon; our squadron insignia had been created.

This insignia was immediately adopted with great enthusiasm by all members of the squadron; the aircraft mechanics worked overtime, day and night, to affix it to all our aeroplanes as quickly as possible.

One day we had firing practice at ground targets. There were only a few planes operational and we had just received a new aircraft. Due to the last minute rush, the squadron insignia had not been affixed to it yet. However, being so short of planes, it also had to participate in the target practice even if the 'Marienkäfer' was missing. As fate would have it, it was precisely that plane that flew too low when trying to fire at the targets. It hit the ground, and the pilot was killed. From that day on, no pilot or radio operator would ever even touch an aircraft that did not bear our insignia!

The war started on 1st September 1939, and we were based in Silesia from where we directed our first attacks against Poland. Without any casualties on our side, the 'Marienkäfer' squadron was highly successful, and press and radio mentioned it for the first time. In my capacity as squadron leader, I had a small square frame painted with a red lady-bug and its black spots on a white background. Whenever I landed, I used to open the cockpit window as soon as the aircraft touched down and fixed this frame to it in a special holder. In addition, we recorded every plane the squadron had shot down by marking a black stroke on the white field of the escutcheon.

After spending some time on the so-called 'West Wall' over the winter, our squadron was transferred to Jever on 17th December 1939. It was the first time we had flown over the sea in the West and we were issued with life jackets, rubber dinghies and emergency radio sets, all in the middle of that exceptionally cold winter.

On the next day, 18th December 1939, we began our first preparatory flight, in groups of four each, to get acquainted with the sea, the coast, and the islands. I was flying in a North-Westerly direction from the island of Borkum in the North Sea, when we suddenly heard, via the radio, that the British were heading for Wilhelmshaven and that we should fly to the Wilhelmshaven Heligoland area immediately. We could see the anti-aircraft bursts from far away, and shortly afterwards also the British bomber formation. They were Wellingtons, and our Me-109 hunters were circling around them. We were just approaching the British, when they deviated onto a North-Westerly heading. We attacked at once and managed to shoot down a few planes in spite of the heavy fire from the British tail guns. My plane had been hit several times, the starboard engine had stopped functioning, fuel was running out of numerous holes on the surface, and the ammunition for the four machine guns contained in the fuselage, was in flames. To make things worse, I had to open the cabin window because of the dense smoke inside the cockpit. Shortly afterwards, the port engine packed up as well. Nevertheless, thanks to our altitude, the light weight resulting from the loss of fuel, the expended and burned-out ammunition, as well as a favourable wind, I was finally able to land smoothly with the accuracy of a glider, onto the aerodrome on the island of Wangerooge.

As it turned out after the battle, the Me-109 squadron led by First Lieutenant 'Mäcki' Steinhoff, who was to become German Air Force Inspector later on, had been the most successful Me-109 squadron, and my own, the best among the Me 110s. The RAF had suffered terrible losses, although they were not quite as enormous as had been initially assumed by the Germans, although these claims had been made in good faith.

Now that the combat was over, on 19th December, the group commodores LTC Schumacher, First Lt Steinhoff and I, as well as two more pilots, were summoned to Berlin to report on those events to the national and international press. Through the neutral countries, our reporting also reached England. This explains why, in my personal opinion, I was honoured with the greatest distinction that could ever have been attained during the war: Mr Grey, editor of the magazine, *The Aeroplane,* whom I had already met before the war, published an article about me! The fact that he should have described an 'enemy', who had victoriously fought against the air force of his own country, with so much fairness and objectivity has always flattered me much more than any piece of coloured ribbon or bit of engraved tin on my uniform.

Thus the lady-bug became famous and we could hardly cope with the multitude of letters and lady-bugs of all shapes and sizes and for all possible and impossible uses we received.

# *Appendix B*

Only two claims can be confirmed with absolute certainty.

*N2936* This Wellington was shot down by Helmut Lent. Records clearly state that the first aircraft he shot down crashed on the island of Borkum. Herbie Ruse has stated, in correspondence with the author, that he was the pilot of the Wimpy that crash-landed on Borkum.

*Me 109* piloted by Leutnant Stiegler. Records again state that it was his fighter that was lost when its wing tip touched the sea and it cartwheeled and disappeared. Peter Lemon has also been in contact with the author to say that it was his rear gunner, Corporal Kidd, who fired a long burst at a pursuing Me 109 and, as the fighter broke off the attack and turned clear, possibly because it had been hit, its wing tip just brushed the surface, and the fighter cartwheeled into the water.

All the other claims can only be supposition based on the evidence from:

(1) The Operations Record Books of No. 149, 9 and 37 Squadrons
(2) No. 3 Group reports on the events of 18th December 1939
(3) *The Luftwaffe War Diaries* by Cajus Bekker
(4) *Les Aiglons, combat aeriens de la Drôle de Guerre* by C. J. Ehrengardt; C. F. Shores; H. Weisse and J. Foreman.
(5) Personal account of the battle by Group Captain P. I. Harris, DFC.

*N2935* Herbie Ruse also confirmed that he was flying as one of a pair with Flying Officer Thompson. They broke away westwards across the Friesian Islands and he and Thompson were still flying together as a pair when they were attacked by an Me 110. Bekker states that Lent spotted two Wellingtons and attacked and shot down the rear one which forced landed on Borkum. Lent then went on to pursue the second Wellington and brought it down in the sea close by Borkum. Ruse confirms that F/O Thompson's aircraft crashed into the sea just to the west of Borkum. Thompson probably fell to Helmut Lent.

*N2889* Bekker relates that the Geschwader Commander, Carl Schumacher, shot down a bomber and: 'For days to come the wreck of the Wellington he had dispatched remained sticking out of the mud-flats off Spiekeroog.' This island is twenty kilometres to the west of the route taken by Kellett's main formation. A body was later washed ashore and identified as A/C Geddes, the rear gunner from N2889. Ruse confirms that both Wimberley and Lewis broke away to port with the rest of No. 37 Squadron. It is therefore probable that N2889 was brought down by Schumacher.

*N2888* Five aircraft from No. 37 Squadron took the course to the west over the Friesian Islands. N2903 was the sole survivor that made it back to Feltwell. This leaves only Wimberley's aircraft to be accounted for. F/O Wimberley was picked up by a German patrol boat after he ditched his aircraft in the vicinity of Borkum. Bekker states that: 'Lent brought down a third Wellington which had already been shot up. This plunged into the sea fifteen miles north-west of Borkum.' It could only have been N2888 as all the others have been accounted for. Because the Wellington had already been badly shot-up, Lent was not credited with this last victory, which was more than likely N2888.

*N2904* Peter Grant observed Squadron Leader Hue-Williams racing far ahead of his formation in an attempt to catch up with Kellett's formation. At 2.45 p.m. (German time), according to Bekker, Oberleutnant Gordon Gollob attacked the rear left Wellington in a formation of *seven*. The only possible way in which seven Wellingtons could have been flying together at that particular time was if Hue-Williams had caught up with and joined Paul Harris's six Wimpys on the starboard side of the big diamond. The stated position of the encounter is however inconsistent with the known course of Harris's formation. It is impossible that seven Wellingtons were flying in formation to the north west of Langeoog, forty kilometres due west of Harris's flight-path. Ten minutes *before* that, Falck and Fresia had broken up the only other formation of six bombers, i.e. F/O Guthrie's two flights, out on the port side of the big diamond. *If* Gollob did attack a formation of seven aircraft, then he must have mis-reported his position and it is possible that his victim was Hue-Williams.

*N2962* Paul Harris was insistent that Flying Officer Speirs was shot down by an Me 110. There were only *four* other Me 110s that reported their position as being anywhere within twenty kilometres of Kellett's main formation. Two of these 110s were engaged in attacking No. 9 Squadron's formation out on the port side of the big diamond. This only leaves Oberfeldwebel Fleischmann or Feldwebel Gröning that could have been responsible for dispatching Speirs.

*N2939 and N2940* Bekker relates how Wolfgang Falck and his No. 2, Fresia, ran into a close formation of returning Wellingtons at 2.35 p.m. (German time). In *Les Aiglons* it describes how Falck attacked the right-hand bomber in the last formation and watched it explode in mid-air. Fresia attacked the plane on the left-hand side of the same section and watched it crash into the sea with its port engine in flames. As Falck and Fresia raced in from the West, Guthrie's six aircraft would have been the first 'close formation' they encountered. In the 3 Group report it states that an aircraft in F/O Allison's section appeared to explode and another was seen to go down with its port engine on fire. Sergeant Petts also reported that an aircraft in Allison's section was seen to receive a direct hit and fell to bits. Pilot Officer Lines was supposed to be in the No. 2 position and Pilot Officer Challes in the No. 3 position. However, Sergeant Murphy in Macrae's plane reported that the aircraft in Allison's section were changing position so it is not possible to be precise about Falck and Fresia's victims.

*N2941* Fresia was credited with two victories and this would have been the remaining aircraft in Allison's Section, possibly Allison himself.

*N2872* Falck was shot down by the last aircraft he attacked. The 3 Group report states that Squadron Leader Guthrie was attacked by an Me 110 which he shot down in flames before he himself went down. If the aircraft of No. 9 Squadron were flying in their allotted positions then it is probable that Falck shot down Lines and Guthrie while Fresia put paid to Challes and Allison.

*Me 109* piloted by Oberleutnant Fuhrmann. This fighter pilot attacked a flight of *four* Wellington bombers as related by Bekker. Paul Harris recalled watching an Me 109 attack Kellett's four Wimpys several times before it curled away seaward trailing a cloud of smoke. There was only one formation of four Wellingtons when the bombers cleared the flak over Wilhelmshaven and that was Kellett's four. Bekker states that Fuhrmann attacked a Wellington that flew on the left of a flight of four. As this was probably the position of Flying Officer Riddlesworth at the time, it is reasonable to presume that Fuhrmann fell to AC2 Gouldson, the rear gunner, assisted by the tail gunners in the adjacent Wimpys.

*Me 110s* piloted by Staffelkapitän Falck and Leutnant Uellenbeck. The fate of these fighters has already been fully discussed in Chapter 5.

With JG1 claiming a total of twenty-seven *confirmed* victories, it must be stressed that the above accounts are only the author's interpretation of the available evidence. It is not intended to be the final word on the battle as other records, not available to the author, may exist which would cast a different light on the events that day. What is known for certain is that *only ten* Wellingtons were shot down during the battle and logic dictates that a Wimpy can only be shot down once.

# *Appendix C*

THE WELLINGTON

In 1936 Barnes Wallis had a plan,
A revolutionary idea so far unknown
to man.
They put their heads together and,
Before the year was done,
A brand new plane – a bomber
Its name – the Wellington.

The plane was made and tested
And took off to the skies.
Soaring, cruising, diving,
A sight for every eye.

The years rolled by and in 39
Before the plane was rested,
A war broke out – a brilliant way,
For the bomber to be tested.

One year later on Hogmanay
At R.A.F. Lossiemouth
Eight men boarded a Wellington
Ready to take flight.

Away they went on exercise
But alas not for long.
A dreadful snowstorm hit the plane
Not far from the Cairn Gorm.

The pilot gave orders to his crew
That they should all bail out
The only way to save themselves
Was this – without a doubt.

The men now gone, the plane
spluttered on
Until the pilot saw Loch Ness.
And without hesitation he ditched it
there
And finally it came to rest.

But in 1985
An effort was made
To lift the Wellington bomber up
From its watery grave.

And now she's up and gone away,
Poor Nessie's in a daze,
Back to her place of origin,
For all the world to gaze.

She's gone back to Weybridge
To the brand new Brooklands
Museum
To the place where Vickers made her,
For all of you to see.

*By Rhiannon Naismith*
*Aged 11 years*

*Drumsmittal Primary School,*
*North Kessock, Ross-shire.*

# References

*Introduction*
1. Hastings, M., *Bomber Command,* Chapter 6, p. 166 (Pan Books – 1981).

(1) *'Hidden away for all time'*
1. Klein, M., *Technology Review* Volume 79, Number 2, December 1976, p. 45 (Edited at the Massachusetts Institute of Technology).

(2) *'A very good cottage on the foundations of a castle'*
1. Webster and Frankland, *The Strategic Air Offensive against Germany,* Volume 1, Trial and Error, p. 191 (HMSO 1961).
2. Penrose, H., *British Aviation Ominous Skies 1935–1939,* p. 231 (HMSO 1980).
3. Hansard, Volume 339, 1937–38, September 28th to October 6th, p. 50.

(3) *La Drôle de Guerre*
1. Ehrengardt, C. J. et al, *Les Aiglons,* p. 26 (Charles-Lavauzelle, Paris-Limoges, 1983).
2. Armand van Ishoven, *Messerschmitt Bf 109 at war,* p. 44–45 (Ian Allan Ltd 1977).
3. Richards, D., *Royal Air Force 1939–1945,* Volume 1, The Fight at Odds, Chapter II, p. 44 (HMSO 1974).
4. Letter to author from Bundesarchiv, Militärarchiv, Freiburg, 3 December 1986.
5. Bottomley, Air Commodore, Report on operation carried out by No. 99 Squadron on 14th December 1939 and covering letter dated 28th December 1939 (AIR files in the Public Record Office).
6. Hastings, M., *Bomber Command,* Prologue, p. 17 (Pan Books – 1981).
7. Webster and Frankland, *The Strategic Air Offensive against Germany,* Volume 1, Trial and Error, p. 192 (HMSO 1961).

(5) *The Battle of Heligoland Bight*
1. Kellett, R., Wing Commander, Narrative report dated 20th December, 1939 (AIR files PRO).
2. Bekker, C., *The Luftwaffe War Diaries,* p. 74 (Macdonald 1967).
3. Bekker, C., *The Luftwaffe War Diaries,* p. 77 (Macdonald 1967).
4. Kellett, R., Wing Commander, Narrative report dated 20th December, 1939 (AIR files PRO).
5. Baldwin to Ludlow-Hewitt, letter dated 19th December, 1939 (AIR files PRO).
6. Ludlow-Hewitt to Baldwin, letter dated 24th December, 1939 (AIR files PRO).
7. Webster and Frankland, *The Strategic Air Offensive against Germany,* Volume 1, Trial and Error, p. 198 (HMSO 1961).
8. Webster and Frankland, *The Strategic Air Offensive against Germany,* Volume 1, Trial and Error, p. 201 (HMSO 1961).
9. Bekker, C., *The Luftwaffe War Diaries,* p. 79 (Macdonald 1967).
10. HQ No. 3 Group report, 22nd December, 1939 (AIR files PRO).
11. Ludlow-Hewitt to Baldwin, 24th December, 1939 (AIR files PRO).
12. Webster and Frankland, *The Strategic Air Offensive against Germany,* Volume 1, Trial and Error, p. 200 (HMSO 1961).

13. Richards, D., *Royal Air Force 1939–1945*, Volume 1, The Fight at Odds, Chapter II, p. 47 (HMSO 1954).

(6) *'Blood, toil, tears and sweat'*

1. Ehrengardt, C. J., Shores, C. F., Weisse, W., Foreman, J., *Les Aiglons, Combats Aeriens de la Drôle de Guerre*, p. 98 (Charles-Lavauzelle, Paris-Limoges 1983).
2. Lumsden, A., *Wellington Special* (Ian Allan Ltd 1974).
3. Bowyer, C., *Wellington at War* (Ian Allan Ltd 1982).
4. Bowyer, C., *The Wellington Bomber* (William Kimber & Co. 1986).
5. Andrews, C. F., *Vickers Aircraft since 1908*, p. 309 (Putnam 1969).
6. Cooksley, P. G., *Wellington, Mainstay of Bomber Command* (Patrick Stephens 1987).
7. Chappel, F. R., *Wellington Wings* (William Kimber & Co. 1980).
8. Webster and Frankland, *The Strategic Air Offensive against Germany*, Volume 1, Trial and Error (HMSO 1961).
9. Bekker, C., *The Luftwaffe War Diaries*, p. 76 (Macdonald 1967).
10. Baldwin to Ludlow-Hewitt, 19th December, 1939 (AIR files PRO).
11. Ludlow-Hewitt to Baldwin, 24th December, 1939 (AIR files PRO).
12. Richards, D., *Royal Air Force*, 1939–1945, Volume 1, The Fight at Odds, Chapter II, p. 47 (HMSO 1954).
13. Musgrove, G., *Pathfinder Force a History of 8 Group*, p. 181 (Macdonald and Janes 1976).

(7) *One of our aircraft comes home*

1. Moran, P., *FlyPast Magazine*, May/June 1981, p. 12.
2. Holmes, R. T., *New Scientist*, 26th August, 1982, Volume 95, No. 1320, p. 546.

# Glossary

Throughout the text, the abbreviations used for ranks in the Royal Air Force are the informal ones taken from the Operations Record Books for 1939 and 1940. The contemporary *Luftwaffe* equivalent is also given where appropriate. Several German ranks, in fact, had no direct equivalent in the Royal Air Force. Other German language terms used in the book are also included.

The list below gives equivalent wartime ranks in the RAF and USAAF.

| | *Luftwaffe* | *Royal Air Force* | *US Army Air Force* |
|---|---|---|---|
| 1. | Generalfeldmarschall | Marshal of the Royal Air Force | General (five star) |
| 2. | Generaloberst | Air Chief Marshal | General (four star) |
| 3. | General der Flieger | Air Marshal | Lieutenant General |
| 4. | Generalleutnant | Air Vice-Marshal | Major General |
| 5. | Generalmajor | Air Commodore | Brigadier General |
| 6. | Oberst | Group Captain | Colonel |
| 7. | Oberstleutnant (Obstlt) | Wing Commander (W/Cdr) | Lieutenant Colonel |
| 8. | Major | Squadron Leader (S/L & S/Ldr) | Major |
| 9. | Hauptmann | Flight Lieutenant (F/Lt) | Captain |
| 10. | Oberleutnant (Oblt) | Flying Officer (F/O) | First Lieutenant |
| 11. | Leutnant (Lt) | Pilot Officer (P/O) | Lieutenant |
| 12. | Stabsfeldwebel | Warrant Officer (W/O) | Warrant Officer |
| 13. | Oberfeldwebel (Ofw) | Flight Sergeant (F/Sgt) | Master Sergeant |
| 14. | Feldwebel (Fw) | Sergeant (Sgt) | Technical Sergeant |
| 15. | Unterfeldwebel | — | — |
| 16. | Unteroffizier (Uffz) | Corporal (Cpl) | Staff Sergeant |
| 17. | Hauptgefreiter | — | Sergeant |
| 18. | Obergefreiter | Leading Aircraftman (LAC) | Corporal |
| 19. | Gefreiter | Aircraftman First Class (AC1) | Private First Class |
| 20. | Flieger | Aircraftman Second Class (AC2) | Private |

*Luftwaffe Formations*

| | |
|---|---|
| Rotte | Two fighters working as a fighting pair. |
| Schwarm | Two Rotte. |
| Kette | A unit of three or four fighters. |

| | |
|---|---|
| Staffel | The nearest equivalent to an RAF squadron, 10 to 12 aircraft. |
| Gruppe | Three, occasionally four Staffeln. |
| Geschwader | The Luftwaffe's largest formation; comprising approximately one hundred aircraft, usually confined to one rôle; normally three Gruppen. |
| Rottenflieger | Wing man, equivalent to the RAF's 'No. 2', also Rottenkamerad/Kaczmarek. |
| Rottenfuhrer | Leader of a rotte. |
| Staffelkapitan (Stfk) | Luftwaffe officer commanding a staffel. |
| Geschwaderkommodore | Luftwaffe officer commanding a geschwader. |
| JG (Jagdgeschwader) | Fighter geschwader. |
| NJG (Nachtjagdgeschwader) | Night fighter geschwader. |
| KG (Kampfgeschwader) | Bomber geschwader. |
| ZG (Zerstorergeschwader) | Literally 'Destroyer' and applied to bomber escorts, heavy fighters including the ME110; thus ZG is a Heavy-Fighter Group. |

For example, the designation I/ZG76 would refer to the first Gruppe of Zerstorergeschwader 76, the Roman I indicating the Gruppe. Individual staffeln within the gruppe would be designated with an Arabic numeral such as 2/ZG76.

# *Acknowledgements*

The successful recovery of Wellington bomber N2980 from the depths of Loch Ness was due entirely to a unique set of circumstances. First and foremost must be recorded the support and encouragement given to the project by the Administration of Heriot-Watt University. Then there was the dedication of a small group of individuals who formed the Executive Committee and gave their time and specialist knowledge to help organise and run the Loch Ness Wellington Association Ltd. To this must be added the generosity of the National Heritage Memorial Fund and those other organisations and individuals who contributed the necessary money. Last, but by no means least, there was the wide range of professional expertise that fused together so harmoniously at Loch Ness to provide the brains and the brawn that eventually wrested old 'R for Robert' from its forty-five years of slumber on the bottom, and then dismantled and transported it home to its birthplace at Weybridge.

Following the recovery of the Wimpy, especially after the first attempt had failed so spectacularly, I was struck by the thought that perhaps the story of this old warrior from a bygone era was worth telling. Never having set pen to paper before on anything so ambitious as a book, I was at first apprehensive about finding enough to write, particularly concerning such an obscure period as the Phoney War. I was greatly encouraged, however, by Paul Harris, who had earlier acquainted me with the full significance of the Battle of Heligoland Bight. With his help I was able to locate Richard Kellett and Bunny Austin. Fortunately, I was also able to track down David Marwood-Elton, Bill Wright, Peter Grant, Wolfgang Falck, 'Cheese' Lemon, Herbie Ruse and Harry Jones. In what can only be described as an incredible stroke of good luck, I located Mrs Sylvia Richardson, Sandy Innes's sister, and found that Sandy had kept a diary. From all these first-hand accounts I was able to put a lot of meat on the bare bones of the official histories. All this personal information, coupled with the positive and helpful response I received from everyone I contacted, greatly encouraged me to persevere with the task of recording the story of 'One of our Aircraft'. As a rank amateur in the field of historical research, I must also tender my apologies to all those professional historians and other more knowledgeable experts for the mistakes and oversights I am bound to have inadvertently made. I trust they will forgive an engineer for his inadequacies as an historian.

Therefore, it is to all those who helped restore N2980 to the nation and to those who provided the wealth of information on its history that I offer my most sincere thanks.

The following is a list of organisations and individuals whose help I gratefully acknowledge.

*Heriot-Watt University Administration*: with particular thanks to Principal Tom Johnston and Professor Colin Davidson, Head of the Department of Electrical and Electronic Engineering. Special thanks are due to Rod Lindsay for acting as the Hon. Treasurer of the LNWA Ltd. A debt of gratitude is owed to Fiona Samson, Paula Ingram, Pamela Meikle and Gillian Swanson for their tolerance and infinite patience while typing up and forever amending the seemingly endless drafts of this book, together with mountains of other correspondence for the LNWA Ltd.

*The Loch Ness Wellington Association Ltd*: Executive Committee – Richard Kellett, Paul Harris, Ken Crichton, Don Storer, David Brown, Bob Allwood and Morag Barton, together with all the members without whose support the Association could not have been formed: John Atkey, David Attrill, Bunny Austin, Sandy Benzies, Spud Boorer, Gary Brindle, Philip Douglas-Cooper, Gillian Dennison, Robert Didwell, Robin Dunbar, Wolfgang Falck, Andrew Gemmell, Paul Harris, William Holmes, Howard Johnson, Marty Klein, Sir Walter Merton, Julian Mitchell, Jeremy Petts, Sylvia Richardson, Mauritz Rossavik, Ruth Stainforth, Cliff Steanson, Paul Vaughan, Paul Wiggins, Gordon Williamson, Joe Zarzynski, Stuart Usher, Ken Hunter, Don Clarke, Leonard Green, Douglas Hamilton, Susan Hamilton, David Morgan, Bill Ranger, G. Sutherland, David Esslemont, Brian Jones, John Johnson, Neil McTaggart, Margaret Vick, Allan Crewe, Tim Harris, James Pow, Dennis Hillman.

*The National Heritage Memorial Fund*: with special thanks to Brian Lang and Clive Jenkins for their support.

Other organisations and individuals who helped to finance the project were The Carnegie Trust for the Universities of Scotland; The MacRobert Trusts; The Highlands and Islands Development Board; RAF Museum, Hendon; *FlyPast* Magazine; Royal Bank of Canada; British Oxygen Ltd; AOC International Ltd; Water Weights Ltd; Gas Supplies Ltd; British Alcan Tubes Ltd; Bernard ('Bootiful') Matthews and A. A. Garside. Many hundreds of people sent donations and contributed by buying our brochure. Thousands of pounds were raised by these means and I would like to thank everyone who thereby helped to fund the recovery. Unfortunately, there are far too many people to name them all individually, but without their help we could not have covered the costs of salvaging the Wellington.

*Oceaneering International Services Ltd*: Chris Jenkins and Tony Pritchard with special thanks to Alfie Lyden and his ADS Team; Andy Griffiths, Eric Hammons, Dave Weddle, David (Lefty) Foot and Neil Brock, together with John McKenzie, David Sinclair and Norman Brown on the M.V. *Work Horse.*

*J.W. Automarine*: with thanks to John Wise, Malcolm Felmingham and Richard Allen.

*British Aerospace. Weybridge*: with special thanks to Norman Barfield and Heinz Vogel, together with the transport drivers Jack Wheeler, Dick Alder, Colin Casemore, John (Jock) Clark and photographers Dave Clark, Dave Price and Cliff Knox. Help was also provided by British Aerospace at Chester and Prestwick.

*Vintage Aircraft and Flying Association (VAFA)*: Spud Boorer, John Mitchell, Hugh Tyrer, Peter Hancocks, Martin Cutler, Alan Jeffcoate, Alex Delaney, Andy Pither, Frank Hack, Tony Large and Dennis Winsor.

*Institute of Offshore Engineering*: Bob Allwood and Alan Crewe.

*James Jack (Evanton) Ltd*: James Jack and George Heggie.

*Brooklands Museum*: Morag Barton, Ann Watson, Mike and Shirley Goodall and Barbara Sants.

Thanks are also due to MacDonald Ferries *Eilean Dubh*; Ecosse Wire Ropes Ltd; Cromarty Firth Engineering Ltd; British Waterways Board; Lord Burton, Dochfour Estate; George Reid, Bona Lighthouse; the VAFA wives; Drew Holmes and Keith Holmes; Elmbridge Borough Council; Highland Regional Council; Northern Constabulary; Meridian International Communications Ltd; Moray Firth Radio (Charlie Stuart); Mr & Mrs McKenzie, Clansman Hotel; Mrs McIntosh, 'The Foich', Drumnadrochit; Loch Ness and Morar Project; UMEL; Osprey Electronics Ltd; Oceonics Ltd; Fiona and Eric Hutchinson, M.V. *John William*; Sonat Subsea Services (UK) Ltd; Hydro Products Ltd; The Royal Navy Fleet Diving Group (formerly called the Fleet Clearance Diving Team); John Turner, M.V. *Conserver*; K.D. Marine (UK) Ltd; Ministry of Defence (Adastral House); Scottish Marine Biological Association, Dunstaffnage, Oban.

The following organisations provided information and photographs on the history of N2980 and the Phoney War in general: The Imperial War Museum, London; Royal Air Force Museum, Hendon; Ministry of Defence, Air Historical Branch (Lacon House); Public Record Office, Kew; London Film Productions Ltd; Bundesarchiv – Militärarchiv, Freiburg; Gemeinschaft der Jagdflieger, Munich; British Libraries, Newspaper Library.

The following individuals provided information on N2980 and its crews or otherwise helped with the recovery of the aircraft or the production of this book: Paul Harris, Richard Kellett, Bunny Austin, Peter Grant, Wolfgang Falck, Cheese Lemon, Herbie Ruse, Harry Jones, David Marwood-Elton, Bill Wright, Sylvia Richardson (*née* Innes), Mrs J. Mullineaux, Mrs Vick (*née* Mullineaux), Jeremy Petts, Tim Harris, Johannes Steinhoff, Robin Dunbar, Joe Watts-Farmer (*née* Frazer-Nash), Joan Tarry, the Rev. Canon M. C. G. Sherwood, Des Lampard, Ruth Stainforth (*née* Douglas-Cooper),

A. A. McIntosh, John MacPherson, Morag Barton, Ann Huckins, Dr Tanner, Jack Bruce, Ken Hunter, Eric Morgan, Marty Klein (USA), Robert Rines (USA), Joe Zarzynski (USA), John Johnston (USA), J. C. Brannam, Angus Grant, Sandy Benzies, Paul Wiggins, Julian Mitchell, Alex Lumsden, P. J. Moran, Norman Didwell, Don Clarke, Bill Ranger, Bob Barnard, Jim Pow, P. Surman, A. Gemmell, A. Spanier, A. W. Cooper, Archie McMillan, Brett Studley, Crawford Grier, Hugh Keith, Mireille Poots, Allan Spence, Duncan Hurst, P. J. Foreman, Sue Brenchley and Andrew Swanson.

Very special thanks are due to Neil McTaggart of Balfour and Manson, Solicitors, Edinburgh, without whose expert help the LNWA Ltd, would not have been formed and the aircraft thereby recovered.

I would like to express my thanks to James Caw for scrutinising my English and suggesting suitable corrections and to Ken Crichton for proof reading my draft manuscript.

I am also indebted to the following for permission to quote from published work and private sources: Jonathan Cape Ltd, for the quotation from *The 'Caine' Mutiny* by Herman Wouk; Sphere Books Ltd, for extracts from *Star Wars* by George Lucas; Michael Joseph Ltd for lengthy passages, particularly in Chapter 5, from the Prologue to *Bomber Command* by Max Hastings; Octopus Books Ltd for an extract from the *History of World War II* by A. J. P. Taylor; Aeroplane Monthly for an extract from a 1939/40 edition of *The Aeroplane*; the Controller of Her Majesty's Stationery Office for extracts from *The Strategic Air Offensive against Germany* by Webster and Frankland, *British Aviation, Ominous Skies* by H. Penrose, *Royal Air Force 1939–45* by D. Richards, and Hansard; extracts from *Bomber Squadrons of the RAF and their Aircraft* by P. J. R. Moyes, published by MacDonald and Jane's 1976, reproduced by kind permission of Jane's Publishing Co. Ltd; Times Newspapers Ltd, for permission to reproduce extracts from 1939 copies of *The Times* and *The Sunday Times*; Jane's Publishing Co. Ltd, for extracts from *The Luftwaffe War Diaries* by Cajus Bekker; the Controller of HM Stationery Office for transcripts of Crown-copyright records in the Public Record Office; (This includes material from the AIR files and the *Operations Record Books* of Number 149, 9 and 37 Squadrons.); C. J. Ehrengardt for permission to reproduce Table 1 in Chapter 5; William Shirer ©1940 by William Shirer; renewed 1968 by William Shirer) for an extract from *Berlin Diary*; Jane's Publishing Co. Ltd for an extract from *Pathfinder Force* by G. Musgrove; Jane's Publishing Co. Ltd for the cutaway drawing of the Vickers Wellington Mk III; Mr A. A. Hillhouse for his drawings of N2980; Mr Sandy Bell for his drawings and sketches; *Jaegerblatt*, Journal of the German Fighter Pilots Association for an article by Oberfeldwebel O. K. Dombrowski; Mrs M. Vick for the article by her father, Flight Lieutenant J. J. Mullineaux DFM; Mr J. B. Petts for the article by his father, Flight Lieutenant F. C. Petts DFC and Bar; Wolfgang Falck for the article on his 'Ladybug' Squadron; Mrs Sylvia Richardson for lengthy extracts from the *Diary of War*

1939 by her brother, Flying Officer H. A. Innes DFC (the addition of this material was greatly appreciated as it brought a close personal insight to the events and helped me to understand a little better the feelings and emotions of the combatants during those very early, and rather overlooked, days of the Phoney War); the late Group Captain Paul Harris DFC for his recollections: after forty-five years, it could not have been an easy task to set down on paper such long forgotten events, and his notes, together with personal discussions and numerous letters were invaluable in helping me to piece together the story of *One of our Aircraft*.

# *Postscripts*

(1) On the 13th May 1987, the front gun turret from N2980 was successfully retrieved from Loch Ness. I would like to express my thanks to the following people for their help in salvaging the last large item of 'R for Robert' from a depth of seventy metres.

*Secretary of State for Defence*; the Right Honourable George Younger, TD, MP

*Royal Navy Fleet Diving Group*; Lt/Cdr 'Pincher' Martin, Lt/Cdr Robin Jack, Lt/Cdr Henry Mark (Canadian Navy) together with all the divers and crew of their support ship, the *Ilchester*. Special thanks are due to Willie Sharpe and Roy New, who were the two divers who went down to seventy metres and attached the recovery line to the front gun turret.

*Heriot-Watt University, Unilink*; Ken Crichton.

*U.D.I. Group Ltd*; Alistair Marshall and Lawrence Smith.

*Ametek Offshore (Scotland) Ltd*; Dave Siviter, Brian Barratt, Doug Huntington, Dave McKeown, Alan Niven, Donald Sandilands and Russell McDonald.

*Caley Cruisers*; Jim Hogan.

The project was financed by contributions from the Highlands and Islands Development Board, the Inverness, Loch Ness and Nairn Tourist Board, Mr A. A. Garside and all those people who responded to the 'It's your round!' appeal in the May 1987 issue of *FlyPast Magazine*.

(2) Over the 1987 Christmas and New Year period the last recoverable pieces from N2980 were salvaged from a depth of ten metres at Lochend. For this, I would like to express my thanks to the following people; *RAF Kinloss Sub-Aqua Team*; Sgt Paul Avant, Sgt Dave Watson, Jun. Tech. Nick Hall, Flt Lt Grizz Fairhurst, Club Diving Officer Marie Pittock and all the other divers involved at Lochend.

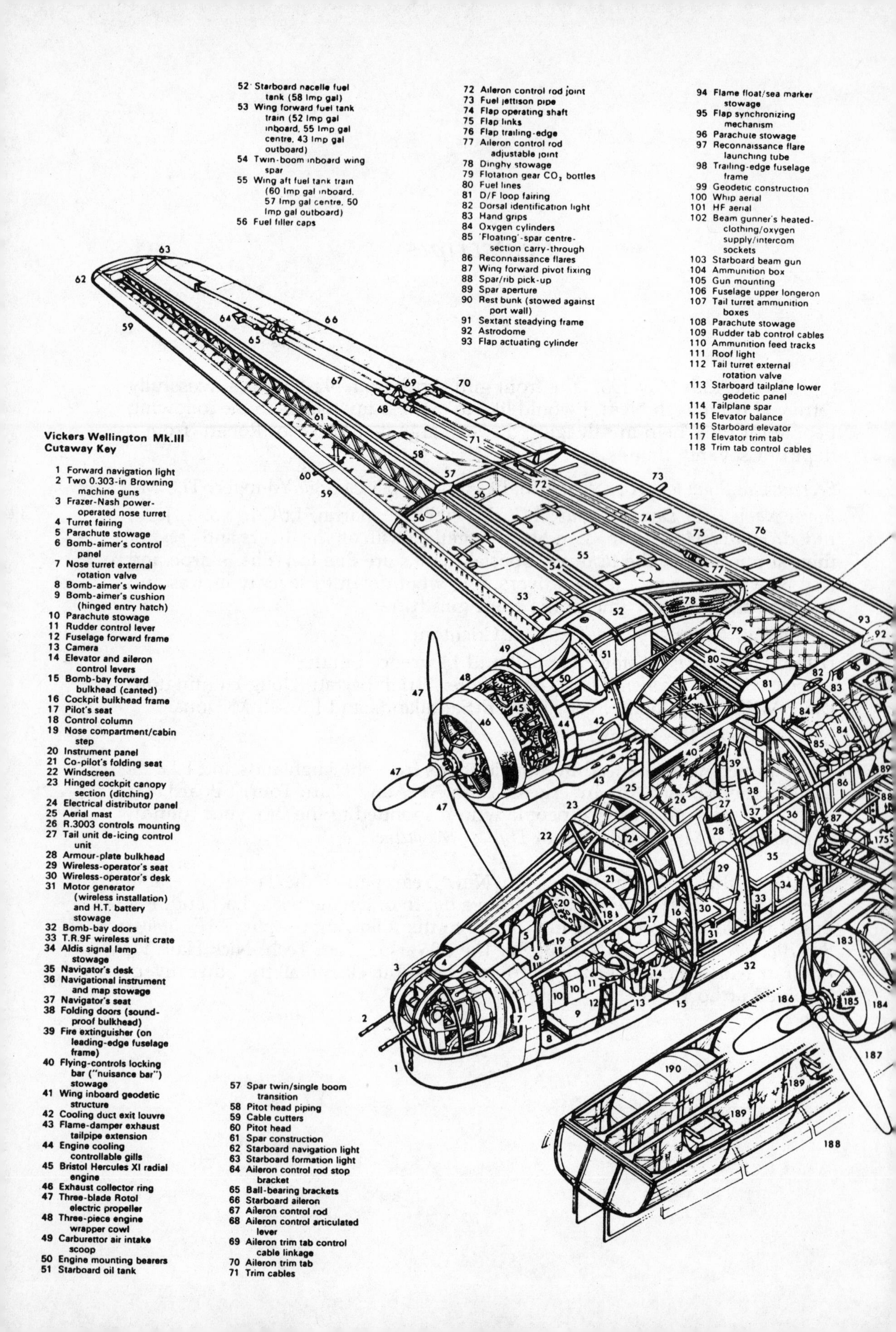

Vickers Wellington Mk.III
Cutaway Key
1 Forward navigation light
2 Two 0.303-in Browning machine guns
3 Frazer-Nash power-operated nose turret
4 Turret fairing
5 Parachute stowage
6 Bomb-aimer's control panel
7 Nose turret external rotation valve
8 Bomb-aimer's window
9 Bomb-aimer's cushion (hinged entry hatch)
10 Parachute stowage
11 Rudder control lever
12 Fuselage forward frame
13 Camera
14 Elevator and aileron control levers
15 Bomb-bay forward bulkhead (canted)
16 Cockpit bulkhead frame
17 Pilot's seat
18 Control column
19 Nose compartment/cabin step
20 Instrument panel
21 Co-pilot's folding seat
22 Windscreen
23 Hinged cockpit canopy section (ditching)
24 Electrical distributor panel
25 Aerial mast
26 R.3003 controls mounting
27 Tail unit de-icing control unit
28 Armour-plate bulkhead
29 Wireless-operator's seat
30 Wireless-operator's desk
31 Motor generator (wireless installation) and H.T. battery stowage
32 Bomb-bay doors
33 T.R.9F wireless unit crate
34 Aldis signal lamp stowage
35 Navigator's desk
36 Navigational instrument and map stowage
37 Navigator's seat
38 Folding doors (sound-proof bulkhead)
39 Fire extinguisher (on leading-edge fuselage frame)
40 Flying-controls locking bar ("nuisance bar") stowage
41 Wing inboard geodetic structure
42 Cooling duct exit louvre
43 Flame-damper exhaust tailpipe extension
44 Engine cooling controllable gills
45 Bristol Hercules XI radial engine
46 Exhaust collector ring
47 Three-blade Rotol electric propeller
48 Three-piece engine wrapper cowl
49 Carburettor air intake scoop
50 Engine mounting bearers
51 Starboard oil tank
52 Starboard nacelle fuel tank (58 Imp gal)
53 Wing forward fuel tank train (52 Imp gal inboard, 55 Imp gal centre, 43 Imp gal outboard)
54 Twin-boom inboard wing spar
55 Wing aft fuel tank train (60 Imp gal inboard, 57 Imp gal centre, 50 Imp gal outboard)
56 Fuel filler caps
57 Spar twin/single boom transition
58 Pitot head piping
59 Cable cutters
60 Pitot head
61 Spar construction
62 Starboard navigation light
63 Starboard formation light
64 Aileron control rod stop bracket
65 Ball-bearing brackets
66 Starboard aileron
67 Aileron control rod
68 Aileron control articulated lever
69 Aileron trim tab control cable linkage
70 Aileron trim tab
71 Trim cables
72 Aileron control rod joint
73 Fuel jettison pipe
74 Flap operating shaft
75 Flap links
76 Flap trailing-edge
77 Aileron control rod adjustable joint
78 Dinghy stowage
79 Flotation gear $CO_2$ bottles
80 Fuel lines
81 D/F loop fairing
82 Dorsal identification light
83 Hand grips
84 Oxygen cylinders
85 'Floating'-spar centre-section carry-through
86 Reconnaissance flares
87 Wing forward pivot fixing
88 Spar/rib pick-up
89 Spar aperture
90 Rest bunk (stowed against port wall)
91 Sextant steadying frame
92 Astrodome
93 Flap actuating cylinder
94 Flame float/sea marker stowage
95 Flap synchronizing mechanism
96 Parachute stowage
97 Reconnaissance flare launching tube
98 Trailing-edge fuselage frame
99 Geodetic construction
100 Whip aerial
101 HF aerial
102 Beam gunner's heated-clothing/oxygen supply/intercom sockets
103 Starboard beam gun
104 Ammunition box
105 Gun mounting
106 Fuselage upper longeron
107 Tail turret ammunition boxes
108 Parachute stowage
109 Rudder tab control cables
110 Ammunition feed tracks
111 Roof light
112 Tail turret external rotation valve
113 Starboard tailplane lower geodetic panel
114 Tailplane spar
115 Elevator balance
116 Starboard elevator
117 Elevator trim tab
118 Trim tab control cables

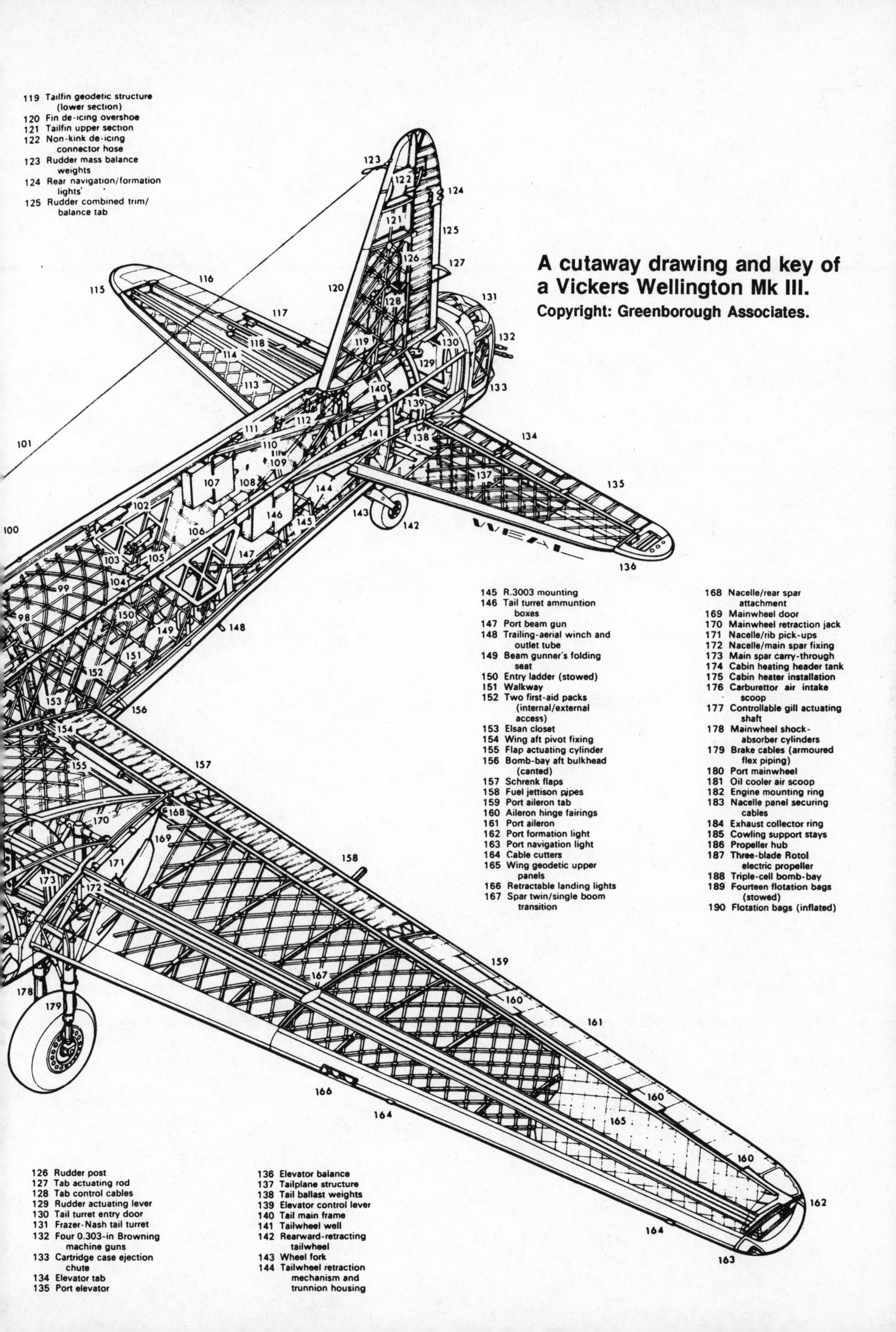


**A cutaway drawing and key of a Vickers Wellington Mk III.**

# Index